Overcoming Gangsterism and Geo-Political Anarchy

"Thought-provoking and timely, this book offers compelling questions and insights amid a shifting world order—perhaps one evolving into a multipolar reality. Its ideas deserve discussion not only among scholars but also at dinner tables around the world and indeed by any one who seeks practically peace and prosperity for humanity."

—Annela Anger, *Professor University of Cambridge and fellow of Emmanuel College Cambridge*

"I wholeheartedly endorse this compelling book that tackles one of the most pressing issues of our time: the failures and inherent violence of the nation-state system. Based on a thought-provoking critique of the current world order it argues skilfully for innovative solutions rooted both in classical theory and current issues building on the notion of a supranational world authority. It will be a valuable source for all those interested in global governance and sustainable peace."

—Paola De Vivo *Professor and Director of the Department of Political Science, Università di Napoli Federico II*

"This timely and thought-provoking work challenges us to rethink global governance structures in an era of shifting influence from West to East. By drawing on lessons from the EU and ASEAN, the authors offer an inspiring vision for a supranational world order grounded in peace, sustainability, and shared human values."

—Vasu Srivibha, *Chair - PRME Chapter ASEAN+ and Chief Impact Officer, Sasin School of Management*

"A bold and provocative work that dares to imagine a world beyond national sovereignty. Built on deep philosophical foundations, this book argues that lasting peace and justice demand a supranational authority capable of enforcing law above the nation state. Whether regarded as visionary or utopian, this is a book of big, necessary ideas. It is an invitation to think anew about humanity's political future at a moment when the old frameworks pose imminent danger."

—J. Peter Clinch, *Jean Monnet Professor of European Environmental Economics and Full Professor of Public Policy, University College Dublin*

Patrick O'Sullivan • Paolo Ricci
Ola Ngau

Overcoming Gangsterism and Geo-Political Anarchy

The Case for a Supranational World Order

palgrave
macmillan

Patrick O'Sullivan
Faculty of Management
University of Warsaw
Warsaw, Poland

Paolo Ricci
Department of Political Sciences
University of Naples Federico II
Napoli, Italy

Ola Ngau
Secretariat, Professors Guild
International
Rimini, Italy

ISBN 978-3-032-22437-8   ISBN 978-3-032-22438-5 (eBook)
https://doi.org/10.1007/978-3-032-22438-5

This Palgrave Macmillan imprint is published by the registered company Springer Nature Switzerland AG.
The registered company address is: Gewerbestrasse 11, 6330 Cham, Switzerland

This book has grown out of a university course developed and delivered over the past five years by Patrick O'Sullivan at Judge Business School, University of Cambridge. The detailed and animated open discussions with some very talented students that were generated contributed immensely to the elaboration and refinement of the ideas that are presented in the work, and so the book is dedicated to all of those lively articulate students who have taken part in the course over the years.

Paolo Ricci, while acknowledging the impassioned and enriching exchanges among the principal authors and with their students over a period of years as the ideas were developed, dedicates the work above all to all of those who daily toil to promote peace and goodwill in our troubled world and to all of those committed students who passionately believe in the possibility of a better world and seek enthusiastically to prepare it.

Ola Ngau dedicates the work to Patrick, who opened the door to Philosophy and taught her the love of a well-reasoned argument; to her family in Sarawak, her unwavering foundation and heart.

And to the leaders and politicians of the future, may this book serve as a catalyst for thoughtful change in the face of their immense responsibilities to the whole of humanity.

Preface

While the argumentation of this book was born from critical reflections in political philosophy on the geographical contours of Hobbes *Leviathan* and on Kant's *Essay on Perpetual Peace,* as the arguments were matured over the course of three years, they have taken on an egregious practical relevance in the light of startling developments in the real-world geopolitical arena. Russia militarily invaded Ukraine in 2022 in an attempted land grab worthy of the nineteenth or early twentieth century, and despite injunctions to desist from the International Court of Justice in Den Haag, it has stubbornly persisted in its military operations, the end goal of which is difficult to ascertain (unless it is annexation of the whole of Ukraine). The events of the past two years in Israel and Palestine become progressively more horrific in a conflict in which both sides have flagrantly violated international law albeit each in different ways. Donald Trump struts the world stage threatening to annex Greenland and perhaps parts of Panama and blowing up boats on the high seas in equally flagrant violation of any national law as well as of the Law of the Sea. With the US-Israeli bombardments of Iran in March 2026 the Middle East has descended into gangsterish chaos causing huge economic dislocation in addition to geopolitical upheaval.

Although the claim outlined in Chap. 1 of this book that the contemporary geopolitical world order is nothing but an anarchic war of all against all worthy of gangland *regolamenti di conti* by the principle of might is right might have seemed a bit exaggerated back in 2021 when the book was first conceived, the tragic outbreak and evolution of so many violent conflicts involving extensive loss of civilian life has given the work a poignant and even urgent relevance. We would not be so pretentious as to claim that we have a formula that will solve all of the world's manifold problems and crises: but we do believe that the significant and perhaps radical institutional innovations that we propose in the form of a supranational world authority with real enforcement powers against recalcitrant nation states have become an indispensable preliminary, even if audacious step, if we are serious about resolving the manifold horrendous conflicts that today scar humanity and its aspiration to a civilised prosperous existence which as Kant rightly understood can only be built on a basis of perpetual peace. For those who are thinking seriously about the institution of a new and better world order given the widely acknowledged demise of the post-1945 set-up our book offers we hope some food for thought and some practical suggestions.

Warsaw, Poland

Patrick O'Sullivan

Acknowledgements

The authors would like to acknowledge the efficiency and helpfulness of the editorial team at Palgrave Macmillan, notably Ambra Finatello, who was always available and flexible for us. Our thanks is also due to Sergio Franceschini of Rimini for the picture collage on the front cover of the book. We should in addition like to thank Abigail Hallowes for the excellent initial suggestion to submit our work to Palgrave Macmillan. We also acknowledge with heartfelt thanks all of the students, colleagues and professionals with whom we have discussed the ideas contained in the book. A certain debt is also due to the work of Guido Montani whose excellent work, *Supranational Political Economy: The Globalisation of the State-Market Relationship,* on the theme of the supranational imperative in the realm of economic policy-making has served as an inspiration. While what is written is entirely our responsibility, all of the above have all made contributions to shaping the final product.

Contents

List of Figures

PART I

The Philosophical and Economic Case for Radical Institutional Innovation: From Contemporary Geopolitical Anarchy Towards a Supranational World Order

CHAPTER 1

The Supranational Argument in the Contemporary Context

Abstract This chapter serves as an introduction to the book as a whole. The book aims to make a modest but important contribution to normative political philosophy drawing on the works of Hobbes and Kant, both of whom wrote their original contributions at times of warfare and political upheaval. Similarly, this work is in part a philosophical response to the conflict that has broken out again in Europe in the Russia/Ukraine war and in the ongoing violence in the Middle East which has plumbed new depths in the past two years. The central question of the book is introduced: how can such conflagrations involving extensive violence in pursuit of territorial annexation be avoided and definitively ended? The answer to be developed in detail in the volume is that the contemporary geopolitical order built around the principle of sovereignty of nation states has not despite the best efforts of international law and of the UN brought peace but rather what today more resembles a Hobbesian war of all against all. Hence, just as in Hobbes argument of the need for a sovereign authority to end the war of all against all, what the world needs today is a supranational World Authority with real powers of enforcement in those areas of policy competence that may be assigned to it (and of which the primordial competence would be arbitration and settlement of disputes among states). While such an arrangement would represent a radical political institutional innovation at world level, a model of this type already exists in the European Union. The chapter includes some reflections on why

P. O'Sullivan et al., *Overcoming Gangsterism and Geo-Political Anarchy*, https://doi.org/10.1007/978-3-032-22438-5_1

there has been such a recrudescence of violent conflicts in recent years linking absolutist claims of national sovereignty for states with the analogous absolutist claims for pursuit of self interest to be found in anarcho-capitalist writings. The chapter concludes with a summary of the main arguments of the book: Part I which outlines the central normative arguments for a supranational World Authority by the principal authors (O'Sullivan, Ngau and Ricci, Chaps. 1–9); and Part II which consists of independent expert insights in relation to the proposals of the book from a number of different perspectives written by independent authors (Chaps. 10–13).

Keywords War of all against all • International law (enforcement) • Balance of powers • Supranationalism • Anarcho-capitalism • Positivism • Normative discourse

Ever since (at least) the time of Plato's classic *The Republic* (c. 380 BC)[1] and Han Fei's partly Confucian inspired reflections on statecraft (Han Feizi c. 250 BC),[2] philosophers have from time to time proffered detailed critical reflections on the form which an ideal state or polity might or should take. But while the matter is assuredly of great consequence for the lives of human beings living together in societies as "political animals" in Aristotle's famous phrase, the field of political philosophy is surprisingly underdeveloped by comparison with other areas of philosophical reflection. While a long and impressive succession of writers can be cited as having made contributions to metaphysics and epistemology as core philosophical disciplines, the lineage of political philosophy is much more thinly populated. In addition to Plato, Aristotle and Confucius, one can mention Cicero, Hobbes, Machiavelli, Locke, Rousseau, Hugo, Montesquieu, Kant, Hegel, Marx, J S Mill, Trotsky, Nozick and perhaps indirectly such great legal theorists as Grotius, Austin and Rawls or the philosophical novelist Ayn Rand. One might argue for the addition of

[1] Plato (2007) *The Republic*, Penguin Classic, London.

[2] Han Feizi (2003) *Han Feizi basic writings* translated by Burton Watson Columbia University Press, New York. available at https://terebess.hu/zen/mesterek/Han-Feizi.pdf. Accessed 9 September 2025.

some other contemporary but perhaps not so famous names as the above such as Michael Sandel, R M Hare or Jürgen Habermas. But with these we would submit that we have a near complete list of the philosophers who have made original and influential contributions to the specific discipline of political philosophy.

This book seeks to make a modest new but not entirely original contribution to political philosophy. Just as many of the earlier political philosophers were actually responding to urgent practical political challenges of their own day (Plato to the crisis of democracy in Athens that led to Socrates' execution; Hobbes[3] to the English civil wars), the motivation for this work is to respond to the brutal challenge to peaceful co-existence in Europe and in the world that has been posed by Russia's invasion of Ukraine. That such a brutal war with extensive and wilful killing of civilians should have broken out in Europe (even if not in the European Union *stricto sensu*) has not only been shocking for EU citizens who had come to take peace, cooperation and freedom of trade and travel very much for granted, it has left Europe's politicians groping around in the dark for an appropriate response to the armed aggression that has occurred. They had simply never imagined that an armed conflict of this type could happen again on European soil. Of course, there has been a large and generous immediate political response in the form of financial and military aid and a willingness to assist and welcome Ukrainians displaced by the war; and the EU has granted candidate status for membership of the EU to Ukraine and Moldova. But in terms of the question of a long-term resolution of the conflict in a way that does not see armed invasion rewarded, Europe's politicians have had little of consequence to say apart from Emmanuel Macron's rather vague initial (and much challenged) assertion that Putin must not be humiliated. That was 2022, and now Macron seems to have changed his mind to become one of the most hawkish EU leaders saying that above all Putin must not be allowed in any sense to "win" the war.[4] But even in Macron's pronouncements, more explicit than those of any other EU leader, at the time of initial conception of this work, the Russia/Ukraine war was the most salient theatre of violent conflict in the world, but there

[3] Hobbes T (1651) *Leviathan* reprinted with an introduction by Plamenatz J (1969) 4th edition, Fontana London. Also reprinted as a Penguin Classic (2017), Penguin Books Harmondsworth.

[4] On this volte-face, see Gatinois C et al. Guerre en Ukraine: "La métamorphose d'Emmanuel Macron, colombe devenue faucon" in *Le Monde* 14 March 2024.

were also smaller conflicts in certain parts of Africa and outfight gang warfare in Haïti. Since 2023, the world has been witness to a shockingly violent Israeli/Palestinian conflict; and most recently in 2026 there has been the US-Israeli invasion of Iran with the resulting political contagion throughout the Middle East and economic chaos worldwide. But whether in Macron's pronouncements on Russia/Ukraine or in the endless disquisitions on the various other conflicts, the focus has largely been on seeking to bring ceasefires while almost nothing concrete has been said by politicians about how such conflagrations can be avoided in the future.

The purpose of this book is to begin to give a critical and some might say radical answer to the following two questions that arise from a serious reflection on all of the above: how can such conflagrations involving extensive violence in pursuit of territorial annexation be avoided and definitively ended; and why are such wars breaking out among nation states (or substates) in so many areas of the world[5] and in particular how could such a war have broken out again in Europe? To the second question, there are no doubt a number of explanatory factors, perhaps most obviously that Putin had long been warning of his intentions, but nobody in Europe took him seriously, dismissing his claims to reconstitute the old Soviet empire as bravado talk for internal Russian consumption.[6] But looking beneath the surface and recognising that recent years have seen similar wars of aggrandisement break out in other parts of the world (most recently in the Middle East) and threats of such wars being bandied around by Donald Trump (in relation to Greenland and perhaps Panama), there are arguably deeper roots to the recrudescence of wars and weakening of the institutions for international cooperation and negotiation that we are witnessing. These roots lie in the rise of increasingly self-centred behaviour and philosophies of life of which the most extreme expression is the "anarcho-capitalism" of Murray Rothbard and the minarchist egoism of Ayn Rand.[7] If the immediate post-1945 period was characterised by the

[5] In 2024, the number of ongoing armed conflicts as measured by the Peace Research Institute of Oslo has reached a level not seen since the Second World War. See PRIO website https://www.prio.org/news/3616. Accessed 27 July 2025.

[6] See, for example, Shinar C (2016), "Vladimir Putin's Aspiration to Restore the Lost Russian Empire" (November 15, 2016). Available at SSRN: https://ssrn.com/abstract=2869863 or https://doi.org/10.2139/ssrn.2869863. Accessed 17 July 2025.

Shinar discusses in particular Putin's now (in)famous assertion in an address to the Russian people in 2005 that the "1991 break-up of the Soviet Union was the greatest geopolitical catastrophe of the (20th) century".

[7] On anarcho-capitalism, see Rothbard M (1993) *Man Economy and State*, 2nd ed., Mises Institute, Auburn. Ayn Rand's work with its radical individualism and adoption of the "trader

construction of the European welfare states and by a widespread willingness to collaborate and cooperate in good faith among states to further peace and common well-being, since the early 1980s, the welfare state has been gradually challenged and mutilated by a thousand cuts in the pursuit of a philosophy loosely described as economic neo-liberalism but which could more accurately be labelled as "market fundamentalism". In this creed, epitomised by John Williamson's Washington Consensus, market economies if left entirely to themselves under laissez-faire are held always to achieve results superior to any kind of regulated economy.[8] Markets will always know best, and the unregulated pursuit of individual wealth will always lead to the best possible solutions. Even if markets are not always perfect, regulated markets subject to interference by inevitably corrupt politicians will only make matters worse. On the back of these ideas and in particular their exaltation in financial economics by the Efficient Markets Hypothesis,[9] globalisation proceeded apace with the liberalisation of large swathes of trade in goods and services, ultra-internationalisation of supply chains and complete liberalisation of international financial markets. And because such market fundamentalism has through the effects of globalisation generated huge increases in wealth and income especially for certain emergent economies who embraced export-led growth and financial openness, it remains the basic credo guiding economic affairs over most of the world.

But perhaps less well appreciated are some of the corollary effects of this headlong market fundamentalism, one of which is arguably the recrudescence of warfare among states. The ultimate motive force of so-called economic liberalism is individual greed, and when carried to its extreme with the dismantlement of all forms of regulation, it leads to an extreme atomistic individualism devoid of any moral sense in the pursuit of

principle" also typifies anarcho-capitalist ideas. Much of her work was actually published in philosophical novels widely read by market fundamentalists such as Rand A (1943) *The Fountainhead*, Bobbs Merrill, New York; Rand A (1957) *Atlas Shrugged*, Random House, New York. But she also wrote a significant ideological defence of capitalism as a moral system in Rand A (1967) *Capitalism, the Unknown Ideal*, 2nd ed., New American Library, New York.

[8] See Williamson J (2000) "What Washington means by Policy Reform" in Frieden et al. (2000) *Modern Political Economy and Latin America*, Routledge, London.

[9] The theory was first propounded by Eugene Fama in his seminal article Fama E (1970) "Efficient Capital Markets: a review of theoretical and empirical work" *Journal of Finance* 25(2): 383–417. The same article has also been subject to various often severe criticisms. See, for example, O'Sullivan P (2018) "The Capital Asset Pricing Model and the Efficient Markets Hypothesis: The Compelling Fairy Tale of Contemporary Financial Economics" *International Journal of Political Economy*, 47:3–4, 225–252.

individual aggrandisement. Ayn Rand at least had the decency to make this clear when she argued that the *only* moral value is a purely self-centred individual enhancement. From this glorification of individual greed and personal aggrandisement, not only did the dismantlement of manifold regulations and of the Welfare State follow logically, the same self-centredness in pursuit of aggrandisement has been transferred to the nation state (even if a strict anarchist should reject any kind of state). But however suspect logically the transference of the ideas of the pursuit of untrammelled self-centredness to the level of nation state, it has certainly occurred and is proudly professed by sovereignist populists of all stripes. It is deemed to be entirely acceptable for nations to pursue aggressively their own interests; and it has even been suggested that successful business tycoons will make the best politicians; and of course in certain cases, tycoons have indeed taken the plunge into politics with at best very mixed results. It is expected that they will apply to a nation's affairs that same ruthless pursuit of narrow self-interest that has brought them profitability in the business realm. But what is being destroyed thereby in the political realm is any sense of collaboration and cooperation in the pursuit of the common good of humanity (and of the planet as a whole) and so it is hardly surprising that this has led not only to the disappearance of any true moral sense in the conduct of governments but also to the outbreak both of trade wars and wars of military invasion.

This is but one of the awkward corollary side effects of the market fundamentalist anarcho-capitalist-inspired globalisation of the past 40 years, a globalisation which we fully recognise has nevertheless made possible huge increases in the world's wealth and income. There are other side effects associated with the abyssal inequalities which it has generated and with the all-embracing financialisation of so many areas of human activity, but these are themes for another day. For now, we wanted to underline how the transference of market fundamentalist individualism to the level of nation states has played a role in legitimising the recrudescence of wars of military conquest and annexation of territories (as well as of course extensive trade wars).

On the first of the questions above (how can the use of violence by nation states to annex territories or settle other disputes be definitively avoided), there has been much talk and hand-wringing by international relations experts about "balance of power", zones of influence of "great" powers and "security architecture". But it is the thesis of this book that none of these have ever worked on a long term basis to restrain violence in the past since they have led inevitably to wars of various kinds to "restore balance" especially in the "security architecture" and to massive conflicts based on little more than jealousy among the "great" powers regarding their zones of influence (the First World War being the prime example). It will also be shown that philosophically speaking these approaches to understanding and organising the relations among states are based on logically defective and in many cases morally reprehensible premises. In the twenty-first century where the fates and fortunes of human beings the world over have never been so intertwined and interdependent (think climate change impacts, globalised supply chains, etc.), a geopolitical organisation of the world around sovereign nation states acting independently in "their own national interest" is disastrously obsolete and urgently needs to be transcended to create a world order based on supranational institutions with real effective power to override the actions of nation states when they enter into conflict with each other and to promote peaceful co-existence and cooperation among the peoples of the world at least in all areas where policies perforce intersect and people's fates and prosperity are interdependent. Like many previous sorties by political philosophers, this may sound nice but Utopian: supposedly realistic cynics will say that it will never happen. But let us right now pin our colours transparently to the mast. A supranational organisation overriding the absolute sovereignty of nation states already exists on a small scale: the European Union, warts and all. That France, Germany and Italy as well now as now 24 other European states have been able to come together to transfer some aspects of their sovereignty to the central EU institutions (Commission, Council, European Parliament and European Court of Justice) to act for the common good of all Europeans and to make war (at least among European states) unthinkable ever again is a living testimony to the fact that a supranational order is not only a theoretical possibility: it can be achieved in reality when there is sufficient good will and rationality in the face of shared challenges. The idea of extending the European Union experiment to world level is not so fanciful when we consider the example of the Association of Southeast Asian Nations (ASEAN) and in particular its Political and Security Community set up under the inspiration of Thanat Khoman (Thai foreign minister) in 1967[10] precisely to make territorial

[10] ASEAN was set up by the Bangkok Declaration of 1967. Thai foreign minister Thanat Khoman had acted as mediator in a number of local territorial disputes in south-east Asia of the time, and he suggested formalising this role in the form of an intergovernmental entity

wars among its members unthinkable. But admittedly the supranational path remains highly challenging: major obstacles litter the way, not least the question of how to secure the participation of the larger and more powerful nations, often those with imperial pasts. In this book, we will frankly face up to these challenges making suggestions as to how they might eventually be overcome. We will insist that a supranational geopolitical order is a real possibility albeit idealistic and far removed from today's realities, but that given the dividend of peace and well-being which it can bring, it is well worth the effort. While the idea of creating a supranational world order to replace the current system based on sovereignty of nation states constitutes a relatively new contribution to geopolitical theory, we freely acknowledge the inspiration that has been drawn from the political philosophy of Thomas Hobbes, from the seminal political essay of Immanuel Kant on the subject of perpetual peace[11] and from the political thought of Jean Monnet and Robert Schuman, architects of the European Union as well as of Thanat Khoman for ASEAN. It is for this reason that we have said earlier that our contribution is new in its application at world level but not entirely original.

Many contemporary academic thinkers will be uneasy if not appalled by a work which sets out such a strongly normative standpoint, sketching in effect how we think that the world's political set-up *ought* ideally to be ordered. This reluctance to deal with normative questions in political science and indeed throughout the contemporary human sciences derives from the influence of logical positivist ideas on said human sciences. Although the positivist epistemology as espoused by Auguste Comte, Alfred Ayer and the Vienna Circle theorists[12] (Schlick, Neurath, etc.) has long since been demonstrated to be untenable as an epistemology (because self-contradictory), it continues to exercise a vice-like grip on human

designed to promote a lasting peace. He was joined by the foreign ministers of Malaysia, Indonesia, the Philippines and Singapore in the founding of ASEAN. See *The Founding of ASEAN* available at https://asean.org/the-founding-of-asean/. Accessed 9 September 2025.

[11] Kant I (1795) *Zum Ewigen Frieden*, Nicolovius, Königsberg. Available in English in Kant I (1991) *Political Writings* 2nd ed., translated by Nisbet H, Cambridge University Press, Cambridge. In this work the essay "*Perpetual Peace: a philosophical sketch*" is contained.

[12] For a very good summary of positivist thinking in general, see Kolakowski L (1972) *Positivist Philosophy from Hume to the Vienna Circle,* Penguin, Harmondsworth. See also Ayer A (1936) *Language Truth and Logic* Reprinted 2001 by Penguin Harmondsworth. For an epistemological refutation of positivism as self-defeating if applied to its own strictures, see O'Sullivan P (1987) *Economic Methodology and Freedom to Choose*, Allen & Unwin, London. Reprinted 2011 as a Routledge Revival, Routledge, London: chapter 3.

scientists who seek to avoid at all costs passing any kind of "(moral) value judgments", that is to say uttering normative discourse of any kind.[13] This readily explains why so few contemporary political theorists have ventured into the field of normative political philosophy outlining how a better political order whether at local or international level can and should be put in place. Once positivism as an epistemology is discarded, there is no logical or epistemological justification for thus eschewing normative political theorising; and on the contrary, given some of the major political problems we face, very good reason to develop such theorising on a rigorously rational basis. Many academic political theorists are both horrified and puzzled at the rise of so many manifestations of simplistic populism in the actual politics of a wide variety of contemporary states including many European democracies with supposedly well-educated populations. But perhaps this has something to do with the almost total ban and avoidance of normative political philosophising which so many academic political theorists have imposed on themselves. Where the academics have feared to tread because of a misplaced self-imposed positivist hang-up, populist thinkers with little or no background in political theory and practice rush in with their simplistic ill thought-out formulae supposedly to improve the world for their followers at least (but usually with the most blinkered of horizons). In short, the failure of academic political theorists to tackle normative questions has left open season for crude populisms of every stripe and to that extent is arguably irresponsible on the academics' part.

It may be useful at this stage to summarise the overall argument of the book. We will begin with a critical examination of the contemporary geopolitical order whose central pillar is the (essentially absolute) sovereignty of nation states, and we will see how this is effectively enshrined in what is called international law and is the organisational cornerstone of the United Nations and its various offshoots. We will then move to a critical philosophical examination of the basis of the sovereignty of nation states showing that philosophically it is ultimately based on the thesis that might is right and therefore of very dubious moral cogency; while economically speaking, the nation state is an increasingly powerless anachronism. With nation states claiming absolute sovereignty, it will be shown that regular outbreaks of wars are inevitable and this despite the Charter of the United Nations which prohibits the use of military force except in self-defence, a

[13] They are quite happy however to make judgements about creation of financial "value" in the form of profitability of investments/production.

charter which we will show has been honoured more in the breach than in the observance even by supposedly developed and civilised nation states. We will suggest that as a result the contemporary geopolitical order resembles more the unstable gangland rivalry and "turf wars" that occur among criminal gangs in many of the world's bigger cities: in effect the contemporary world order is an anarchic war of all against all such as Hobbes described in *Leviathan* (referring to the civil wars in England of the seventeenth century). We will also note that since the inception of Donald Trump's aggressively unilateral trade policies, the whole realm of international commerce has equally come to resemble an anarchic economic war of all against all in which might is ultimately deemed to be right.

From that perspective, drawing explicitly on the Hobbesian line of reasoning regarding resolution of the war of all against all, we move to construct the argument for replacement of the contemporary order of international law of the United Nations and World Trade Organisation (WTO) with a supranational institutional framework in which nation states (as in the EU) would surrender part of their sovereignty to supranational entities charged with acting for the common good of all. Most basically, such a supranational entity would have the requisite powers of enforcement to prevent wars among nation states in a "peace-enhancing union";[14] but once constructed, such a union could also be used as the locus of policy-making for a variety of other contemporary policy challenges which demand strong common policy responses from wide ranges of nation states simultaneously if those policies are to have any chance of being effective. The most obvious example of such is of course climate change policy, but we could also mention such problems as international financial stability, free trade, immigration and energy flows.

We will suggest that the institutional structure of such a supranational order could be built up learning from the experiences both good and bad of the European Union with such structures. One perhaps immediately obvious challenge when drawing on European experience is that of the democratic deficit of supranational institutions with decisions being taken at a level very far removed from those who will be affected. And yet on certain policy topics, such supranational decisions are indispensable for the common good of all (preservation of peace, climate change mitigation, etc.). But for those policy issues which do not require a concerted world level response, there will be no need for supranational policy articulation,

[14] A phrase used by Robert Schuman at the founding of the European project.

and decision-making can be at a more local level. This is known as the principle of subsidiarity in policy-making. We will make the at first sight radical suggestion that in application of subsidiarity and in order to address fully effectively the democratic deficit challenge, the next level of political institutions below the supranational should be entities small enough to be governed by direct democracy as in the Swiss cantons or the Greek city states of old. That would indeed involve the abolition of nation states as we know them; but given their moral bankruptcy and economic obsolescence, why not?

The book will close with some reflections on the most significant practical challenges which such a supranational project would face. In addition to the reflections of the principal authors on the practical aspects in Part I of the book, we have in Part II at the end of the volume included a set of appendices on specific aspects of practicability from a number of independent specialist scholars with whom we have discussed the project. These specialist contributions can only enrich the discussion and include: one from a professional economist's point of view (Alojzy Nowak); one offering an insight into how the project may be viewed through the eyes of Asian wisdom (Francis Kim); one from a jurist looking at the project of institutional reform in terms of international law (Alexandru Zgardan); and finally a reflection on the rhetoric of war as an obstacle to promotion of a lasting peace (Daniela Russo). Possibly the biggest practical challenge to our proposals would arise from the suggested elimination of nation states and their replacement with direct democracy cantons which would be hotly contested by the bigger nation states of the world, but ironically in many of them, a fragmentation is already occurring along these lines. One only has to consider the polarisation on a whole range of policy questions among the more conservative and more "progressive" states of the USA, the urban rural divide in France, the drive for independence of various separatist leaning regions within certain larger nation states: Scotland and Catalunya.[15] Another somewhat related and intensely practical question is how precisely this supranational world order should be put in place. Given that the fundamental philosophical impulse and motivation is

[15] Incidentally and very interestingly, if Scotland did break from the UK, they would immediately apply to re-join the supranational EU. This unusual concatenation of views actually shows rather clearly that our proposition for a supranational set of institutions with below them much smaller entities than the bigger nation states is actually potentially rather attractive.

to avoid the anarchic war of all against all in a peace-enhancing union, there can be no question of using military force to corral people into this supranational order we are seeking to construct. People or communal entities would join this order of their own free will just as nation states have joined the European Union (and as Kant had envisaged for his perpetual peace project[16]). But this leaves the awkward question of what to do about states or entities which do not want to become part of the supranational order. It must be recalled that for the supranational order effectively to promote peace and put an end to the anarchic war of all against all that we face today, all of the world's political entities must be part of the new set-up. As in Hobbes' argument for the social contract, there can be no exceptions if the peace is to be fully effective. What we will suggest to face this challenge is that once the supranational order is partially put in place, it should maintain the strictest policy of non-engagement with political entities which do not join the peace-enhancing union with supranational powers of dispute resolution; in short, an iron curtain across which no interaction of any kind would be permitted: no trade, no migration, no cross-border travel or tourism, no cross border financial flows of any kind, no overflight; nothing at all. If that may seem too extreme in the globalised world economy in which we find ourselves today, then perhaps one could envisage working gradually towards this within the context of the United Nations whereby subgroups of states could proceed within the UN framework along an irrevocable supranational path while leaving the door always open to those more reticent while stressing that the supranational commitment once made would be irrevocable (that irrevocable character being the guarantor of perpetual peace). Such arrangements have been used to great effect in the European Union under its "enhanced cooperation" principle.[17]

We are the first to admit that there would be other major challenges of detail to such a supranational project such as rules on internal migration within the union (if any), the detailed definition of a constitution for the union and of the rights of citizens, the delimitation of the supranational competences and of how the principle of subsidiarity is to be applied, the restriction of the abuses of lobbying power which would inevitably emerge

[16] Kant I, op. cit. See the Second Definitive Article in his essay.

[17] For the definition of this principle, see European Union EU-Lex *Enhanced Cooperation* available at https://eur-lex.europa.eu/EN/legal-content/glossary/enhanced-cooperation.html. Accessed 17 September 2025.

at the level of the supranational decision-making institutions and no doubt others as well. Some treatment of these practical challenges will be offered in Chaps. 6–8 without however any claim to being exhaustive. We believe that the peace dividend and the immense contribution to human well-being which an end to warfare would represent offer good reasons and incentives to face all of these challenges; and we reiterate that if the European states with their age-old rivalries have been able to construct a supranational union, why not one day the world. In a quintessentially Hegelian moment relying on the logic of the Hobbesian and Kantian arguments, the march of Reason in the world can take us there.

Bibliography

ASEAN. *The Founding of ASEAN.* Accessed September 9, 2025., from https://asean.org/the-founding-of-asean/

Ayer, A. (1936). *Language truth and logic* (Reprinted 2001 by Penguin Harmondsworth).

Fama, E. (1970). Efficient capital markets: A review of theoretical and empirical work. *Journal of Finance, 25*(2), 383–417.

Gatinois, C., et al. (2024). Guerre en Ukraine: "La métamorphose d'Emmanuel Macron, colombe devenue faucon". *Le Monde*, 14 March 2024.

Han Feizi. (2003). *Han Feizi basic writings* (B. Watson, Trans.). Columbia University Press. Accessed September 9, 2025, from https://terebess.hu/zen/mesterek/Han-Feizi.pdf

Hobbes, T. (1651). *Leviathan* reprinted with an introduction by Plamenatz J (1969) 4th ed. Fontana London. Also reprinted as a Penguin Classic (2017), Penguin Books Harmondsworth.

Kant, I. (1795). *Zum Ewigen Frieden*, Nicolovius, Königsberg. Available in English in Kant I (1991) *Political writings* (2nd ed., H. Nisbet, Trans.). Cambridge University Press.

Kolakowski, L. (1972). *Positivist philosophy from Hume to the Vienna circle.* Penguin.

O'Sullivan, P. (1987). *Economic methodology and freedom to choose.* Allen & Unwin, London. Reprinted 2011 as a Routledge revival, Routledge.

O'Sullivan, P. (2018). The capital asset pricing model and the efficient markets hypothesis: The compelling fairy tale of contemporary financial economics. *International Journal of Political Economy, 47*(3–4), 225–252.

Peace Research Institute Oslo (PRIO) website available at https://www.prio.org/news/3616. Accessed 27 July 2025.

Plato. (2007). *The republic.* Penguin Classic.

Rand, A. (1943). *The fountainhead.* Bobbs Merrill.

Rand, A. (1957). *Atlas shrugged.* Random House.

Rand, A. (1967). *Capitalism, the unknown ideal* (2nd ed.). New American Library.
Rothbard, M. (1993). *Man economy and state* (2nd ed.). Mises Institute.
Shinar, C. (2016). *Vladimir Putin's aspiration to restore the lost Russian empire* (November 15, 2016). Available at SSRN. Accessed July 17, 2025, from https://ssrn.com/abstract=2869863 or https://doi.org/10.2139/ssrn.2869863
Williamson, J. (2000). What Washington means by policy reform. In Frieden et al. (Eds.), *Modern political economy and Latin America*. Routledge.

CHAPTER 2

The Nation State as the Basis of the Contemporary International Order: Ethically Questionable and Economically Obsolete

Abstract The nation state with its proclaimed sovereignty (absolute right to self-determination) is the key pillar both *de jure* and de facto of the contemporary international order built around the UN and international law. This chapter reflects critically on the foundations of such a claim showing first of all that nations are in effect what international law accepts as a nation (already a circular argument) and that the territorial boundaries as recognised in international law are ultimately the resultants of past military conquests, of "might is right". This is in effect no more than the law of the gangland urban jungle and hardly constitutes a morally convincing basis for nation states and their proclaimed sovereignty. But if the moral basis of national sovereignty is dubious, in economic terms in an intricately interdependent world economy where sovereign nation states nonetheless retain control of economic policy-making and regulation, the nation state has become largely irrelevant if not entirely obsolete. In our era of free trade, freedom of movement of factors of production, globalised financial markets and interdependence of all markets in globalised supply chains, many if not most of the major economic policy challenges that governments face require a coordinated supranational response reaching far beyond the competences of most of the world's nation states. Because of its moral bankruptcy and economic obsolescence, the world needs to move beyond a geopolitical order built around sovereign nation states.

P. O'Sullivan et al., *Overcoming Gangsterism and Geo-Political Anarchy*, https://doi.org/10.1007/978-3-032-22438-5_2

Keywords Nation state • National sovereignty • Might is right • Transnational economic policy challenges • Obsolescence of nation states • International Court of Justice (ICJ) • Enforcement (of international law)

We begin from an outline of the nature and structure of the contemporary international order in the course of which we shall also subject it to a critical philosophical appraisal of its foundations. The international geopolitical order as we know it today is built on the nation state and its sovereignty, and this is the first premise and starting point of what is called international law. When an entity claims sovereignty, this means an absolute right to self-determination, a complete freedom to make and to enforce its own laws as it sees best fit; or put slightly more bluntly, a sovereign entity recognises no law higher than those it makes for itself. One may now reasonably ask what about the United Nations and international law; and has not the UN got its own court in Den Haag in Netherlands: the International Court of Justice? The UN has indeed a Charter which includes a Declaration of Human Rights and even a prohibition of the use of military force by member states against each other except in self-defence. But the Charter also recognises the sovereignty of the member states and that no state should seek to make any interference in the "internal" affairs of any other member states.[1] This set-up is to say the least ambiguous and is unfortunately ineffective when it really matters.

The UN Charter and Declaration of Rights undoubtedly set out great ideals for all nations to respect and implement, and every member state has signed up to these ideals. The problem is their **enforcement**. As long as it suits self-determining sovereign nation states to obey the Charter, there is no difficulty: but what happens when a member state clearly and wilfully violates the UN Charter? Well there is the International Court of Justice (ICJ) in Den Haag which can pass judgements on such matters,

[1] This principle of non-interference is also known as the Westphalian principle, so-called after the Peace of Westphalia (1648) that brought an end to the Thirty Years War and the Eighty Years War in Europe of the time and sought to establish the principle of non-interference in the affairs of sovereign states by others. The aforementioned wars had been prolonged precisely because of persistent attempts at such interference.

but it has no power whatever of enforcement. Indeed normally before a case can even be heard before the court, the sovereign nation states concerned must have a priori agreed to the jurisdiction of the court; and even then they may simply decide to ignore judgements against them. The Russian invasion of Ukraine was judged by the ICJ to be illegal under international law on 16 March 2022,[2] but the Russians have not paid the slightest attention to this. In theory by the UN Charter, the Security Council could also be invited to review the legitimacy of the use of military force and could even apply sanctions for such cases, but the well-known veto power of the five permanent members (USA, UK, France, Russia and China) almost invariably means that this sanctioning power remains a dead letter, especially in the most diplomatically sensitive cases (and in particular in the case of Russia in 2022; any action of condemnation of the Russian invasion was blocked by…the Russian veto power on the Security Council).[3] At least for the great English jurist Austin for whom law is a system of commands emitted by a sovereign and backed by threats,[4] international law and the ICJ in particular as currently set up cannot be considered properly speaking to be law at all.

To the extent that there is a growing awareness of the limitations of international law and the jurisdiction of the ICJ in recent times, we also hear much talk of a "rules-based" international order presumably as some sort of fallback when the ICJ is ineffective in enforcement. But the definition of this order and how if at all it differs from or goes beyond international law is not at all clear. Generally speaking, it is presumed that international law as emanating from the UN Charter and various international treaties is part of this rules-based order, but it is also held to encompass various other types of agreement seeking to regulate and "order" the relationships and interactions among sovereign nation states. For example, the United Nations Association of Australia adopts the following definition "*this means a shared commitment by all countries to conduct their activities in accordance with agreed rules that evolve over time, such as international law, regional security arrangements, trade agreements,*

[2] See International Court of Justice *Order of 16 March 2022* available at https://www.icj-cij.org/node/106135. Accessed 6 September 2025.

[3] There have of course been sanctions, but they are not universal and backed by UN authority. They are entirely an initiative of the EU states and certain others (USA, Canada, UK, Switzerland, etc.).

[4] Austin J L (1832) *The Province of Jurisprudence Determined*, John Murray, London. See pp. vii–x.

immigration protocols, and cultural arrangements" (UNAA, 2017: 1). But quite what exactly the rules-based order is, what is its extent, who exactly makes/recognises/codifies the rules and how if at all it can be enforced in the event of disputes remain ill defined. Interestingly, China as much as the major Western states explicitly supports such an order (Vylegzhanin A et al. 2021). The perplexity is also clearly present in the declaration by Stefan Talmon of the German Practice in International Law Institute at University of Bonn that "*Germany is a champion of the so-called 'rules-based order'... Germany has not defined what it means by a 'rules-based order' and has not explained whether and, if so, to what extent it differs from the traditional 'international legal order' or, in short, 'international law'. A rules-based order may generally be understood as a shared commitment by States to conduct their activities in accordance with an existing set of rules. The rules-based order is underpinned by a system of global governance that has developed since the Second World War. The United Nations is considered to be at the heart of this rules-based order*".[5]

Pressing our philosophical critique of the contemporary geopolitical order somewhat further, one may ask in all of this set-up how we are to recognise what is a sovereign state to which self-determination of its laws is to be assigned; and what is the moral or political philosophical basis for such assignment? How do we recognise a nation in the first place? Is it by race (racial homogeneity)? Surely not because there are many completely coherent nation states which are multi-racial in the world today: all of the European nation states, for example, are a racial hodgepodge that stretches back over centuries of migration and interaction. Can it be language? Again surely not because there are plenty of examples of multi-lingual nations (Canada, Switzerland...). Can it be culture? Apart from the fact that culture is an ill-defined swamp, there are clearly examples of multi-cultural nation states that seem to function reasonably well (Germany, Britain). And of course it is manifestly not geography as a cursory glance at the political map of Europe or of South-East Asia (to take just two examples) will readily testify. In fact, the best that can be said is that nation states are whatever international law at any time recognises as nation states, a formulation which is blatantly inadequate for the vicious circularity of its

[5] Talmon S (2019) Rules-based Order v. International Law at *German Practice in International law* blog, GPIL University of Bonn available at https://gpil.jura.uni-bonn.de/2019/01/rules-based-order-v-international-law/. Accessed 9 September 2025.

definition. Worse, what international law recognises as states is almost invariably the resultant of borders that were drawn on maps after various past military conflicts: *might is right* and *winner takes all.* This last may appeal to *realpolitik* cynics, but it is certainly not a morally valid or even sustainable footing on which to define the most fundamental elements of international law. It implies that the moment a sovereign nation state decides that it wishes to redraw the borders then if this cannot be done by a negotiated agreement, the aggrandising nation will do so by military force if it thinks it can get away with it. And for all of the handwringing in the contemporary supposedly rules-based international order "*who shall say them nay*"?

However, it is true that the question of the legitimacy of war as a method of solving disputes among sovereign states has been much debated over the past 100 years with major efforts having been made actually to outlaw war, to make war in some sense and in certain scenarios at least illegal. The first such attempt was the Paris Peace Pact of 1928 (Briand-Kellogg pact) set up at the instigation of France and the US: the signatories of the pact for the first time in human history in effect declared wars to be illegal; that they were not a legally acceptable way of solving disputes among sovereign states.[6] Even Germany and Japan had signed the pact, but that of course did not prevent the outbreak of the Second World War. As that brutal war with its massive destruction and loss of human life drew to a close, the construction of the United Nations with its Charter made very specific commitments on the unacceptability of wars within the framework of international law. Echoing the Peace Pact, the Charter of the UN (binding on all members) stipulates clearly at article 4 that "*all members shall refrain in their international relations from the threat or use of force against the territorial integrity or political independence of any state, or in any other manner inconsistent with the purposes of the United Nations*".[7] Only a very small number of exceptions are allowed: war may be waged in self-defence against an armed aggressor; or if the Security Council unanimously approves use of military force to keep the peace.

[6] For the original text, see Avalon Project *Kellogg Briand Pact*, Yale University Law School Archive available at https://avalon.law.yale.edu/20th_century/kbpact.asp. Accessed 9 September 2025.

[7] United Nations Charter Full Text available at https://www.un.org/en/about-us/un-charter/full-text. Accessed 9 September 2025. See article 2.4.

The trouble with these fine sounding initiatives can be expressed in one simple word as noted earlier: **enforcement**. When there are breaches of the UN Charter who or what institutions are to bring the breakers of international law into line? The International Court of Justice as already mentioned has no power of enforcement; and while the Security Council has some theoretical power of punishment by economic sanctions, these are rarely used because of the vetoes that the "great" powers have on that Council. Also unless said sanctions are swingeing and upheld to the letter by a wide range of states against a violator, their deterrence potential is limited as violators circumvent the sanctions in various ways. Moreover, as the years have passed, a variety of states have flagrantly broken the Charter's prohibition of war as a way of resolving disputes, and in some cases, the states in question have been among those who actively instituted the UN and its Charter for promotion of peace and outlawing of war. The examples have multiplied as the years have passed: Turkey's annexation of a part of Cyprus, Israel's annexation of parts of Palestine, NATO's entry to the war in Kosovo in 1999, US and UK invasion of Iraq in 2003, Russian annexation of Crimea from Ukraine in 2014. These sorties have no doubt been given various sorts of justification (pre-emptive strike in self-defence, humanitarian grounds to avoid genocide, will of the people, etc.), but in the absence of Security Council approval, they remain illegal under the UN Charter. Unfortunately, far too many sovereign nation states still in practice remain ready and willing to use war as a way of settling their various disputes, and might remains right when defining all too many territorial borders.

The above arguments have focussed on the moral and political legitimacy of the nation states as the basic sovereign entities at the basis of the international order. But it can also be argued that the nation state is not only morally dubious, it is to a significant extent obsolete as an economic entity in terms of its ability to be effective in implementation of many aspects of economic policy.

It is a truism to note that today the world economy constitutes a single highly interdependent system with vast flows of trade in goods and services, huge international flows of funds among the world's financial markets and large-scale migratory flows motivated by the search for better economic opportunities. Some of the latter are of course problematic and illegal, but there are also major flows of economic migration between nation states today that are entirely legal and accepted (e.g. the freedom of movement of labour within the EU). Moreover, there is large-scale tourism, and in the internet age, people from anywhere in the world can not only instantly be in contact; they may engage in trading with each other. We are not the first to note that economic globalisation is very much a pervasive and largely irreversible reality even if in certain respects it may be crying out for a greater degree of regulation.[8] In the context of such an intense degree of interdependence, the nation states can be seen as an economic anachronism; economically speaking, they rarely represent any kind of useful unit of economic decision-making. The reason is simple: in such a highly interdependent world economy, many of the challenges of economic policy reach well beyond national frontiers, and so for economic policy efforts to meet these challenges, they must be collaborative and international in character to have any hope of being effective.[9] The most obvious of these policy challenges are those to do with greenhouse gas emissions/climate change where one nation state acting independently can have only a very limited effect unless almost all of the other states of the world are acting in a similar manner. A nation state cannot hope to be able to reduce global warming, for example, within its own frontiers by its own policies acting on its own. That point can be made for a variety of other policy areas where there is manifest economic interdependence. Given the level of interdependence of the world's financial markets, the same can be said of policies designed to promote financial stability. Where certain naturally occurring resources are scarce (and often localised as with oil wells, rare earth mines, etc.) and where these same resources are drawn upon by the whole of humanity, economic policies regarding exploitation and stewardship of such resources again need to be international in character to be effective. For example, in relation to preservation of fish stocks, if one nation state decides out of a concern for good stewardship of said stocks that it will limit its fishing of certain species on the high seas (i.e. outside its own protected waters), this policy is pointless unless all other countries fishing in the same high seas also restrain their activities in a

[8] Without wishing to take any ideological stance specifying the type or extent of regulation, we can say that the areas of migratory flows, of (international) financial market stability and environmental pollution demand at least a debate on regulatory questions amid a galloping and irreversible globalisation.

[9] For an excellent discussion of this, see Montani G (2019) *Supranational Political Economy: the Globalisation of the State-Market Relationship*, Routledge, London. See Chaps. 1 and 3 especially.

similar way.[10] It can be seen therefore that over a wide and indeed widening range of economic policy challenges, the nation state is largely powerless if it seeks to act entirely on its own as a locus of policy-making. Its sovereignty is in effect neutered over large areas of economic policy-making that have a huge impact on people's lives. This compromise of supposed economic sovereignty may also come into play when countries with large or increasing public sector debt burdens sell significant amounts of that debt to bondholder investors in other sovereign states if for whatever reason the foreign holders of the debt lose confidence and refuse to roll over the debts at maturity.[11] Worse still where nation states in pursuit of their sovereignty make economic policies that are at variance with or even contradict those of other states, they may be contributing to economic instability for many others. The manner in which the US Federal Reserve under Alan Greenspan maintained a strongly laisser-faire approach to financial regulation of banking and mortgage lending in the USA between 2000 and 2006 contributed directly to the sub-prime mortgage crisis starting in 2007 and eventually from that to the financial crash of 2008, the effects of which spread out over much of the world generating a major economic downturn even in countries who had never deregulated their mortgage markets…and which none of the countries wanted. Our point here is not that financial crashes would never happen if we had supranational financial regulation; rather the point is that where each state pursues its own economic policies independently of others, it may generate in an interdependent world economy damaging effects on other state's economies which were certainly not wished by these others; and worse still, the policies of different states may contradict and frustrate each other. If, for example, Donald Trump's trade policies are intended to create or restore jobs in the USA, when pursuing this goal by reducing imports, this in effect means destroying jobs and employment in those countries which exported on a large scale to the USA (China, Vietnam, Thailand, EU…). Hence, we would conclude that the nation state as an economic policy-making unit is not only powerless over many of the most important policy areas where international economic interdependence is inevitable, in some

[10] Indeed to the extent that fish do not recognise national boundaries of exclusive economic zones even restraint within protected waters of nation states may have little point unless other nations are exercising similar restraint.

[11] On the topic of government debt rollovers and explosion of debt burdens, see O'Sullivan P & Ricci P (2025) *The Political Economy of Debt Financing*, Routledge, London: Ch 7.

cases the independent economic policy action of a nation state may be positively damaging for other states. In short, the nation state as an economic policy-making unit is largely obsolete.

While it may be true that economic globalisation from the late 1980s onwards was seen by certain commentators as the prelude to the emergence of some kind of parallel globalised democratically inspired political order in which military confrontations and conflicts of all kinds would fade away under the weight of ever-increasing economic interdependence through globalised supply chains,[12] this manifestly has not happened.[13] Nation states remain firmly in place as cornerstones of international law and the geopolitical order, and they jealously guard their sovereignty however theoretical it may be, and this has been reinforced by populisms both of left and right varieties.[14] As a result apart from the exceptional case of the EU for its 27 member states, there is no overarching economic regulatory authority to oversee the workings of the world economy; and as noted above, while the nation states may have in principle sovereignty to regulate economic affairs/policies, the exercise of this remains problematic and vacuous in the face of the global scale challenges thrown up by the interdependencies of economic globalisation. The result has been that economic globalisation, far from being accompanied by a parallel political globalisation, has rather been accompanied by political anarchy in relation to matters requiring global economic policies and exacerbated by often stridently nationalist populisms.

The policy anarchy has been clearly and often explicitly underpinned and encouraged by the philosophies of market fundamentalism with its advocacy of wholesale de-regulation of all aspects of the economy. Indeed, one can even detect the influence of the minarchism and anarcho-capitalism of Ayn Rand[15] and others which has reached its apogee in the wholesale destruction of state regulation epitomised by the Trump–Musk shadow

[12] This thesis was nurtured by such works (among others) as Fukuyama F (1992) *The End of History and the Last Man* Free Press, Glencoe.

[13] On the realities of globalisation as opposed to the political hype, see Guttal S (2007) Globalisation, *Development in Practice* 17(4–5): 523–531.

[14] On the role of populisms in this, see Rodrik D (2017) Economics of the Populist Backlash in Vox EU CEPR, 03 July 2017 available at https://cepr.org/voxeu/columns/economics-populist-backlash. Accessed 20 August 2025.

[15] Rand A (1967) *Capitalism: the Unknown Ideal* Signet Books, New York: intriguingly given what has been noted above about Alan Greenspan's role in the lead-up to the 2008 crash, Rand's book includes an essay by…Alan Greenspan.

Department of Government Efficiency (DOGE) in the USA and the progressive withdrawal of the same USA from a whole array of intergovernmental institutions such as WHO and UNESCO (from end of 2026) which have tried, however ineffectually, at least to promote a collaborative approach to common global socio-economic policy challenges.[16] Massimo de Carolis in his work *Convenzioni e Governo del Mondo* (DeCarolis, 2023)[17] makes a similar point convincingly noting how over the past 100 years many of the implicit everyday rules and ethical conventions that governed people's behaviour in the global marketplace have seriously broken down giving way to what one may aptly dub a Wild West style global economy.[18]

The conclusion of this chapter is therefore that the nation state as a foundation stone for the world geopolitical order has no moral or political legitimacy being nothing more than the expression of brute force (might is right), and entities such as the UN have not been able to counter this; while in economic terms, the nation state is effectively obsolete over large areas of economic policy-making and in some cases actually destabilising. Globalisation far from being accompanied by any commensurate advance in world governance evolved in an unregulated anarchic manner in a war of competing nationalist populisms. Arguments such as these have led certain theorists to conclude that the notion of national sovereignty for all its centrality in international relations and international law is little more than "*organised hypocrisy*" (Krasner, 1999).[19] In the next chapter, we will see what we may be able to do to pass beyond the nation state to put in place a more civilised, and we would argue more rationally founded geopolitical order.

[16] See, for example, (in relation to WHO) US White House Executive Order *Withdrawing US from the World Health Organisation*, 20 January 2025 available at https://www.whitehouse.gov/presidential-actions/2025/01/withdrawing-the-united-states-from-the-world-health-organization/. Accessed 20 August 2025.

[17] DeCarolis M (2023) *Convenzioni e Governo del Mondo*, Quodlibet Macerata.

[18] Not for nothing has the term "cowboy capitalism" been coined.

[19] See Krasner S (1999) "*Sovereignty: Organised Hypocrisy*", Princeton University Press, Princeton. See Chaps. 1 and 8.

Bibliography

Austin, J. L. (1832). *The province of jurisprudence determined.* John Murray.

Avalon Project. *Kellogg Briand Pact*, Yale University Law School Archive. Accessed September 9, 2025., from https://avalon.law.yale.edu/20th_century/kbpact.asp

DeCarolis, M. (2023). *Convenzioni e Governo del Mondo.* Quodlibet.

Fukuyama, F. (1992). *The end of history and the last man.* Free Press.

Guttal, S. (2007). Globalisation. *Development in Practice, 17*(4–5), 523–531.

International Court of Justice. *Order of 16 March* 2022. Accessed September 6, 2025., from https://www.icj-cij.org/node/106135

Krasner, S. (1999). *Sovereignty: Organised hypocrisy.* Princeton University Press.

Montani, G. (2019). *Supranational political economy: The globalisation of the state-market relationship.* Routledge.

O'Sullivan, P., & Ricci, P. (2025). *The political economy of debt financing.* Routledge.

Rand, A. (1967). *Capitalism: The unknown ideal.* Signet Books.

Rodrik, D. (2017). Economics of the Populist Backlash. *Vox EU CEPR*, 03 July 2017. Accessed August 20, 2025, from https://cepr.org/voxeu/columns/economics-populist-backlash

Talmon, S. (2019). Rules-based order v. international law. *German Practice in International law* blog, GPIL University of Bonn. Accessed September 9, 2025, from https://gpil.jura.uni-bonn.de/2019/01/rules-based-order-v-international-law/

United Nations Association Australia UNAA. (2017). *The UN and the International Rules Based Order.* Accessed April 25, 2026, from https://www.unaa.org.au/2017/03/21/unaa-argues-for-rules-based-international-order-in-paper/

United Nations Charter Full Text. Accessed September 9, 2025., from https://www.un.org/en/about-us/un-charter/full-text (See article 2.4).

US White House Executive Order. *Withdrawing US from the World Health Organisation*, 20 January 2025. Accessed August 20, 2025, from https://www.whitehouse.gov/presidential-actions/2025/01/withdrawing-the-united-states-from-the-worldhealth-organization/

Vylegzhanin A et al. (2021). The Term Rulse-based Order in International Legal Discourse. *Moscow Journal of International Law, 2*, 35–60.

CHAPTER 3

The Hobbesian Argument and the Supranational Alternative

Abstract In making the case to pass beyond the contemporary geopolitical order based on sovereign nation states to some form of overarching supranational World Authority with enforcement powers, we can draw inspiration from the political philosophy of Hobbes *Leviathan*. Therein, Hobbes argued that people in an anarchic state of nature which in the absence of restraints would descend into a war of all against all and people would be led rationally to surrender all of their natural rights to a sovereign authority with real enforcement powers with a view to instituting a peaceful, law abiding and civilised community. We argue that the Hobbesian argument can be applied to the war of all against all that in effect characterises the geopolitical order today based as it is on absolute sovereignty of nation states and despite the efforts of international law. Hobbes never really defined the geographical extent of his supreme sovereign charged with keeping the peace: but in the context of the cotemporary world with its heightened interdependence and manifold shared policy challenges, we argue that today the Hobbesian *Leviathan* needs to be conceived as a World Authority. Following Kant, we argue moreover that the world sovereign does not need to be a full-blown centralised world state but rather some kind of supranational authority with enforcement powers over precisely defined supranational competences. These competences would most basically include binding and enforceable dispute settlement powers but could also include a variety of policy

P. O'Sullivan et al., *Overcoming Gangsterism and Geo-Political Anarchy*, https://doi.org/10.1007/978-3-032-22438-5_3

competences designed to deal with suitable regulation of certain aspects of the globalised world economy and the shared policy challenges which it throws up, for example, in respect of environmental sustainability and of international financial stability.

Keywords Hobbes Leviathan • Geographical extent of Hobbes sovereign state • War of all against all (among nation states) • World sovereign authority • Enforcement power • Kant's essay on perpetual peace

As a prelude to the effort to sketch the outlines of a geopolitical order that would pass beyond the severe moral, political and economic limitations of the contemporary order based on sovereign nation states, we will first of all take a look at a centuries old political philosophy which can offer us powerful insights in the matter: that of the great English political philosopher Thomas Hobbes.

We start from a fundamental insight which is not in itself particularly original regarding the contemporary international order: in the end and despite the efforts of the UN, the contemporary order is little more than a "war of all against all" such as Hobbes described in his seminal work *Leviathan* (1651) as being typical of a pre-political "state of nature", a hypothetical state of total anarchy in society before any government of any kind is formed. Hobbes argument was cast in terms of individual persons (or gangs of individuals) living in a pre-political anarchic society with no government of any kind as yet in existence, and he argued that in such a society human interactions would degenerate into a war of all against all which would render the lives of people "*solitary, poor, nasty, brutish and short*"[1] (sometimes summarised in Latin as *homo homini lupus*). Hobbes

[1] Hobbes T (1651) *Leviathan* reprinted with an introduction by Plamenatz J (1969) 4th edition, Fontana London: p. 143. We may note *en passant* that many critics of Hobbes have held that his view of human beings in a state of nature is far too pessimistic: he portrays human beings as ruthlessly self-seeking individualists apparently incapable of any sense of compassion and/or solidarity. There is indeed some merit in this criticism, but we must point out that unfortunately Hobbes vision is true for at least significant segments of the population and that alone is good enough reason for his line of argument. For as long as there are some ruthlessly greedy individualists in a state of nature, they will indeed prey on others, and the more decent compassionate people will find themselves dragged into a war of all against

went on to argue that in virtue however of our rationality, our power to reflect and reason critically, people living in such an anarchic state of nature would be led by reasoning in relation to their situation and their interdependence to surrender all of their inherent natural rights and freedoms such as prevail in a total anarchy to a "sovereign" (the very word used by Hobbes); and in turn, the sovereign would be expected to initiate at the very least a system of defence and policing for the state so formed and a system of courts to resolve disputes backed by the power of the state to enforce the resulting verdicts and punishments. Indeed for Hobbes (foreshadowing in a way Austin),[2] if the "sovereign" cannot enforce the resolution of disputes, people would take the law into their own hands, and we would soon be back in the war of all against all. Hobbes saw these arrangements as constituting a hypothetical social contract between individual citizens and the state/sovereign; and where a sovereign government fails to protect its citizens against the war of all against all, the social contract becomes void and the sovereign in question loses its political legitimacy for Hobbes. It is for this reason that power of enforcement is fundamental; and where a sovereign state cannot enforce peaceful resolutions, it loses its legitimacy.

Intriguingly, Hobbes did not at any point discuss the geographical extent of this sovereignty; and no doubt in the context of his times with a raging civil war in England, he was arguing for an English sovereign state to put an end to the wars in England. The most he says on this question is the uncharacteristically vague (for Hobbes) statement that "*the multitude* [extent of the sovereign state] *sufficient to confide in for our security is not determined by any certain number but by comparison with the enemy we fear*".[3] Hence, it will be clear that the Hobbesian logic is intended to be applied over any geographic area and any arena of human existence where there is a real threat of a war of all against all. Today after the experience

all if only to defend themselves. Indeed, the impulse and initiative to form a strong government will emanate precisely from those decent segments of the population who wish to protect themselves. The gangsters for their part will merrily continue their lawless depredations until a stronger authority is put in place to maintain a peaceful civilised order. If we were all selflessly loving beings, we would not need a Hobbesian sovereign; but Hobbes prefers to start from a realistic recognition of a lowest common denominator segment in the population.

[2] Austin J L (1832) *The Province of Jurisprudence Determined*, John Murray, London.

[3] Hobbes (1651) op. cit. p. 174.

of two world wars and a possibly imminent third such war, and with an increasingly anarchic disruption of international commerce and of globalised supply chains as a result of Trump's tariffs and indeed outright trade wars, the geographical extent of the sovereign could be argued to be the whole world: a world sovereign. It may also be noted that Hobbes did not take any definitive position on the extent of the policies that the state so formed might implement: debates about the ideal size of the state especially in relation to the economy were for later centuries.[4] However, it will be clear that the Hobbesian reasoning could be applied to any area of human affairs where people's actions are interdependent and where action in relation to a desired outcome presupposes collaboration (e.g. climate change policy). It is also intriguing to note that Hobbes did not say anything about the institutional structure of this "sovereign": would it be a monarch or an Assembly/Parliament or whatever? He would accept whatever was most effective to maintain a peaceful, harmonious law-abiding state.[5]

What is now interesting is to see how the Hobbesian argument can be applied to the kind of anarchic war of all against all that we observe in the international order today in the absence of any effective overarching sovereign authority above the nation states. Nation states which claim an absolute right to self-determination by analogy with notions of individual personal liberty should surely on a rational reflection recognise that the anarchic situation which prevails in the contemporary international order is mutually damaging and leads only to insecurity for all. Of course, it will be retorted there is such a recognition, and it is embodied in the UN Charter with its outlawing of the use of military force or violence to settle

[4] Already in Locke's version of the social contract that appeared some 40 years after Hobbes work, the state is considered primarily as a vehicle for the protection of private property rights. As he bluntly summarises, "The chief purpose of men's uniting into commonwealths and putting themselves under governments is the preservation of their property" (Locke J 1988 *Two Treatises of Government*, Cambridge University Press, Cambridge; Second Treatise chapter 9 paragraph 124). Wider debates about the appropriate role of the state in relation to economic policy especially began in earnest with Adam Smith, notably in his seminal work Smith A (1776) *An Enquiry into the Nature and Causes of The Wealth of Nations*, Strahan & Cadell London.

[5] It is in this formalism of Hobbes argument for enforcement of order by a sovereign whose format is not prescribed in detail that the similarity with Han Feizi's thought is most evident. See Han Feizi (2003) *Han Feizi basic writings* translated by Burton Watson Columbia University Press, New York. available at https://terebess.hu/zen/mesterek/Han-Feizi.pdf. Accessed 9 September 2025.

interstate disputes. Yes indeed: but the UN and its court, the ICJ, being intergovernmental in their constitution,[6] lack the power of enforcement, a power which for Hobbes is indispensable and essential to the sovereign for effective keeping of the peace and avoidance of the war of all against all. The same can be said of the WTO since it too is ultimately intergovernmental in character; and although it has a dispute resolution body for its members, it has been rendered inoperative by US refusal to appoint judges to that body.[7]

Speaking of trade policy, we may recall that in Chap. 2 we have explained how alongside the effective war of all against all that prevails in respect of actual and potential military conflicts among nation states, there has developed an equally anarchic situation in terms of a regulatory framework for economic globalisation; one could even speak of the globalised un- or de-regulated world economy as being in effect an anarcho-capitalism.[8] But this anarcho-capitalist war of all against all is crying out as much as are ongoing geopolitical conflicts for a World Authority capable of bringing order and perhaps above all fairness to the inevitable processes of economic globalisation. Globalisation has unleashed huge increases in prosperity under the logic of comparative cost advantage. In order to ensure that those benefits are shared equitably by all, we need a corresponding state power in the form of a supranational World Authority to implement suitable economic regulation at world level in response to anarchic excesses and to shared world-level challenges as well as to ensure a fair (re)distribution of the gains from trade. The World Authority that we have envisaged for the purposes of generating most basically world peace could also be a powerful actor for meeting other world-level policy challenges associated with economic globalisation such as climate change, financial stability and equitable trade policy.[9]

[6]The precise meaning of an intergovernmental structure is discussed below at p. xx.

[7]For an incisive explanation on this, see Bown C & Keynes S (2020) Why did Trump end the WTO appellate Body? Available at *Peterson Institute of international Economics* website https://www.piie.com/blogs/trade-and-investment-policy-watch/2020/why-did-trump-end-wtos-appellate-body-tariffs. Accessed 21 August 2025.

[8]The term is particularly associated with the thinking of Ayn Rand. See Rand A (1967) *Capitalism: the Unknown Ideal* Signet Books, New York.

[9]This would follow closely the suggestions made by Montani in his work Montani G (2019) *Supranational Political Economy: the Globalisation of the State-Market Relationship*, Routledge, London. See Chap. 3, especially the conclusions at pp. 77–78.

Of course, we recognise that there are centrifugal forces at work in today's world which in response to the extensive globalisation of the economy and of supply chains would advocate a very different if not polar opposite set of responses. Various forms of identitarian populism however chaotic and confused (coming in both extreme left and extreme right varieties) are an expression of this. There is also the siren call of localism, proximity economics and job protectionism which have a powerful appeal, not just in Trump's USA.[10] Teamed up with aggressively identitarian politics, these latter have become a staple of the appeal of right wing populism in Europe and in many parts of Asia as well. Yet, none of these populists want to stop trading completely with the rest of the world (that would be rather inconvenient especially in the case of smaller states) nor do they want to initiate complete bans on inward and outward flows of funds or of people. Illegal immigrants they do not want for sure but they are keen to have "productive" immigrants, ideally who share their values, and of course, they want to be able to travel wherever they wish for tourism purposes. In short, the localists and protectionists do not actually want to stop all interaction with the rest of the world. Like it or not, they want to live lives of interaction with other people trading, travelling, exchanging… The challenge is not how best societies can close in on themselves and protect their identity and culture in an autarchic isolationist manner but rather how one can learn to live in a peaceful respectful co-existence with other peoples and other societies. In this process, "identities" will almost certainly evolve, and it is one of the cardinal errors of identitarian political advocates to assume that cultural identity and values are fixed constants.[11] A casual glance around Europe and South-East Asia will quickly illustrate how cultures and values have evolved through time in a process of fruitful cross-pollenisation as people of different backgrounds and religions and from different parts of the world met and interacted.

It would therefore be a mistake to interpret our above endorsement of economic globalisation as somehow an attack on identity and values. Rather what we have been arguing is that economic globalisation is inevitable, and there will be no going back to an isolationist world as we have now tasted (in some cases almost literally) the exotic forbidden fruits of

[10] See, for example, Foroohar R (2022), *Homecoming: The Path to Prosperity in a Post-Global World*, Crown New York.

[11] On this theme, see Segre G (2024), *La cultura della convivenza*, Bollati Boringhieri, Torino.

said globalisation. But what we are emphasising is that the manner in which economic globalisation has proceeded from the 1990s onwards has been accompanied by a progressive and insidious process of (nation) state capture by powerful business interests and a resultant wholesale deregulation of extensive areas of economic interaction inspired by an anarcho-capitalist market fundamentalism. Hence, what we now need is not any kind of a retreat into protectionist isolationism but rather, recognising the inevitability of economic globalisation, to match it with a political globalisation in the form of a supranational World Sovereign or World Authority of some kind which would have the power effectively to define a suitable and equitable framework of economic regulations for the world economy taken as a whole...and which would of course need to be proof against state capture at world level.[12] And we believe that when such a geopolitical order is instituted by means of peaceful rational persuasion as opposed to any kind of military force, cultural identities will themselves evolve through interaction towards mutual respect and peaceful co-existence.

Hence, the Hobbesian argument for a world sovereign constitutes a rationally based collaborative response not only to the potential and actual war of all against all that prevails in respect of armed conflicts in a world of sovereign nation states, it is equally applicable to the often mutually frustrating economic policy anarchy that has accompanied economic globalisation. While we have been critical of the various intergovernmental UN institutions as set up after the Second World War, it might be argued with some justification that they were introduced into a world considerably less interconnected and interdependent than that of today, and it is true that there are policy challenges at world level today that simply did not exist and were not foreseen back in 1945. In addition to the dramatic forces of globalisation in trade, finance and supply chains there are also the challenges associated with environmental sustainability and climate change; and while there may be some tendencies of pushback on trade and supply chain interdependence or denial in relation to climate change, these challenges will not evaporate. All of these new and increasingly complex interdependencies together with the controversies that have surrounded them only further strengthen the case for a Hobbesian sovereign at a supranational level.

[12] We will return to this point in Chap. 8 dealing with the possible corruption of a supranational World Authority.

While the analogy between the Hobbesian argument and the attempted outlawing of warring among nation states of the UN might be recognised by some politicians, political and (international) legal theorists even if Hobbes is not mentioned by name, what is certain is that the full Hobbesian implications regarding the indispensability of strong enforcement powers for the overarching sovereign charged with maintaining peace and security is almost entirely overlooked (as is all too clearly illustrated by the case of the UN). In effect, the full set of conclusions that Hobbes drew from his insights in the *Leviathan* are not being applied in the realm of international relations and international law. Partly, this can be explained by Hobbes effective silence on the geographical extent of the sovereign state as already noted, and partly, it was because Hobbes clearly spoke of an absolute and indivisible sovereignty for the effectively national state authority set up by the (hypothetical) social contract.[13] If the sovereign power as thus set up by Hobbes basic social contract among individuals in a state of nature is to be absolute and indivisible, that would point to rejection of any kind of supranational authority above the nation states so constituted and so inevitably to the anarchic war of all against all among these sovereign (nation) states and many followers of Hobbes seemed to accept such conclusions.[14] *But Hobbes argument for an all-powerful sovereign could also imply all of the world's peoples collectively recognising their interdependence and setting up a world sovereign, a world state!*

Of course, there are also no doubt practical political reasons for the failure to draw out the logical conclusions of the Hobbesian argument in international relations and international law. Enforcement is a highly sensitive matter for national politicians being central to the power they can exercise over the affairs and citizens of their sovereign states, and it is therefore jealously guarded, especially the power of taxation. Nonetheless, the failure to draw the logical conclusion of a supranational authority to

[13] It may be remarked that in Kant's incisive essay *Perpetual Peace: A Philosophical Sketch*, he did not envisage an all-powerful world sovereign entity but rather some sort of federal state or confederation. But it is debatable how much practical influence Kant's ideas have had, for example, in the formation of the UN. See Kant I (1795) *Zum Ewigen Frieden*, Nicolovius, Königsberg. Available in English in Kant I (1991) *Political Writings* 2nd ed., translated by Nisbet H, Cambridge University Press, Cambridge.

[14] This is the interpretation offered by Eva Boka in her illuminating article Boka E (2012) The European Idea of a Supranational Union of Peace, in *Society and Economy* 34(3): 387–397.

put an effective end to the war of all against all in international relations is at once careless and tragic.

To understand more precisely this failure, we need to consider the different ways in which institutions for international collaboration may be constructed. This analysis will be elaborated in more detail in Chap. 5, but it is worth giving already an indication of what is involved. Most international collaboration as we know it today is undertaken on an intergovernmental basis. What this means is that the nation states involved do not surrender any of their sovereignty in the collaboration process. They collaborate only as long as it suits them; and as absolutely sovereign entities they can withdraw from the collaboration at any time. Most international treaties and pacts are set up on just such an intergovernmental basis (which explains why they are so regularly broken), and it is in practice the basis on which the UN and its various component agencies are organised. This can be contrasted with supranational forms of collaboration where the nation states agree to surrender defined areas of their sovereignty to an overarching institution charged with carrying out in an effective long-term manner the desired collaboration. In short in supranational collaboration, the central institutions constructed have powers of enforcement. Such surrender of sovereignty in turn when engaged without coercion is actually binding in international law. The strongest form of supranational collaboration would be a situation where the states decide to form a new federal state, but there can also be lesser degrees of supranational collaboration whereby states agree on a menu of policy areas over which they surrender their sovereignty to central institutions while retaining sovereignty in other areas.

In the context of the previous discussion of the failure to apply the Hobbesian conclusions in the contemporary geopolitical order, what we can say is that to ensure enforcement of peace and security the sovereign to which power should be transferred in order to put an end to the war of all against all must be supranational in character embodying at the very least the powers to resolve disputes among states through a legal process of negotiation and arbitration and to enforce the adjudicated solutions. Such a supranational entity could also of course act on other areas of policy where to be effective a collaborative response across the world's nation states is required. As noted previously in an increasingly interdependent world, there are other areas of policy, most notably of economic policy, which require a strongly collaborative approach if they are to be effective for the states pursuing them. Environmental policies regarding global warming and policies for promotion of financial stability and fair trade are the most obvious examples. Once a supranational entity is put in place following the Hobbesian logic to prevent the war of all against all, this same body complete with its enforcement powers could also be a powerful actor in any of these policy areas that require a supranational response in order to have any realistic chance of being effective.

It should be remarked that in the argument we have just put forward we have departed in one key respect from Hobbes original. Whereas Hobbes in dealing with the case of individuals living in total stateless anarchy argued for the transfer of individual rights to the sovereign to be total[15] in our application of the argument at the level of relations among nation states as opposed to individual persons, we have held that the transfer of policy competences (hence rights to self-determination) by states can be partial: only those policy competences that are necessary for keeping the peace and regulating the globalised economy need to be transferred to a supranational authority with enforcement powers. On that point, our argument is closer to Kant in his essay *Perpetual Peace: A Philosophical Sketch*: the Second Definitive Article as proposed therein suggests that the federal or confederal authority which is to keep the peace should not be an all-powerful world state.[16] Many if not most areas of policy competence which do not generate international conflicts of interest can be left with the nation states (or indeed at even lower regional levels within these). This is what is known as the Principle of Subsidiarity in the structuring of supranational organisations and as we shall later see it is epitomised by the organisation of the European Union's institutions (in particular since the Lisbon Treaty of 2009).[17]

There is therefore a strong normative argument drawing on political philosophy and political economy for the construction of a world-level supranational government to promote peace and security and to deal with other world-level policy challenges. Here, we have based ourselves on the Hobbesian argument because of its logical cogency and immediacy in the contemporary context of war once again in Europe (Russia's invasion of Ukraine), but we may acknowledge the work of other thinkers such as Ernst Haas who have made similar arguments for levels of governance

[15] The only exception for Hobbes might be the right to defend one's life, but even on that, it seems that the sovereign has the ultimate say; he would accept the death penalty.

[16] Kant (1795) op. cit.

[17] For a detailed exposition of supranationalism, subsidiarity and their role in the EU, see Boka E (2012) op. cit.

above and beyond the nation state invoking functional interdependence of policies as a driver of international cooperation.[18] But we find that while the literature that has been launched by functionalist, neo-functionalist and more recently constructivist analyses of international relations represents a welcome passage beyond realist and purely positivist theories focussing on territoriality and the crude exercise of national sovereignties, almost all of this literature skirts around the question of the enforcement powers to be assigned to international institutions. For the reasons we have cited from Hobbes work, we believe this question to be primordial to effective success of international cooperation especially in the longer term. This might lead some to say that we are ultimately realists or neo-realists since we emphasise keeping our feet firmly on the ground by insisting (following Hobbes and Austin) on enforcement powers. But where we differ decidedly from all realists is that we **cannot** accept the contemporary geopolitical order based as it is (in reality and indeed in most of the alternative approaches) on nations states as sovereign units. We have argued normatively for the imperative of passing beyond such an order based on (absolutely) sovereign nation states through a transfer of certain sovereign enforcement powers to a supranational authority.

An obvious question that now arises is regarding the practicality of such a normative project. This we believe breaks down into two separate questions: what would be the precise nature and *modus operandi* in practice of the supranational governing entity; and as a preamble, what is the nature of the current arrangements for maintenance of international peace and security and how defensible and effective are they? The reason that the latter question is important is partly because it is always useful to understand the *status quo* in detail when seeking to pass beyond it and partly because the current arrangements have not at all been effective in maintaining peace and security. Worse, echoing some of the themes of Chap. 2, we shall show that they are based on some philosophically dubious if not indefensible premises. We will deal with this preamble question in some detail because in that way while the proposal for a supranational government may appear idealistic to some, once we recognise in full detail the

[18] Ernst Haas has written on the theory of international cooperation over the past 50 years starting from his seminal work Haas E (2008) *Beyond the Nation State*, Rowman & Littlefield, London and Washington. See also on this theme Schmitter P (2003) Neo-neo-functionalism in Wiener A & Diez T eds. *European Integration Theory*, Oxford University Press, Oxford.

severe deficiencies (as we shall argue) of the contemporary geopolitical set-up, the imperative of the effort to pass beyond it will become much more compelling.

Bibliography

Austin, J. L. (1832). *The province of jurisprudence determined*. John Murray.
Boka, E. (2012). The European idea of a supranational Union of Peace. *Society and Economy, 34*(3), 387–397.
Bown, C., & Keynes, S. (2020). Why did Trump end the WTO appellate body? Available at *Peterson Institute of international Economics* website. Accessed August 21, 2025, from https://www.piie.com/blogs/trade-and-investment-policy-watch/2020/why-did-trump-end-wtos-appellate-body-tariffs
Foroohar, R. (2022). *Homecoming: The path to prosperity in a post-global world*. Crown.
Haas, E. (2008). *Beyond the nation state*. Rowman & Littlefield.
Han Feizi. (2003). *Han Feizi basic writings* (B. Watson, Trans.). Columbia University Press. Accessed September 9, 2025, from https://terebess.hu/zen/mesterek/Han-Feizi.pdf
Hobbes, T. (1651). *Leviathan* (reprinted with an introduction by Plamenatz J (1969) 4th edition, Fontana).
Kant. (1795a). op. cit.
Kant, I. (1795b). *Zum Ewigen Frieden*. Nicolovius, Königsberg. Available in English in Kant I (1991) *Political writings* (2nd ed., translated by Nisbet H). Cambridge University Press.
Locke, J. (1988). *Two treatises of government*. Cambridge University Press. Second Treatise.
Montani, G. (2019). *Supranational political economy: The globalisation of the state-market relationship*. Routledge.
Rand, A. (1967). *Capitalism: The unknown ideal*. Signet Books.
Schmitter, P. (2003). Neo-neo-functionalism. In A. Wiener & T. Diez (Eds.), *European integration theory*. Oxford University Press.
Segre, G. (2024). *La cultura della convivenza*. Bollati Boringhieri.
Smith, A. (1776). *An enquiry into the nature and causes of the wealth of nations*. Strahan & Cadell London.

CHAPTER 4

Balance of Powers: What Balance? Zones of Influence: Who Said So?

Abstract In this chapter as a prelude to outlining the details of a possible supranational World Authority, the theories which underlie the contemporary set-up of the geopolitical world order are examined critically. This philosophical critique expands on the basic criticisms of the nation state as morally dubious and economically obsolete by going into the detail of what influential realist International Relations theories have proposed regarding the organisation of a world order based on sovereign nation states. The two predominant theories in this field are those regarding balance of ("great") powers and zones of influence for the aforesaid "great" powers. It is shown that both theories are completely indefensible and even reprehensible in philosophical terms. Balance of powers theory has signally failed to bring peace to the world and is moreover based on a cynical premise of implacable hostility among nations and so among human beings, and this implacable hostility is even celebrated in tales of (violent) heroism and in educational curricula. Such a theory cannot recognise that while human beings are often evil and violent, they are also capable of love and peaceful cooperation. In the world of implacable hostility, the "great" powers claim a right to zones of influence so that they can feel secure, a claim very much on display in our own day. But zones of influence again assume irreducible implacable hostility among peoples, and they cannot but involve supremacist presumptions on the part of the self-appointed "great" powers in relation to smaller states.

P. O'Sullivan et al., *Overcoming Gangsterism and Geo-Political Anarchy*, https://doi.org/10.1007/978-3-032-22438-5_4

Keywords Contemporary (post-1945) world order • Theoretical justifications of international relations • Balance of powers • Zones of influence • Challengeable supremacist premises • Financing of wars

In the previous chapter, we noted that in dealing with the practicalities of our proposed setting up of a world-level supranational governing entity on the Hobbesian argument, it is important given its perhaps Utopian flavour to look first of all at the contemporary set-up with a view to establishing why it is so imperative to pass beyond it. Our task in this chapter will therefore be to outline in more detail the manner of functioning of the contemporary geopolitical order and in particular the political theories and philosophies which have underpinned it while subjecting these to a probing philosophical critique.

We have already referred to the institutional aspects of the contemporary geopolitical order when outlining the United Nations Charter and the framework of international law. Our conclusion on the operation of these was not at all favourable. Despite the lofty ambitions of the UN Charter seeking to outlaw the use of military force to settle international disputes, in practice, military force continues to be used by members of the UN against each other (and in some cases by supposedly reputable founding members of the UN as we saw). We emphasised that apart from the inconsistency and even hypocrisy of such actions, what is most glaringly absent from the UN set-up is precisely the power of enforcement of the Charter. Supposedly, there is the UN Security Council with a limited degree of enforcement powers but because of the veto powers of the permanent members and of the cynical manner in which they have used the veto in pursuit of their national interests and global ambitions, the Security Council has rarely been able to enforce anything of consequence by way of resolution of conflicts, in particular in some of the major cases where exercise of its theoretical enforcement powers would have been useful and beneficial to preservation of peace. More recently, there has as we have seen in Chap. 2 been a lot of talk about a supposed rules-based international order, but nobody is quite sure what that means nor of who exactly makes the rules let alone enforces them.[1]

[1] See Chap. 2, p. 20.

Lying behind the cynical behaviour of the permanent members of the Security Council are certain theories of international relations which were influential at the time of the set-up of the UN and continue to exercise a major influence: balance of powers theory and the notion of zones of influence for "great powers". Both of these theories feature prominently in what is known as International Relations theory, and they are regularly cited in the practice of international diplomacy. Balance of Powers featuring the USA and the Soviet Union was the *leitmotiv* of the Cold War era,[2] and the theory is being cited today by Russia and China in arguing for a multipolar world order. Zones of Influence (for "great" powers) have in our own day been explicitly cited by Russia as a reason for its invasion of Ukraine. Both theories are associated with a supposedly realistic approach to international relations and diplomacy often dubbed as "*realpolitik*". Realists whose approach can ultimately be traced back to the political thought of Nicolo Machiavelli[3] eschew grand moral principles for guidance of foreign policy preferring to base policy on a recognition of the national interests of sovereign nation states. They argue that international diplomacy must start from where we are in the real world with all of its rivalries, jealousies, inequalities and skewed power relations and work as best we can with that mess as opposed to dreaming about Utopian solutions that for realists will never be attained in practice due to human frailty and criminality.[4] The best we can hope for is somehow to balance off the "great" powers against each other so as to restrain their depredations; and to keep them (relatively) happy by according them a zone of influence or security buffer in their immediate geographical neighbourhoods supposedly to guarantee their security. We will now examine and develop a philosophical critique of each of these theories.

Taking the balance of powers theory, this is the idea that peace and security from warfare can be maintained by having a balance of military might at least between the biggest nation states; and that as long as that balance is maintained, none of the "great" powers will go to war against

[2] For a good account, see Snyder G (1960) Balance of Power in the Missile Age, *Journal of International Affairs* 14(1): 21–34.

[3] Machiavelli's most famous work is Machiavelli N (1532 & 2011) *The Prince*, Penguin Classics, London.

[4] For a good account of *Realpolitik* past and present, see Bew J (2016) *Realpolitik: a history*, Oxford University Press, Oxford.

each other for fear of the mutually destructive consequences.[5] As noted above, balance of powers theory was very clearly present in the Cold War era between 1946 and 1989 with the balance concerning the USA and its allies on the one hand and the Soviet Union and its allies on the other. (There were of course also many non-aligned and neutral countries in that era.) In the nineteenth and early twentieth centuries, this approach was epitomised by the search for balance among the "great" European (and often imperial) powers of the time: Britain, France, Germany, Austria-Hungary, Russia and the Ottoman Empire. Whereas the cold war was characterised by an arms race between the USA and Soviet Union whereby each maintained a similar level of military prowess (and stocks of nuclear weapons), in the nineteenth century, the balance was more often adjusted by shifting patterns of alliances.

While we have concentrated here on the rivalry among big power nation states as a persistent source of warfare, this is not to suggest that there may not be other factors that can give rise to warring among states. For example, where there are serious internal imbalances within nation states in the form of inequalities of opportunity, racial or religious tensions and so on, these can give rise to warring, for example, when outside powers seek to intervene in a state's internal affairs on behalf of some disadvantaged group or when a nation makes war abroad in order to distract attention from its own internal problems. Furthermore, where significant levels of economic inequality among nation states develop in the course of economic expansion, these can also contribute to envy and a sense of injustice which can fan the flames of nationalistic sentiment especially where inequalities in access to critical resources are present. But if we look at historical facts, it is clearly not the case as certain dialectical materialists would suggest that all wars derive ultimately from economic inequalities. Moreover, it is still nation states that make wars, not economic classes: and so what these reflections in fact suggest is that if we put in place a supra-national authority charged with eliminating wars and keeping the peace, one of its perhaps further major policy concerns will be to ensure a high degree of equity in respect of equality of opportunities for all within the

[5] For a detailed discussion of balance of powers theory, see Sheehan M (2004) *The Balance of Power: History and Theory* 3rd ed., Routledge London; or Paul T et al. eds. (2004) *Balance of Power: Theory and practice in the twenty-first Century,* Stanford University Press San Francisco. See also Nexon D (2009) The Balance of Power in the Balance, *World Politics* 61(2) 330–359.

areas of competence of the supranational authority. This would be especially true in terms of access to natural resources.

While this theory of balance of powers remains popular among diplomats, security experts and International Relations theorists, it has to be said that it is highly challengeable on political and moral philosophical grounds. First of all, it is entirely focussed on "great" powers, large nation states with big military capability (and up to comparatively recently, empires). What about the place of smaller nation states in this "big bully" order? Are they just minions or pawns to be pushed around at will by the big powers and their alliances and if so how much sovereignty or right to self-determination have those smaller states then got in practice? This awkward question was very much present at the foundation of the United Nations when despite the assertion of the rights to self-determination of all member states large or small, the UN decided that in what is in some ways its most important organ, the Security Council, five "great" powers (allies of the Second World War as it happens) were to have a permanent veto power: USA, Britain, France, Soviet Union (today Russia) and China. This position reminiscent of an older era and redolent with balance of "great" powers thinking is increasingly challenged by scholars such as David Bosco[6] and by political critics, most recently and overtly by President Zelensky of Ukraine.[7] But leaving aside that dilemma of fitting smaller states into the balance of "great" powers, there is a much more fundamental philosophical problem. Balance of powers theory presumes a backdrop of hostility among the great powers: they are a permanent threat to each other, and they keep the peace only by balancing these threats.[8] Nowhere in balance of powers theory is there room for the idea of a permanent abandonment of hostilities among states to form instead a peace-enhancing union such as the Schuman Declaration of 1950[9] envisaged for the

[6] Bosco D (2011) Uncertain Guardians: the UN Security Council's Past and Future, *International Journal* 66(2): 439–449.

[7] Financial Times (2022) "Volodymyr Zelensky ratchets up criticism of UN Security council", *Financial Times* 06 April 2022.

[8] The analogy can be made with gangland turf wars such as occur in many of the world's big cities between rival criminal gangs and the uneasy "balance" that is maintained by routine violence whenever a gang "invades" the territory of another gang.

[9] Schuman R (1950) *Founding of the means of gathering the European Nations into a Peace Enhancing Union* available at https://www.schuman.info/9May1950.htm. Accessed 17 August 2022. Kant in his seminal *Essay on Perpetual Peace* argued with great acuity that as long as states (especially larger states) retain large armies (and today we might add stockpile of weapons), they represent a constant danger of relapse into warfare, a lawless war of all

EU. Balance of powers theory can only be based on a premise of implacable hostility among nation states; it accepts as inevitable the war of all against all as between nation states. It cannot possibly imagine a world where nation states might decide by whatever means to abandon irrevocably their hostilities and constant threats to each other to live in peace (and prosperity perhaps as a result).

It is true that in challenging the implicit backdrop of permanent hostility that perforce underpins balance of "great" powers theory, we are making the presumption that people in the world can see the benefits of living in a peaceful harmonious society both intrinsically for the peace of mind and tranquillity that it engenders (Hobbes…) and also for the prosperity that has typically accompanied periods of peaceful co-existence (as in Europe after 1945). An interesting question that arises in this connection is why the benefits for all of peace and security do not seem to be more widely appreciated and why belligerent stances by nation states and especially by "great" powers can command so much popular support despite the manifest horrors of war that do not get any better with technological progress. Rare are the voices like those of Kant calling for a universal and perpetual peace. The allure of supremacist ideologies no doubt makes its contribution (making people feel more important or even divinely appointed saviours) as also perhaps does the brutish predatory instinct that Hobbes had highlighted. But there may also be a more prosaic element of explanation present in our educational systems. While history courses in our schools in many countries focus to a greater or lesser extent on past military exploits celebrating supposedly great military victories, far less attention is paid to the horrors of warfare. Moreover, how often by comparison with the paeans to past military escapades do we find in our schools courses that seek to educate our young people in the merits of peaceful co-existence and in the manners, tolerance, respect and benevolence to all (including arguably to all living beings) which it requires? The question is perhaps rhetorical.

Speaking of the damages and disruption generated by warfare, we may also mention one aspect that is rarely mentioned despite the fact that historically it has been almost inevitable: the problem of the financing of military spending in general and in particular in periods of war. It is obvious

against all. See Kant I (1795) *Zum Ewigen Frieden*, Nicolovius, Königsberg. Available in English in Kant I (1991) *Political Writings* 2nd ed., translated by Nisbet H, Cambridge University Press, Cambridge.

enough how military spending will crowd out other types of spending (guns vs. butter) while such spending will only generate macroeconomic multiplier effects in countries that already have a major armament industry; and even then there are other peaceful types of infrastructural spending that can equally generate such multiplier effects in the domestic economy (guns vs. railways and hospitals) so there is no valid fiscal stimulus type of argument in favour of military spending. Some idea of the size of military spending both in absolute terms and as a proportion of country's GDP can be gleaned from the annual tables produced by the Stockholm Institute for Peace Studies,[10] and below is a table of the top 40 countries in absolute terms for 2024 (see Table 4.1).

Moreover, governments typically borrow extensively (issuing government bonds) to finance wartime spending, but such spending manifestly does not generate any type of income stream from which the interest on the bonds let alone the principal can be paid back. As we have shown in the *Political Economy of Debt Financing*,[11] such spending beyond a certain point[12] therefore leads inevitably to debt explosion. Moreover, it is a matter of historical fact that most of the world's hyperinflations leading to currency collapses have been associated with massive borrowings by governments from their own central banks and the huge money supply expansions which that engendered. The most well-known examples are the two German hyperinflations after the First and Second World Wars.

The presupposition of implacable hostility that underpins balance of "great" powers theory is in any case in philosophical terms completely untenable for the simple reason that as well as of war and destruction human beings are also capable of love and cooperation; and these impulses mean that implacable hostility is not after all totally inevitable. The argument may seem staggeringly simple but in fact the philosophical refutation of Balance of Powers theory really is that basic: a better more peaceful world than such an approach has ever yielded us is not only logically possible and within the reach of human beings of good will who recognise

[10] See Stockholm International Peace Research Institute (2025) *Trends in World Military Expenditure 2024*, SIPRI, Stockholm.

[11] O'Sullivan P & Ricci P (2025) *The Political Economy of Debt Financing*, Routledge London. See Chapter 7 passim.

[12] It is difficult to pin down where exactly this point is reached. Certainly when government debt is equal to 100% of GDP or more then unless and economy is growing very rapidly, the debt will be exploding at rollovers. See O'Sullivan and Ricci (2025) op. cit. ch 7.

Table 4.1 The 40 countries with the highest military expenditure in 2024

Rank			*Spending ($ b.), 2024*	*Change in spending (%)*		*Spending as a share of GDP (%)*[b]		*Share of world spending (%), 2024*
2024	*2023*[a]	*Country*		*2023–24*	*2015–24*	*2024*	*2015*	
1	1	United States	997	*5.7*	*19*	*3.4*	*3.5*	*37*
2	2	China	[314]	*7.0*	*59*	[1.7]	[*1.8*]	[*12*]
3	3	Russia	[149]	*38*	*100*	[7.1]	[*4.9*]	[*5.5*]
4	7	Germany	88.5	*28*	*89*	*1.9*	*1.1*	*3.3*
5	4	India	86.1	*1.6*	*42*	*2.3*	*2.5*	*3.2*
Subtotal top 5			**1635**	..	..	..	..	***60***
6	6	United Kingdom	81.8	*2.8*	*23*	*2.3*	*2.0*	*3.0*
7	5	Saudi Arabia	[80.3]	*1.5*	*−20*	[*7.3*]	[*13*]	[*3.0*]
8	8	Ukraine	64.7	*2.9*	*1 251*	*34*	*3.8*	*2.4*
9	9	France	64.7	*6.1*	*21*	*2.1*	*1.9*	*2.4*
10	10	Japan	55.3	*21*	*49*	*1.4*	*0.9*	*2.0*
Subtotal top 10			**1981**	..	..	..	..	*73*
11	11	South Korea	47.6	*1.4*	*30*	*2.6*	*2.4*	*1.8*
12	14	Israel	46.5	*65*	*135*	*8.8*	*5.4*	*1.7*
13	16	Poland	38.0	*31*	*159*	*4.2*	*2.1*	*1.4*
14	12	Italy	38.0	*1.4*	*45*	*1.6*	*1.2*	*1.4*
15	13	Australia	33.8	*1.9*	*25*	*1.9*	*2.0*	*1.2*
Subtotal top 15			**2185**	..	..	..	..	***80***
16	15	Canada	29.3	*6.8*	*38*	*1.3*	*1.2*	*1.1*
17	19	Türkiye	25.0	*12*	*110*	*1.9*	*1.8*	*1.0*
18	17	Spain	24.6	*0.4*	*35*	*1.4*	*1.3*	*0.9*
19	21	Netherlands	23.2	*35*	*111*	*1.9*	*1.1*	*0.9*
20	20	Algeria	21.8	*12*	*69*	*8.0*	*5.6*	*0.7*
21	18	Brazil	20.9	*−0.4*	*−14*	*1.0*	*1.4*	*0.7*
22	24	Mexico	16.7	*39*	*129*	*0.9*	*0.5*	*0.6*
23	22	Taiwan	16.5	*1.8*	*48*	*2.1*	*1.9*	*0.5*
24	26	Colombia	15.1	*14*	*35*	*3.4*	*3.1*	*0.5*
25	23	Singapore	15.1	*3.0*	*32*	*2.8*	*3.0*	*0.4*
26	28	Sweden	12.0	*34*	*113*	*2.0*	*1.1*	*0.4*
27	25	Indonesia	11.0	*−0.4*	*31*	*0.8*	*0.9*	*0.4*
28	27	Norway	10.4	*17*	*79*	*2.1*	*1.5*	*0.4*

(*continued*)

Table 4.1 (continued)

Rank			*Spending ($ b.), 2024*	*Change in spending (%)*		*Spending as a share of GDP (%)*[b]		*Share of world spending (%), 2024*
2024	*2023*[a]	*Country*		*2023–24*	*2015–24*	*2024*	*2015*	
29	29	Pakistan	10.2	*−5.1*	*−0.7*	*2.7*	*2.7*	*0.4*
30	30	Denmark	10.0	*20*	*154*	*2.4*	*1.1*	*0.3*
31	39	Romania	8.7	*43*	*143*	*2.3*	*1.5*	*0.3*
32	32	Belgium	8.6	*7.4*	*58*	*1.3*	*0.9*	*0.3*
33	34	Greece	8.0	*11*	*45*	*3.1*	*2.5*	*0.3*
34	33	Iran	7.9	*−10*	*21*	*2.0*	*2.6*	*0.3*
35	31	Kuwait	7.8	*−2.6*	*10*	*4.8*	*5.0*	*0.3*
36	36	Finland	7.0	*16*	*73*	*2.3*	*1.5*	*0.3*
37	35	Switzerland	6.7	*3.1*	*26*	*0.7*	*0.7*	*0.2*
38	44	Czechia	6.5	*32*	*129*	*1.9*	*0.9*	*0.2*
39	40	Iraq	6.2	*4.4*	*−41*	*2.4*	*5.4*	*0.2*
40	43	Philippines	6.1	*19*	*67*	*1.3*	*1.1*	*0.2*
Subtotal top 40			**2521**	..	..	..	..	***93***
World			**2718**	***9.4***	***37***	***2.5***	***2.3***	***100***

Spending figures and GDP are in US dollars, at current prices and exchange rates. Changes are in real terms, based on constant (2023) US dollars. Percentages below 10 are rounded to 1 decimal place; those over 10 are rounded to whole numbers. Figures and percentage shares may not add up to stated totals or subtotals due to the conventions of rounding

.. = data not available or not applicable; [ ] = estimated figure; GDP = gross domestic product

[a] Rankings for 2023 are based on updated military expenditure figures in the current edition of the SIPRI Military Expenditure Database. They may therefore differ from the rankings for 2023 given in *SIPRI Yearbook 2024* and in other SIPRI publications released in 2024

[b] The figures for military expenditure as a share of GDP are based on estimates of 2024 GDP from the International Monetary Fund World Economic Outlook and International Financial Statistics databases

Sources: SIPRI Military Expenditure Database, Apr. 2025; International Monetary Fund, World Economic Outlook Database, Oct. 2024; and International Monetary Fund, International Financial Statistics Database, Sep. 2024

Source: Stockholm International Peace Research Institute (2025) *Trends in World Military Expenditure 2024*, SIPRI Stockholm: p. 2

their interdependence; it has to an extent been tried and tested in the supranational arrangements of the European Union and in the ASEAN Political and Security Community. No wonder that Vladimir Putin and Donald Trump have been so suspicious of the EU and done so much to undermine it: it represents a direct refutation of one of the theory that is central to their geopolitical standpoint and foreign policy approach.[13]

A second often related theory that is widely found in contemporary International Relations theory and diplomatic discussions is the idea that "great" powers should have their wider "zones of influence" consisting of (usually) neighbouring states with whom they would form an alliance or even install subordinate regimes amenable to the great powers wishes and diktats; and ideally with suitable small buffer states committed to neutrality inserted between them and other "great" powers or alliances who might threaten them. This was of course the essence both of the Molotov–Ribbentrop Pact (1939) between Soviet Union and Nazi Germany with its Secret Protocol that divided up large tracts of Eastern Europe into zones of influence for Nazi Germany and the Soviet Union. The same idea was very evidently present also in the pact for zones of influence in Europe reached by Churchill, Stalin and Roosevelt at Yalta (1945).[14] Germany would be divided up into four zones under military occupation by Britain, France, the USA and the Soviet Union. Stalin also considered that the whole of Eastern Europe was to be his sphere of influence as in the earlier Molotov–Ribbentrop Pact, but the Yalta agreement was not explicit on that point. In any case, soon after the end of the war, Stalin de facto achieved this through the installation of pro-Soviet communist regimes in a whole array of Eastern European states (Poland, Hungary, Czechoslovakia, Romania and Bulgaria) and through the subsequent military alliance of all of these states with the Soviet Union in the Warsaw Pact military alliance.[15]

Turning to the critique of this theory, it will first of all be evident that the zone of influence idea makes exactly the same presumption of inevitable implacable hostility between states and especially between "great" powers which we have detected in balance of power theory and which we have already shown to be philosophically indefensible. But there is also a

[13] Putin was not always so opposed to the EU as he has become in recent years. On the evolution of his views and relations with the EU, see Sakwa R (2017) *Russia against the Rest: the post-cold war crisis of world Order*, Cambridge University Press, Cambridge: chapter 5.

[14] For the Molotov–Ribbentrop Pact, see International Relations and Security Network *The Molotov Ribbentrop Pact* ETH Zürich available at https://www.files.ethz.ch/isn/125339/1393_Molotov-Ribbentrop_Pact.pdf. Accessed 11 September 2025. On the Yalta pact see Avalon Project *The Yalta, Conference* Yale University Law School Archive available at https://avalon.law.yale.edu/wwii/yalta.asp. Accessed 9 September 2025.

[15] For a recent commentary on all of this this, see Allison G (2020) The new Spheres of Influence: sharing the globe with other great powers *Foreign Affairs* March/April 2020: 1–6.

much more insidious presumption implicitly present in the "zones of influence" idea. The "great" powers are arrogating to themselves to decide on the politics and policies of smaller nation states in their zones of influence. This has been most evident in Soviet activities in Eastern Europe during the Cold War (1946–1989), but the USA has clearly subscribed to a similar approach (known as the Monroe doctrine was exemplified in the Cuban missile crisis of 1962. This attitude of "great" powers towards their satellites betrays at best an insufferable arrogance and superiority complex of those supposedly "great" powers if not a downright racism in certain cases. Hitler's whole construct of conquest and subjugation was based on the presumption of the superiority of the Aryan race. While not wishing to suggest that the attitudes of the great powers of today's world are just another form of Hitlerian racism since they may have such motivations as "defending democracy" or "defending civilisation", we will leave it to readers to judge for themselves the extent to which racist or other superiority presumptions may also in part underpin the activities of certain "great" powers of the contemporary era.

These ideas about zones of influence being perhaps susceptible to possible accusations of implicit supremacism of various stripes, they are often couched in terms of coded diplomatic language about "security architecture". The "great" powers need these zones of influence and buffers in order that they can feel safe rather than constantly threatened. One could be forgiven for wondering how on earth the much smaller states are to feel in all of this: do they too need zones of influence in their neighbourhoods since they are also sovereign states after all? Or if they find themselves in a zone of influence what say have they about that? Who said that they should be in such a zone and on what authority (other than might is right)?

Indeed, if the "great" powers really thought through the issues of security architecture, they would arrive through a Hobbesian line of argument similar to that developed in this work, at a conclusion that the only truly effective guarantee of security lies in the initiation of some kind of authority akin to a Hobbesian sovereign to keep the peace with real powers of enforcement. Far from seeking their ill-defined zones of influence within which they can feel secure (a perspective which reveals how close zones of influence theory is to criminal gangland phenomena), these "great" powers would do better to lay aside their gangsterish "big boss" posturing and seek to cooperate in some form of supranational geopolitical order. To put the point simply and bluntly: as long as there are rival gangsters with their armies/militias vying to be the "greatest" of the powers (*capo di tutti i capi*),[16] there can never be a lasting peace so true security together with the tranquillity and prosperity that can accompany it require not some ever-precarious balance of "great" powers but rather a supranational order based on comprehensive cooperation and respect among peoples under a single world authority acting as a Hobbesian sovereign.[17] Of course today that may seem a distant ideal and would imply huge efforts at genuine cooperation among politicians and peoples combined with mutual respect and benevolence (fostered as we have hinted inter alia through a transformation in education), but there is no doubt at all that for any rational mind that would be the ultimate security guarantee. It would also as we have noted promote a greater financial stability given the often disastrous consequences of government borrowings to make wars. "Security architecture" is often said to be about ensuring a balance among states and military alliances such that states do not feel unduly threatened by others. But this once again presumes an implacable hostility in particular among "great" power states; and the idea is that the opposing sides maintain sufficiently similar stockpiles of weapons and armaments that no side "feels" threatened by the other. Fiammenghi has documented rather well the paradoxes that arise in the resultant arms races that can develop: ever more weapons pile up on either side but nobody is really getting any more secure (and so huge amounts of resources are being completely wasted in manufacturing the stockpiles).[18]

Having thus surveyed some of the most prevalent theories that underpin contemporary realist International Relations theory and diplomatic practice, our conclusion is pretty damning. These theories are based on philosophically untenable premises such as that of implacable hostility among peoples and on morally repugnant supremacist premises such as those we find in the Zones of Influence for "great" powers. It is precisely because of the supremacist presumption irretrievably present in the very idea of great powers that throughout this work we have placed "great" in

[16] Italian for the "boss of the bosses", the mafia boss who is (temporarily) recognised as being the de facto strongest due to having the greatest willingness and capacity to deploy violence in pursuit of his goals of domination in certain areas of criminal activity.

[17] The same can be said incidentally of putting an end to gang warfare and violence within sovereign nation states.

[18] Fiammenghi D (2011) The Security Curve and the structure of International Politics: a Neo-realist synthesis, *International Security* 35: 126–154.

quotation marks. Who other than those powers themselves ever said or accepted that they were so great?

Not only have we by now shown that the nation state is devoid of any plausible moral foundation and economically obsolete in the interdependent world economy of the twenty-first century; we have also seen that the theories which have been proffered to defend the kind of war of all against all that is the geopolitical reality today despite the best efforts of the UN—the realpolitik theories based on Balance of Powers and Zones of Influence—are logically indefensible as formulated and wreaking of implicit supremacist presumptions on the part of supposedly "great" powers. It is therefore long overdue that humanity passes beyond this war of all against all in the international order to put in place the perforce supranational institutional structures required for a lasting peace and a more civilised world. In the next chapter, we will look in more detail at the form which such institutions might take.

There is one small parenthesis which we should perhaps enter *en passant* at this stage. While we are extolling the virtues of supranational collaboration, we are aware that human beings also have a competitive urge and will seek to outperform each other in various areas; and indeed, competitive endeavour has often underpinned innovation and social progress (at least over certain areas of human activity). Rivalries and competition will always be present for as long as people are different (and *vive la différence*). The point is that these rivalries can and should be channelled into scientific endeavour and innovation and of course into non-violent essentially friendly but still highly competitive activities such as sporting events, musical competitions, and gastronomic competitions and rankings. The point is that when competing with each other as individuals or groups in a civilised society, we should draw the line at engaging in violence against each other for such violence when generalised in wars leads only to massive mutual destruction; rather, we should compete in a manner whereby mutual respect is at all times preserved.[19] In short faced with the twin urges of competition and collaboration in a civilised society, the ideal

[19] It will be admitted that one of the authors has a strong sporting background, in fact in rugby union; first as a player and after some 15 years of playing experience, 10 years of experience as a referee. This sport is rightly reputed for its sense of fair play and respect of opponents despite the tough and even violent action on the pitch, and of course, it is infamous for the post-match festivities in which both sides joyfully take part together despite the ferocity which may have unfolded on the field of play. No team sport perhaps illustrates the Middle Way we have described better than this.

should be a kind of Middle Path between extreme and even violent competition on the one hand and an extreme of collaboration in which everyone would be the same, and we would never have any occasion to compete.

Bibliography

Allison, G. (2020). The new spheres of influence: Sharing the globe with other great powers. *Foreign Affairs* March/April 2020: 1–6.

Bew, J. (2016). *Realpolitik: A history*. Oxford University Press.

Bosco, D. (2011). Uncertain guardians: The UN security council's past and future. *International Journal, 66*(2), 439–449.

Fiammenghi, D. (2011). The security curve and the structure of international politics: A neo-realist synthesis. *International Security, 35*, 126–154.

Financial Times. (2022). Volodymyr Zelensky ratchets up criticism of UN security council. *Financial Times*, 06 April 2022.

Kant, I. (1795). *Zum Ewigen Frieden*, Nicolovius, Königsberg. Available in English in Kant I (1991) *Political writings* 2nd ed, translated by Nisbet H, Cambridge University Press.

Machiavelli, N. (2011). *The prince*. Penguin Classics.

Molotov Ribbentrop Pact. See International Relations and Security Network. *The Molotov Ribbentrop Pact* ETH Zürich. Accessed September 11, 2025., from https://www.files.ethz.ch/isn/125339/1393_Molotov-Ribbentrop_Pact.pdf

Nexon, D. (2009). The balance of power in the balance. *World Politics, 61*(2), 330–359.

O'Sullivan, P., & Ricci, P. (2025). *The political economy of debt financing*. Routledge.

Paul, T., et al. (Eds.). (2004). *Balance of power: Theory and practice in the 21st century*. Stanford University Press San Francisco.

Sakwa, R. (2017). *Russia against the rest: The post-cold war crisis of world order*. Cambridge University Press.

Schuman, R. (1950). *Founding of the means of gathering the European Nations into a Peace Enhancing Union*. Accessed August 17, 2022, from https://www.schuman.info/9May1950.htm

Sheehan, M. (2004). *The balance of power: History and theory* (3rd ed.). Routledge.

Snyder, G. (1960). Balance of power in the missile age. *Journal of International Affairs, 14*(1), 21–34.

Stockholm International Peace Research Institute. (2025). *Trends in world military expenditure 2024*. SIPRI.

Yalta pact see Avalon Project. *The Yalta, Conference*. Yale University Law School Archive. Accessed September 9, 2025., from https://avalon.law.yale.edu/wwii/yalta.asp

CHAPTER 5

Outline of the Details of a Possible Peace-Enhancing Supranational Order

Abstract Given that our proposal constitutes a supranational world order that would replace the war of all against all among nation states claiming absolute sovereignty, it is incumbent on us to sketch out how such a rationally based ideal can be achieved in practice. In this chapter, some tentative suggestions are made as to the practical organisation of such a world order in terms of its legislative, executive and judicial functions. Based on the model of the EU's institutions which have worked reasonably well even if not perfectly for nearly 70 years by now, we suggest a High Authority as executive; initially a World Council of Ministers making decisions in the area of competence of the supranational authority by qualified majority voting; and a World Court of Justice with real enforcement powers analogous to the European Court of Justice. Since such an arrangement could involve some real challenges in scaling up from the EU case to world level, notably the problems of democratic deficit, a radical suggestion is made to address this issue: the state units below the World Authority although they may initially be the 193 members of the current UN could eventually be broken up into much smaller units with populations never in excess of 10 million people; and in these cantons or city states, direct democracy would be practised. The World Council of Ministers would then evolve into a World Parliament with approximately 1000 MWPs (one per canton/city state) as legislative organ for the World authority.

P. O'Sullivan et al., *Overcoming Gangsterism and Geo-Political Anarchy*, https://doi.org/10.1007/978-3-032-22438-5_5

Keywords Constitutional proposals • Limited transfers of national sovereignty • Supranational world government • EU as model • World High Authority • World Council or Parliament • World Court of Justice • Democratic deficit • Limitation of size of states • Direct democracy

In this chapter, we will outline in more depth the practicalities of the institutional format which we believe that a supranational geopolitical order might take. A significant source of inspiration on which we draw will be the European Union because whatever one may think of its foibles and areas for improvement it has now existed for some 67 years as an explicitly supranational entity which has brought sustained peace and relative prosperity to its member states. The project for construction of a supranational entity which would bring a lasting peace to European states after a half century of often extreme violence (two World Wars arising from conflicts among European states) was enunciated in the Schuman Declaration of 1950. Robert Schuman, French foreign minister of the time, had worked closely with the Head of the French Commissariat du Plan (hence chief civil servant of France) Jean Monnet, first of all to promote the idea of a federal United States of Europe; but when it became clear that Europe was not yet ready for a full-blown federal experiment, they turned their attention to less ambitious forms of collaboration but always of a supranational character. After Europe's constant warring over 40 years, they were adamant that the old essentially intergovernmental order based on nation states with absolute sovereignty had signally failed to keep the peace in Europe and so that some kind of supranational entity with powers of enforcement even if not a federal state was needed. Bearing in mind that the two world wars had involved as a central element, particularly violent conflict between France and Germany, it is worth quoting the Schuman Declaration directly as it goes right to the heart of the argument which we have been elaborating for the geopolitical order in the world today. This remarkable declaration was delivered by the French Foreign Minister Robert Schuman in the Quai d'Orsay Foreign Office building in the form of a surprise press conference on 09 May 1950.

[The declaration] "*proposes that Franco-German production of coal and steel as a whole be placed under a common High Authority, within the framework of an organisation open to the participation of the other countries of*

Europe. The pooling of coal and steel production should immediately provide for the setting up of common foundations for economic development as a first step in the federation of Europe and will change the destinies of those regions which have long been devoted to the manufacture of munitions of war, of which they have been the most constant victims. The solidarity in production thus established will make it plain that any war between France and Germany becomes not merely unthinkable, but materially impossible…".[1]

Monnet and Schuman described this as essentially a proposal for a "peace-enhancing union" in which the participating states would pool their sovereignty in certain defined areas by transferring it to an overarching high authority with powers of execution and enforcement.[2] The analogy with the Hobbesian argument for escaping from the war of all against all will be evident even if Monnet and Schuman may not have mentioned Hobbes by name and envisaged only a partial transfer of policy competences to the supranational European institutions. Equally although not explicitly mentioned by Monnet or Schuman, there are clear echoes of Kant's *Perpetual Peace: A Philosophical Sketch*,[3] and there is even an echo of Cicero's observations on the moral duties of statesmanship in *De Officiis* when he noted that "*Since military achievements are very commonly regarded as outranking civil service this opinion needs to be refuted: for wars have often been encouraged from the desire of fame…Yet if we look only at facts there have been many civic transactions that have surpassed feats of arms in importance and renown*".[4]

The first fruit of the Declaration was the setting up in 1951 of the European Coal and Steel Community with its supranational High Authority and involving as well as France and (West) Germany, Italy, Belgium, Netherlands and Luxembourg. Within seven years, these

[1] Schuman Project available at https://www.schuman.info/9MayProp.htm. Accessed 13 September 2025.

[2] For further detail on the peace-enhancing union and on the various other politicians of the time who supported the initiative (such as Hallstein, Adenaurer, Spaak, De Gasperi, etc.), see Boka E (2012) The European Idea of a Supranational Union of Peace, in *Society and Economy* 34(3): 387–397.

[3] Kant I (1795) *Zum Ewigen Frieden*, Nicolovius, Königsberg. Available in English in Kant I (1991) *Political Writings* 2nd ed., translated by Nisbet H Cambridge University Press, Cambridge. In this work, the essay "*Perpetual Peace: A Philosophical Sketch*" is contained.

[4] Peabody A (1887) *Cicero: De Officiis* (Translation), Little Brown, Boston. The quotation is from Peabody's translation at p. 26 available at https://oll.libertyfund.org/titles/cicero-on-moral-duties-de-officiis. Accessed 27 July 2025.

founding members initiated an even more ambitious economic integration in the form of the European Economic Community (EEC). The EEC has subsequently evolved both horizontally in the sense of geographical enlargement to include today 27 states and vertically in the sense of ever closer forms of integration over an ever wider area of common supranational policies, the most prominent of which is the monetary union with its single currency, the Euro (although this so far is shared by only 21 states[5]). Since the Maastricht Treaty of 1992, the EEC has become the European Union (EU), and it is equipped with a range of supranational institutions to make and enforce by now a wide range of common policies. The key supranational institutions are the European Commission which is the executive arm of EU government; the Council of Ministers which is the legislative arm and which passes legislation normally by qualified majority vote (ministers of larger states having in effect more weight in the vote[6]); and the European Court of Justice as the judicial arm of EU government, which in crucial contrast to the International Court of Justice (ICJ) in Den Haag (UN court) has strong powers of enforcement of its decisions. In fact, decisions of the ECJ in matters of the assigned supranational competences of the EU take precedence over any decisions of national courts (even though there are some nationalist politicians who fail to understand this). There is also the 720-member European Parliament which has a role in the legislative process: before any new legislation can be passed by the Council of Ministers, the said legislation must also have been approved by the Parliament. This unusual set-up in effect gives the Parliament a veto power over any new legislation other than new treaties. The European Central Bank is a politically independent supranational institution charged with overseeing the single currency and controlling the Euro money supply.

What we are now suggesting is that the geopolitical order of the world as a whole should be reconstructed with a set of supranational institutions similar to those of the EU capable at the very least of putting an end to warfare among nation states (or other sovereign entities) by peaceful resolution of any such disputes through negotiation and arbitration with

[5] Twenty states since Croatia adopted the Euro in 2023. Bulgaria is due to adopt the Euro in January 2026.

[6] This is achieved by the qualified majority voting rule on Council. Each minister has one vote and initially for a motion to pass at least 55% of the votes cast must be in favour. If that condition is met, a population check is made: the votes in favour must be representative of at least 65% of EU population: otherwise the motion fails.

strong and effective powers of enforcement.[7] In the spirit of the Schuman Declaration war among nation states would become "unthinkable ever again". If the solution to the war of all against all that we currently face is perhaps rationally obvious in theory, and if we have the blueprint for how one might proceed in the EU experience, we have to recognise that in extending such a supranational political model to the world as a whole, there would be massive practical challenges. These are partly to do with scaling up from a reasonably homogeneous region (Europe) to a much more culturally heterogeneous world with a vastly greater population; and partly from what we might call *realpolitik* considerations, most notably how to get those dreaded "great" powers on board. For our proposals to be taken seriously, it is important that we offer at least some tentative answers to these practical questions, and this is what we will endeavour to do. We do not claim to have necessarily the best answers since this to an extent is a speculative exercise given the radical nature of the departure we propose but at least we will have identified the obstacles and suggested possible ways forward. In this chapter, we shall seek to deal with the scaling challenges while in the next we shall look at the *realpolitik*.

In respect of scaling up to world-level supranational institutions, it should first of all be borne in mind that what we are proposing is nothing like as ambitious as the European integration project in terms of the range of policy competences that would be transferred from nation states to the supranational high authority. In fact in order to address the specific geopolitical problem of the war of all against all that has been our central concern in this book, the only policy competence that would at the very least need to be transferred to supranational level is that of dispute resolution among the nation states (or other sovereign entities in the world). This would involve world-level executive and legislative organs to deal with all matters of defence and global (as opposed to local level) policing and a World Court of Justice whose decisions would be enforceable and take precedence over any national laws/courts. An interesting implication of this would be that if one day we managed to get the whole of the world on board for such an initiative, wars among states would become entirely a thing of the past, although of course there could still be civil wars and

[7] Guido Montani in his work Montani G (2019) *Supranational Political Economy: the Globalisation of the State-Market Relationship*, Routledge, London, similarly makes the suggestion that in moving away from the relative powerlessness of nation states to a Supranational Political Economy, the EU can serve as a useful even if not entirely perfect model.

gang warfare in certain places. This would imply a fundamental rethinking of the role of armies, the military and of weaponry which might not be such a bad thing. But while nation states would no longer be able to make wars and would have to bow to a higher authority in dispute resolution, that is in fact all that they would need to surrender in terms of sovereignty to promote a lasting peace. Wide areas of policy would still be decided at national, regional or local levels (the Principle of Subsidiarity), although, as noted earlier, there might be other areas of policy which nation states might wish to make a world-level supranational policy competence if a suitable world authority existed (climate change, trade policies, financial stability, etc.). It may be noted that in arguing thus for a surrender only of certain specific policy competences to a supranational authority rather than all areas of policy, we could be said to be fleshing out in detail the suggestions of the great German philosopher Immanuel Kant in his fascinating (for the time: 1795) essay *Perpetual Peace: A Philosophical Sketch*.[8] Kant had argued that if mankind were to put an end to the war of all against all among states (of which there were plenty in his era), nation states would need to form a supranational or federal arrangement of some kind in which there would be a central authority with enforcement powers in respect of dispute resolution, but states would still retain freedom over policy areas that would not compromise world peace;[9] Kant did not advocate a full-blown world (federal) state. However, an inexorable implication at least if such a supranational arrangement were to get all of the world's states on board would be that all states would have to disband their standing armies and renounce forever the supposed right to make wars against each other. As Kant so nicely put it with merciless rationality, as long as states maintain standing armies, they are in effect reserving the right to use warfare to settle their disputes and thereby constitute an ever present threat to each other that is inconsistent with perpetual peace.[10]

If the step to supranational authorities for maintaining the peace and for dispute resolution is not too drastic in terms of the degree of surrender of sovereignty, the next question of scale is how such a world entity should

[8] It should be acknowledged that there are also in our argument echoes of the great contemporary German philosopher Jürgen Habermas who has argued for supranationalism in the twenty-first century. See his work Habermas J (2001) *The Post-national Constellation*, Polity Press, Cambridge.

[9] Kant I (1795) *Zum Ewigen Frieden*, Nicolovius, Königsberg, op. cit. Second Definitive Article

[10] Kant I (op. cit), Article 3.

be structured and make decisions. If we followed the EU model, we would have an executive in the form of a High Authority for Maintenance of Peace and a Council of Ministers for the legislative function. This World Council of Ministers could as a starting point be composed of the foreign ministers of each of the 193 member states of the United Nations, and it would take decisions by the same qualified majority rules as those of the European Union:[11] 55% of individual ministerial votes in favour representing at least 65% of the world population for a motion to pass. In order to prevent China and India which between them account for approximately 36% of the world's population from having too preponderant an effect in the voting procedure, there could also be a sub-requirement similar to that in the EU stipulating that a blocking minority when rejecting a motion on the 65% population criterion must include at least let us say 30 states representing at least 40% of world population. If one wished these qualified majority voting rules to be more inclusive and likely to command easy consensus, one could have, for example: 60% of individual ministers in favour representing at least 70% of world population; and with the sub-requirement that a blocking majority must include at least 40 states representing at least 45% of world population.

This World Council of Ministers would among other things choose by qualified majority vote the members of the High Authority, the Executive arm of the world government we are proposing. Given the narrow policy remit that we are envisaging for the Authority at least in the first instance (maintenance of peace and order), this High Authority could be composed of 24 members with four each from North America, South America, Europe and Africa; six from Asia and two from Australasia/Oceania. The Secretariat of this High authority should be physically located in a country with a long established record of neutrality and non-violent behaviour: for example (and these are only sugestions that come to the authors' minds), Genève or Bangkok. The Secretariat of the World Council of Ministers would also be located in the same city as the High Authority (for reasons of convenience); but the regular meetings of the World Council should be chaired on a rotating basis every 6 months (as with the EU Council) among the 24 Council members in a manner which follows roughly a continental sequence, so North America, then South America, Europe,

[11] On EU Council voting rules see EU Consilium *Qualified Majority* available at https://www.consilium.europa.eu/en/council-eu/voting-system/qualified-majority/. Accessed 19 September 2025.

Africa, Asia and Australasia.[12] The location of the meetings of the World Council could rotate in line with the chair.

As for the World Court of Justice, it too could consist of 12 judges representing the various continents as with the High Authority. The World Council of Ministers would select the judges and designate a presiding judge who would have a casting vote in the event of a 6–6 tie among the 12 judges. To our mind, the ideal location for this court could be Singapore with its established law abiding tradition, but Den Haag and Luxembourg could also be suitable homes given their well-established legal reputation (ICJ in Den Haag and ECJ in Luxembourg). If one wanted to have one key institution in the Americas, then Montréal could also be a plausible candidate. But these are only illustrative suggestions, and what is important is not the location but the enforcement powers of the various supranational institutions that would be set up, in particular enforcement power of the World Court of Justice.

It will be remarked that in our proposal none of the organs of the supranational world authority are located in any of the contemporary "great" power states. This is deliberate because in the setting up of an authority to promote peace for all in an equitable manner, we want to break decisively with the dominance of the so-called great powers and anything which symbolises their pretensions. We have already seen in the previous chapter that these "great" power ideas are morally unfounded and wreak of supremacism and their institutionalisation in the United Nations in the form of the Security Council permanent members with veto power has vitiated the operation and even the credibility of the UN from the very outset. Indeed, the setting up of the Security Council at the inception of the UN in the aftermath of the Second World War can justly be described as the original sin of that body. In effect, at the UN, all nations and/or peoples are declared to be equal and to have equal rights in the UN Declaration of Rights…but some in the end are more equal than others (the Security Council permanent Five). This may be explicable in terms of the *realpolitik* of the time, but it represents a running sore in terms of supposedly democratic values as well as having paralysed decision-making in relation to the peaceful resolution of conflicts as the "great"

[12] Given that Australasia would only have two Council members while Asia has six, then, after the first two rounds of rotation as described above, rounds 3 and 4 of the sequence would have two Asian chairings at the end of these sequences. So sequences 3 and 4 would be North America, then South America, Europe, Africa, Asia and Asia.

the world sovereign by ensuring that the political units below the world sovereign should be sufficiently small to allow **direct democracy**, that is to say a democracy in which every citizen votes on every piece of legislation either by participation in a large assembly (as in ancient Athens) or by referendum as in today's Swiss cantons. We could consider breaking up the bigger nation states that we know today into smaller more governable units in which direct democracy could be practised, ensuring thereby that every citizen feels implicated in the decision-making process. In short, we would have the World Authority as described above and below it a large array of city states or Swiss style cantons in which direct democracy could be easily and effectively practised. Being realistic, it is clear that such a radical change in the geopolitical order is not for tomorrow, and it would render our World Council of Ministers as described above very unwieldy and in need of a redesign. However, in view of some of the serious problems that contemporary representative democracies are facing especially in bigger democratic nations such as the USA, the UK, France, Germany, Poland and Brazil (to name but a few) where polarisation is feeding both discontent and policy paralysis and where abstention from voting is reaching levels that challenge the legitimacy of those elected, the case for breaking down into smaller units in which direct democracy could be practised is actually compelling. Simply put, in a direct democracy, people can feel that their vote actually counts, while polarisation is addressed partly by physical proximity of the opposing groups and their obvious need therefore to compromise and co-exist peacefully in the cantons and partly by allowing like-minded fringe groups to coalesce into their own small cantons.

We should perhaps remark that we are not necessarily seeing direct democracy here as a panacea for all political ills: rather we see it as an institutional device which can address the participatory challenges especially of the bigger representative democracies of today. For direct democracy to work effectively, it presupposes what Jason Brennan (2012) has called "ethical voting". The voter participating in the direct democracy (and arguably in any kind of democracy) needs to exercise their vote in an ethical manner: that is to say that they take the time and care to inform themselves of the issues and that they respect certain universal moral principles regarding the substance of that for which they vote (it is not ethical to vote

as will be seen, our solution is somewhat different and more detailed than that proposed by Kant.

for genocide, for example, or at least one would hope so). Direct democracy perhaps reduces these dangers because of the immediate visibility of the consequences of the vote in the small communities of the cantons (while trans-cantonal issues would be the prerogative of the supranational World Authority). At the same time, there remains the danger that individual voters even in a direct democracy may be deliberately manipulated by corruption, lobbying, fake news and distortions leading to ill informed if not downright ignorant voting but manipulation of an assembly of all of the citizens of a state is rather more challenging than manipulation of a few hundred parliamentarians. Nonetheless, Plato had already warned against this in the context of the direct democracy of ancient Athens: the danger of manipulation of the Assembly by sophistry, and indeed Plato never forgave the Athenian Assembly for having voted to put Socrates to death. We are reminded even in respect of direct democracy of Churchill's (2008) remark *"No one pretends that democracy is perfect or all-wise"*;[19] but we can say that perhaps direct democracy for the reasons we have outlined fares better than representative democracy.

Other advantages of a geopolitical order based on a World Authority for keeping the peace with small direct democracy practising cantons or city-states as the next level below can also be mentioned. First of all, there is ample evidence that in politics as well as economics "small is beautiful" as Edwin Schumacher long ago so cogently argued.[20] Among the strongest alternative indices to GDP for measurement of socio-economic performance, we can find the Social Progress Index (SPI) which seeks to measure and compare well-being across the world by a comprehensive index built on three dimensions of such well-being: meeting Basic Human Needs such as access to water and sanitation and level of personal security; Foundations of Well being such as wellness, environmental quality; and Opportunities for self-actualisation such as freedom of expression, inclusiveness and access to higher education. Under each dimension, four components are in turn identified before an attempted measurement of each component from various pre-existing statistical indicators (SPI does not collect any of its own data preferring to use existing data and thereby avoiding potential accusations of data constructivism or massage). See Fig. 5.1 for the structure and statistical indicators as used for each

[19] See footnote 17, this chapter.

[20] Schumacher E (1973) *Small is Beautiful: a study of Economics as if people mattered*, Blond & Briggs, London.

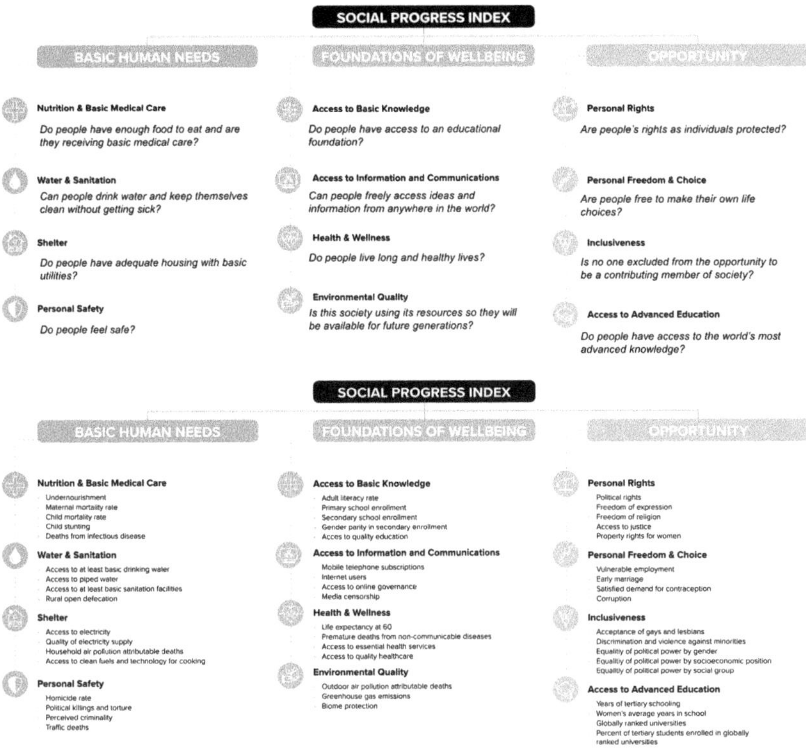

Fig. 5.1 Social Progress Index structure and indicators (Source: Social Progress Imperative (2024) available at https://cdn.prod.website-files.com/6650cb66e461b93f1a906cf2/667c5a2410e6e419272df71a_Global%20Social%20Progress%20Index%20Executive%20Summary%20.pdf. Accessed 30 May 2025)

component of the index. Figure 5.2 gives the 2023 world rankings of social progress, and it is strikingly evident that smaller states do very much better in terms of social progress.

What we can see in these results for 2023 is that of the top 15 states in terms of social progress (with really very high scores), 11 of the 14 are small states. Moreover, if we look back over the years at how states have ranked on Social Progress Index, we find a persistently similar pattern with the top 10 states varying hardly at all. We find for all years since the SPI was first measured in 2013 Norway, Finland, Iceland, Denmark and Switzerland invariably in the top 10. Of course, there will for sure be other

TIER 1

Rank	Country	Score	Annual change
1	Denmark	90.38	↔
2	Norway	90.32	↓
3	Finland	89.96	↔
4	Iceland	89.57	↔
5	Sweden	89.09	↓
6	Switzerland	88.88	↓
7	Luxembourg	87.86	↑
8	Australia	87.77	↑
9	Netherlands	87.73	↔
10	Germany	87.64	↔
11	Austria	86.73	↓
12	Ireland	86.57	↓
13	Belgium	86.13	↔
14	New Zealand	86.06	↔
15	Canada	86.00	↓
16	Japan	85.52	↔
17	Republic of Korea	85.26	↓
18	Estonia	85.17	↓
19	Czechia	84.82	↔
20	Slovenia	84.60	↑

TIER 2

Rank	Country	Score	Annual change
21	United Kingdom	84.49	↔
22	Singapore	84.21	↔
23	Portugal	84.10	↓
24	France	83.88	↓
25	Spain	83.87	↓
26	Italy	83.61	↔
27	Malta	82.68	↔
28	Cyprus	81.88	↔
29	United States	81.70	↓
30	Israel	81.68	↔
31	Lithuania	81.51	↓
32	Latvia	81.12	↑
33	Croatia	80.25	↓
34	Greece	80.09	↔
35	Slovakia	79.54	↓
36	Poland	79.53	↔
37	Chile	78.43	↔
38	Uruguay	78.33	↓
39	Costa Rica	78.03	↔
40	Hungary	77.47	↔
41	Argentina	77.19	↓
42	Barbados	76.54	↔
43	Bulgaria	76.25	↑
44	Romania	75.24	↓
45	Montenegro	75.08	↑
46	Serbia	74.32	↓
47	Malaysia	73.83	↑
48	Kuwait	73.44	↔
49	Moldova	73.24	↔
50	Armenia	73.21	↔
51	United Arab Emirates	72.92	↔
52	Georgia	72.62	↑
53	Mauritius	72.54	↓
54	Jamaica	72.36	↓
55	Panama	72.10	↔
56	Trinidad and Tobago	71.96	↓
57	Albania	71.70	↔

TIER 3

Rank	Country	Score	Annual change
58	Thailand	70.67	↑
59	Ukraine	70.47	↓
60	Republic of North Macedonia	70.24	↔
61	Belarus	70.09	↓
62	Bosnia and Herzegovina	70.01	↔
63	Kazakhstan	69.73	↔
64	Ecuador	69.56	↔
65	Qatar	69.29	↔
66	Vietnam	69.09	↑
67	Brazil	68.90	↔
68	Oman	68.52	↓
69	Mexico	68.49	↔
70	Colombia	67.97	↑
71	Suriname	67.95	↔
72	Dominican Republic	67.92	↔
73	Peru	67.81	↓
74	Cuba	67.78	↓
75	Maldives	67.75	↔
76	Russia	67.68	↓
77	China	67.61	↔
78	Cabo Verde	67.54	↓
79	Paraguay	67.34	↓
80	Indonesia	67.22	↑
81	Uzbekistan	66.88	↔
82	South Africa	66.69	↓
83	Sri Lanka	66.67	↓
84	Jordan	66.27	↔
85	Turkey	66.23	↓
86	Kyrgyzstan	66.20	↓
87	Philippines	66.16	↔
88	Mongolia	66.15	↓
89	Bahrain	66.10	↓
90	Saudi Arabia	65.58	↔
91	Tunisia	65.53	↓
92	West Bank and Gaza	65.52	↑
93	Bhutan	65.49	↓
94	Fiji	65.24	↓

TIER 4

Rank	Country	Score	Annual change
95	Guyana	64.52	↓
96	Lebanon	64.30	↔
97	Algeria	64.22	↔
98	Bolivia	64.11	↔
99	Azerbaijan	62.67	↓
100	El Salvador	62.25	↓
101	Morocco	61.71	↓
102	Botswana	61.57	↓
103	Ghana	60.50	↔
104	Turkmenistan	60.47	↔
105	Iran	60.30	↓
106	Sao Tome and Principe	59.84	↔
107	Honduras	59.01	↑
108	Egypt	58.77	↑
109	Namibia	58.21	↓
110	Nepal	58.10	↔
111	India	58.06	↓
112	Timor-Leste	57.94	↑
113	Iraq	57.76	↑

TIER 4 *(continued)*

Rank	Country	Score	Annual change
114	Guatemala	57.50	↓
115	Nicaragua	57.49	↓
116	Tajikistan	57.45	↑
117	Venezuela	57.23	↔
118	Gabon	56.58	↔
119	Libya	56.39	↑
120	Cambodia	55.36	↔
121	Bangladesh	54.60	↑
122	Senegal	54.53	↔
123	Kenya	53.62	↑
124	Laos	53.05	↑

TIER 5

Rank	Country	Score	Annual change
125	Tanzania	51.94	↔
126	Solomon Islands	51.30	↔
127	Myanmar	51.19	↓
128	Zambia	50.53	↑
129	The Gambia	50.10	↔
130	Malawi	49.85	↔
131	Côte d'Ivoire	49.31	↔
132	Benin	49.08	↓
133	Lesotho	49.01	↔
134	Pakistan	48.87	↓
135	Rwanda	48.82	↔
136	Comoros	48.82	↓
137	Zimbabwe	48.35	↔
138	Syria	48.14	↔
139	Eswatini	48.11	↓
140	Togo	47.81	↔
141	Djibouti	47.43	↔
142	Nigeria	46.97	↑
143	Cameroon	46.05	↔
144	Uganda	45.51	↑
145	Mozambique	45.32	↔
146	Burkina Faso	44.75	↓
147	Mauritania	44.74	↔
148	Sierra Leone	44.73	↓
149	Equatorial Guinea	44.70	↔
150	Papua New Guinea	44.50	↑
151	Republic of Congo	44.45	↔
152	Madagascar	44.21	↑
153	Angola	43.90	↔
154	Liberia	43.80	↔
155	Sudan	43.79	↑
156	Guinea-Bissau	43.60	↓
157	Mali	43.46	↑
158	Ethiopia	43.33	↓
159	Haiti	41.57	↓

TIER 6

Rank	Country	Score	Annual change
160	Guinea	40.61	↔
161	Niger	40.29	↑
162	Burundi	39.90	↔
163	Yemen	39.88	↔
164	Democratic Republic of Congo	37.63	↔
165	Eritrea	36.76	↑
166	Somalia	33.87	↔
167	Afghanistan	32.15	↓
168	Chad	30.20	↔
169	Central African Republic	27.37	↓
170	South Sudan	25.93	↑

↑ Improving country (increase of > 0.25 points)
↔ Stagnating country (change between -0.25 and 0.25 points)
↓ Declining country (decline of < -0.25 points)

Fig. 5.2 Social Progress Index rankings for 2023 published 2024 (Source: Social Progress Imperative (2024) available at https://cdn.prod.website-files.com/6650cb66e461b93f1a906cf2/667c5a2410e6e419272df71a_Global%20Social%20Progress%20Index%20Executive%20Summary%20.pdf. Accessed 30 May 2025)

factors contributing to social progress than simple population size (or population density given that Australia also features in the top 10 and Canada in the top 15), and it would be fascinating to develop a comprehensive statistical study of what these might be once enough years of data for SPI become available (the sample as yet is just 12 years). But it would appear that size is one of the contributing factors to high SPI performance, and the reasons are not perhaps far to seek. In smaller states, individual citizens are more aware of how their own behaviour and votes in elections can make a difference and so they are more likely to behave in socially responsible ways for the common good. Moreover, in smaller states (and in particular when population density is low), criminal elements find it more difficult to hide and to thrive unless of course the government of the state is taken over by criminals themselves (as in certain tax havens).

In short, what all of this means is that smaller states are more governable and participatory. There is no magic figure at which we can say that a state has become too large, no easily definable threshold between what is beautiful/small and what is too big but a threshold there is. If we focus on the theme of participation to address democratic deficit problems, then the threshold could be argued to be that at which direct democracy is still practicable. As a benchmark of a properly functioning direct democracy, the biggest Swiss canton today (Zürich) has a population of 1.5 million. But in the internet age with the possibility of remote voting, the maximum size for an effective direct democracy can be much higher. Relating this to the size of the SPI top 10 (2023) where 7 of the top 10 or 11 of the top 15 are states with population at or below 10 million; and assuming that in a country of 10 million people or less, a direct democracy can function effectively through use of the internet for directly democratic voting one can make the following calculation: if the world's nation states were broken down into units of 10 million or less at today's total world population of approximately 8 billion people, we would have between 800 and 1000 canton-states. (We say between 800 and 1000 because some of the nation states are already much smaller than 10 million people and would probably wish to retain their size as now given that small is beautiful.) Relating this in turn to our earlier proposal for a World Council of Ministers with one minister per member state, it would imply a gathering of up to 1000 ministerial representatives of the 800–1000 canton states. This would be more akin to a parliament than to a council of ministers and so we would suggest eventual replacement of the World Council of

Ministers as described earlier in this chapter by a World Parliament if and when the breakdown into small direct democracy units were achieved. Given that the current EU Parliament has 720 members and functions reasonably well, the idea of a World Parliament of 1000 members is not so shocking or unfeasible. The World Parliament would have one member per canton elected by each canton in a directly democratic vote; and given that there would still be heterogeneity in the size of the cantons qualified, majority voting as earlier described above would be the order of the day (but less complicated because of the lesser degree of variation in the size of the component states).

There may be further advantages of moving to a geopolitical order based on much smaller units below the World Authority that would practise direct democracy. One advantage which we believe would be very significant for direct democracy by comparison with the representative democracies that are the norm today and even more so by comparison with oligarchic or tyrannical states is that corruption would be significantly reduced and the power of lobbyists considerably curtailed. We are not saying that either of these closely related phenomena would disappear completely; but they would become very significantly more expensive for those who would try to sway government decision-making. Giving financial or other sweeteners to a decision-making population of 10 million people is altogether in a different scale from giving sweeteners to say 300 parliamentarians. Of course even a direct democracy can be hijacked by special vested interests, and this is particularly true in the internet age with troll farms and fake news: but it would be considerably more challenging and expensive to mount such hijacks. We will return to this theme of potential corruption of a supranational world order in Chap. 8.

We have suggested that the challenge of democratic deficit (already well known to the supranational EU) or indeed Kant's worries about tyranny of a world state can best be addressed in the peace-enhancing supranational structures of world government that we have proposed by the institution of direct democracy as the next level of decision-making below the supranational World Authority. While certainly radical as a suggestion in relation to the contemporary geopolitical order, when examined rationally and dispassionately devoid of any vested interests, we believe that there is a compelling logic to such a proposal. The biggest objections would be raised by the bigger nation states of the contemporary order and especially by the supposedly "great" powers. In the next chapter, we will examine how these state actors can be brought on board for such a plan. This rather than any inherent weakness of the direct democracy proposal itself is the biggest challenge to its potential implementation.

Bibliography

Boka, E. (2012). The European idea of a supranational union of peace. *Society and Economy, 34*(3), 387–397.

Brennan, J. (2012). *The Ethics of Voting*, Princeton University Press.

Churchill, W. (2008). In R. Langworth (Ed.), *Churchill by himself; the definitive collection of quotations.* Rosetta Books.

EU Consilium. *Qualified majority.* Accessed September 19, 2025., from https://www.consilium.europa.eu/en/council-eu/voting-system/qualified-majority/

Habermas, J. (2001). *The post-national constellation.* Polity Press.

Habermas, J. (2012). *The crisis of the European Union: A response.* Polity Press.

Kant, I. (1795). *Zum Ewigen Frieden*, Nicolovius, Königsberg. Available in English in Kant I (1991) *Political Writings* 2nd ed, translated by Nisbet H. Cambridge University Press.

Montani, G. (2019). *Supranational political economy: The globalisation of the state-market relationship.* Routledge.

Peabody, A. (1887). *Cicero: De Officiis* (Translation). Little Brown. The quotation is from Peabody's translation at p. 26. Accessed July 27, 2025, from https://oll.libertyfund.org/titles/cicero-on-moral-duties-de-officiis

Plato. (2007). *The republic.* Penguin Classics.

Schumacher, E. (1973). *Small is beautiful: A study of economics as if people mattered.* Blond & Briggs.

Schuman Project. Accessed September 13, 2025., from https://www.schuman.info/9MayProp.htm

Social Progress Imperative. (2024). Accessed May 30, 2025, from https://cdn.prod.website-files.com/6650cb66e461b93f1a906cf2/667c5a2410e6e419272df71a_Global%20Social%20Progress%20Index%20Executive%20Summary%20.pdf

CHAPTER 6

Getting All Aboard

Abstract Continuing the discussion of the major practical challenges which implementation of the proposals for a supranational World Authority would face, this chapter considers the question of how all of the world's states might be persuaded to come on board with the initiative. To attempt to bring states aboard by military force would be a contradiction of the whole project, and so it must occur by the persuasive force of rational argument. The world's smaller states would perhaps have little difficulty in joining up because of the manner in which their sovereignty is often in practice limited by the machinations of great powers in their zones of influence and because they have little or no supremacist baggage. But larger states, in particular "great" powers with imperialist tendencies, would probably refuse outright to be involved. Hence, we propose that those states who are willing should proceed with the supranationalist initiative without those "great" powers which do not wish to participate (the EU+ASEAN could be a powerful starting point); and once up and running and capable of financial and energy self-sufficiency, these states should erect an iron curtain, a total blockade of all interactions of any kind with those who do not wish to participate. This may not be ideal in certain respects, but we argue that once the use of military force to attain the supranational order is renounced (much as did the EU in 1950) to rely on rational persuasion, there is little other realistic alternative. The chapter closes by noting that our proposals are not some panacea that will cure

P. O'Sullivan et al., *Overcoming Gangsterism and Geo-Political Anarchy*, https://doi.org/10.1007/978-3-032-22438-5_6

today's manifold problems (the polycrisis of Edgar Morin) but is rather a necessary political institutional innovation to addressing the polycrisis.

Keywords Rationality of Cooperation • Gradualism • Voluntary adhesion • Institutional innovation • EU+ASEAN as nucleus • Human rights (and responsibilities) • Polycrisis • Cosmopolitanism (true meaning) • Hegel • Rational progress in human history

In the previous chapter, we looked at the problems of scalability in seeking to build a supranational geopolitical order drawing inspiration from the experiences in this domain of the European Union. This led us into what was admittedly a relatively speculative discussion regarding institutional structures which whatever about its logical cogency will still seem to many to be Utopian because there remains what we described as the *realpolitik* challenge: how to get all of the world's nation states and in particular those supposedly "great" powers to come on board and collaborate to put in place a supranational geopolitical order for the promotion of peace, in Schuman's words a peace-enhancing union. In this chapter, we examine how that challenge might be tackled.

Returning for a moment to first principles there is no doubt that in Hobbes original argument whereby individuals would surrender their rights to an all-powerful sovereign for the purpose of ending the war of all against all Hobbes does not see any exceptions: all individuals must participate for the peace to be effective. Nobody can reserve the right to remain outside of the social contract because otherwise these people would continue to prey on others destroying the peace that the sovereign authority is constructed to maintain. Carrying this logic over to our World Authority for the promotion of peace among the peoples and states of the world it means that to be properly effective all of the world's contemporary states must come on board for the peace-enhancing union to be truly effective. This we freely admit constitutes a major practical challenge to our project of instituting a supranational geopolitical order and so it is incumbent upon us to make some practical suggestions as to how this obstacle might be overcome.

The guiding principle which we would adopt in elaborating elements of an answer to the immense practical challenge is that of gradualism. It is just extremely unlikely that every nation in our world today will overnight or in a short period of a few years suddenly be convinced of the merits of a supranational world order such as we have outlined; and of course to try to enforce such a revolution of the geopolitical order by military force would be in direct contradiction of the aim of promoting peace and harmony among peoples which inspires the whole project. Nations would have to come aboard entirely of their own volition on the basis of the rationality of the Hobbesian/Kantian arguments deployed and this inevitably would be a gradual process and indeed to an extent a learning process. The first steps would of course be the primordial moves to transfer sovereignty in respect of use of military force to settle disputes to a supranational World Authority for dispute resolution with enforcement powers. But after that first primordial step states could afterwards be left to experiment as to which further areas of sovereignty they may be ready to transfer to a World Authority (e.g. how much of policies in respect of climate or financial matters) much as in the EU not all member states are members of the Eurozone. Meanwhile the old nation states could be encouraged to experiment with greater decentralisation and even break-up into smaller regional entities within which people through a more participatory democracy might better appreciate how "small is indeed more beautiful".[1] Thus, the process of change that we are envisaging would be decidedly gradualist and in this, as well as in its formal institutions, it would resemble the EU and build on its experiences. However, in one key way, it would be different from the EU of the Lisbon treaty: there could be no possibility of divorce (no article 50 of the Lisbon Treaty). In order to produce a truly lasting "perpetual" peace, such surrenders of areas of sovereignty to the World Authority as are made even if in gradual steps would be completely irrevocable: there would be no possibility of seceding from the World Authority once on board since the whole point of the exercise is precisely to put an end forever to those areas of exercise of sovereignty by nations which generate wars of all kinds including trade wars as waged by Donald Trump.[2]

[1] The phrase is of course from Schumacher E (1973) *Small is Beautiful: a study of Economics as if people mattered*, Blond & Briggs, London.

[2] Indeed, it could be said that one of the greatest mistakes of the EU in its over 65-year history is that it allowed Article 50 (Right to Withdraw from the EU) to be inserted in the Lisbon Treaty (2009). Not only did this article open the door to the fiasco of Brexit, it is directly at variance with the principle of supranationalism precisely because it still recognises the ultimate sovereignty of the nation states. This may render it consistent with International

Given the logical cogency of the Hobbesian argumentation and more broadly of Kant's proposals regarding the conditions of a perpetual peace as mentioned in Chap. 5, the obstacles to getting all states on board are emotional or at least blinkered rather than rational in nature but they are nonetheless real and difficult to overcome (perhaps even more difficult to overcome) for being thus based. Smaller states devoid of the supremacist pretensions to political hegemony will have little difficulty in agreeing a partial surrender of their sovereignty in the pursuit of world peace. These smaller states in theory have sovereignty at present and so a right to self-determination in policy matters and a right to defend themselves militarily against attack but in many cases they are at the mercy of "greater" powers in whose zone of influence they may happen to be. This in practice limits considerably their sovereign freedom of political action and so such states may well feel even safer than they now feel as sovereign states by becoming part of a supranational order with an overarching World Authority. So the smaller states will have little difficulty in agreeing to a new supranational order provided it is credible and has unambiguous enforcement powers in respect of maintaining peace among the world's states.

The difficulty arises with the larger states whose rights to self-determination and freedom of military action are much more real rather than theoretical. Such states by agreeing to surrender various rights in respect of foreign policy and military action to a supranational world sovereign will be sacrificing a rather more significant degree of freedom of action than would the smaller states. Even if the ultimate goal is laudable they will no doubt hesitate and resist especially if there is strong nationalist sentiment or if the state has an imperialist past. This problem is at its maximum in the case of the supposedly "great" powers since they will be surrendering their power to dictate (or to attempt to dictate) the terms of world peace as at present and of course it would spell the end for their cherished but ultimately supremacist inspired "zones of influence". As Daniel Esty has remarked in his discussion of good governance above the national level "*An enduring commitment to the principle of national sovereignty is most strongly visible among national political leaders whose power would be constrained by the presence of a layer of governance above them…Those in strong states are most likely to object to any regime of global*

Law as currently understood, but it is in direct contradiction with both the principle of transfer of sovereignty to the EU institutions and with the act of surrender of sovereignty in a peace-enhancing union that was central to the Treaty of Rome.

governance that limits their control".[3] Putting the matter even more bluntly, how can we ever expect the USA, the UK, Russia and China (and no doubt certain others as well) to participate in our proposed supranational order since at least in their eyes to do so would involve a considerable loss of geopolitical power on the world stage and of course a loss of face (of sorts)?

To this challenge we offer a number of elements of response. First of all, if one were to proceed to the break-up of the larger nation states into smaller units capable of functioning effectively as direct democracies as we suggested in the last chapter, this problem of the "great" powers and their pretensions would *ipso facto* fade away. But as noted, being realistic, any such initiative is a long way off and in fact would be resisted even more fiercely by the "great" powers than the suggestion of having a supranational World Authority for effective promotion of peace.[4] Hence, in suggesting practical ways forward, we must presume that in the first instance we are stuck with roughly the current set of nation states as recognised today by the UN. Hence, there remains the challenge of persuading the "great" powers to participate. One interesting observation immediately comes to mind: while getting them on board seems very difficult it would not be entirely impossible; after all in the aftermath of the Second World War three of the main belligerent powers of that war, France (West) Germany and Italy did come together transferring their sovereignty over defined areas in a peace-enhancing union; initially in the European Coal and Steel Community and later in the EEC and eventually the European Union. So as one might say "stranger things have happened".

The European project was born of the horrors of cataclysmic violence which had characterised the First and Second World Wars in Europe and one would not wish to have another such conflagration of violence before "great" powers might be brought to their senses to recognise the rational cogency of the Hobbesian argument for a supranational authority that we have developed. As hinted earlier, a peace-enhancing union cannot be built up by military force since that would imply an outright contradiction

[3] Esty D (2006) Good Governance at the Supranational Scale, *The Yale Law Journal*, 115: 1490–1562.

[4] Imagine if we pressed for a break-up of the USA or China into smaller political units; or more concretely consider the actual resistance of Spain and of the UK to current pressures for their break-up. The latter case is of course highly ironic since while the UK broke out of the EU, the London government does not want to accord the same prerogative of breakaway to Scotland.

in its formation. The supranational order we are proposing must be built up by the power of rational persuasion culminating as in Hobbes in some kind of world level social contract to which all states would freely subscribe with a view to promoting peace and ending the war of all against all among states in an effective manner. As noted, however, many of the world's smaller states could probably already agree in principle to follow such a supranational path voluntarily and might even feel, rather more secure by so doing amid the contemporary context. If we follow such an approach and if a significant number of the world's current states were already to agree to transfer peace-keeping power (among themselves in the first instance) to a supranational World Authority, then in the presence of such a partial attainment of the supranational objective the question would become: how are we to deal with and to persuade the recalcitrant non-members to join given that military force is out of the question?

We believe that once the supranational authority has reached a sufficient critical size it should put in place a total blockade on interaction of any kind, economic, financial, political or cultural, with the recalcitrant states, in effect an Iron Curtain. There would be no freedom of trade in goods and services, strict and total prohibition of flows of funds of any kind, absolutely no freedom of movement of people whether for migration or for tourism and probably not even rights of overflight or navigation. In short, a policy of complete ostracisation of the "great" powers or any others that do not wish to join the supranational order. Such total blockades on interaction are entirely possible and Europe at any rate has experienced such in the period of the Cold War (1946–1989) with the Iron Curtain between the Soviet Union's sphere of influence and Western Europe. However, it is true that for such a blockade to be practicable, the set of states participating in the supranational World Authority needs to be sufficiently large to be entirely self-sufficient in every respect: in terms of food supply, meeting energy needs, financially in the sense of having financial markets capable of meeting the borrowing and investment needs of all of the participating states and finally through a fully integrated transport system. It is interesting to note that if the European Union as it is today and the Association of South-East Asian Nations (ASEAN) were to join up as blocks to the supranational arrangements we are describing then many of the requisite aspects of self-sufficiency for a painless blockade would already be in place; and the more successful the EU and ASEAN become in the development of truly renewable energy sources (wind, water, solar), the more this will be the case.[5]

Of course, some of the "great" powers at least would fight tooth and nail against such a blockade and more generally against the supranational World Authority. In some cases, this might take the form of outright military conquest as certain "great" powers aggressively seek to increase their "zones of influence" and we are living through just such an episode at present with Trump's expansionist activities and threats and Russia's invasion of Ukraine. This means that with the peace-keeping function having been transferred to the World Authority by the participating states they would have to maintain a common army and a common defence policy to protect against such attacks. This after all is one of the most fundamental roles of the Hobbesian sovereign, protection of the citizens against external attacks. Once again if the EU and ASEAN were to come aboard as blocks the common army of the World Authority would offer a powerful deterrent to invasions given the military capabilities of France, Germany, Italy, Poland, Sweden, Finland, Spain, Thailand, and Vietnam (among others). It should be noted *en passant* that the EU today has not got a common army and common defence is provided through the North Atlantic Treaty Organisation (NATO) which includes Canada and the USA as well as an array of EU states.[6] NATO however is patently dominated by the USA as a "great" power with explicit pretensions to hegemony[7] and the USA certainly is not committed to the promotion of a supranational world sovereign such as we have outlined in this book. It would be likely to be one of the major opponents of such an order. Hence, quite apart from the fact that NATO is focussed on the USA and Europe while we are talking about a supranational authority for the world as a whole, NATO because of US hegemony cannot be considered as an embryonic common army for our World Authority. It is true as we remarked earlier that if one day the supranational World Authority is completed and embodies all of the world's states as in Kant's ideal for

[5] For the record, in 2024, the population of EU+ASEAN was 1.15 billion, so 14% of total world population of about 8.2 billion. Of that world total, India had 1.41 billion and China 1.40 billion.

[6] But note that Austria and Ireland remain outside of NATO, whereas Finland and Sweden have just joined NATO for the first time.

[7] See Allison G (2020) The new Spheres of Influence: sharing the globe with other great powers *Foreign Affairs* March/April 2020: 1–6 for a frank discussion of this pretension.

perpetual peace,[8] then the role of armies would be fundamentally transformed to peace-keeping functions and weapons stocks could be drastically reduced (and nuclear weapons perhaps eliminated entirely). But until such time as the World Authority is entirely inclusive the threat of military invasion from outside remains and an army in its classical functions would need to be maintained; but logically with peace-keeping functions having been transferred to the World Authority as per the Hobbesian argument it would be a common army with a common supranationally defined defence policy, not a hegemonically dominated military alliance like NATO (or the old Warsaw Pact alliance dominated as it was by the Soviet Union). Two years ago such ideas of common supranational defence in Europe (or anywhere else) might have seemed Utopian and unfeasible but Russia's invasion of Ukraine and US vacillations in its commitments to NATO under Donald Trump have put such ideas once again on the table of the European Union. France under Emmanuel Macron[9] has been particularly keen.[10]

In our day of course, the external threats to the supranational World Authority from recalcitrant "great" powers would not only come from classic military invasions and attempted annexations of territory; there would also very likely be extensive cyber warfare. Cyberattacks of all kinds and in particular efforts by "great" powers to intervene in the politics and decision-making processes of smaller states have become so commonplace that they are now rarely reported unless the attack has been on a massive scale. Hence, the blockade that we have described would also need to extend to the internet and all forms of electronic communication; and would in effect imply that the World Authority would have to create and oversee its own internet completely independently of any of the "great" powers which have systematically tried to manipulate the internet as we know it for their own narrow nationalistic ends. The Russian troll farms

[8] Kant I (1795) *Zum Ewigen Frieden*, Nicolovius, Königsberg. Available in English in Kant I (1991) *Political Writings* 2nd ed., translated by Nisbet H Cambridge University Press, Cambridge. In this work the essay "*Perpetual Peace: A Philosophical Sketch*" is contained.

[9] Consider Macron's speech on March 2022 as reported in The Guardian (03 March 2022) available at https://www.theguardian.com/world/2022/mar/03/europe-must-become-more-independent-shore-up-defence-emmanuel-macron. Accessed 12 September 2025.

[10] It is interesting to note that if as a "great" power the USA remained outside of the effort to construct a supranational World Authority in which its power and geopolitical influence would be significantly reduced and if the World Authority constructs its own common defence, that would in effect spell the end of NATO as a military alliance. But if the common army of the World Authority is powerful and duly resourced to deal with external threats, that might not be such a bad thing for European states.

are by now famous but the insistence of the US government to have back door access to everything that the US internet giants (Google, Facebook/ Meta, etc.) put in place shows that manipulative intent is not just a Russian obsession.[11] In the construction of an entirely new supranational internet, an effort could also be made to render it significantly more equitable than the in the present set-up which entrenches the dominant positions of the biggest commercial enterprises in the manner of presentation of search results.[12]

Some readers will be troubled by certain of the implications of the all-embracing blockade on engagement by the nascent world authority with those who remain outside of it which we have proposed. There is no doubt that the blockade would in some instances violate certain human rights such as asylum (there could be no possibility of this in a total blockade) and it would also run counter to Kant's Principle of Hospitality as outlined in his essay *Perpetual Peace: A Philosophical Sketch* and more widely to what has come to be known in geopolitical theory as cosmopolitanism.[13] These are fair points and we would not seek to dodge such implications. On the question of human rights, we believe that whatever about the UN or other declarations of these they are neither absolute nor axiomatic. They are not absolute for the simple reason that every human right as exercised by any individual human being can only be so exercised to the point or degree that it does not infringe the exercise of the same or of other declared rights by other human beings. Hence, any right encounters limitations to its exercise (unless one is living alone on a desert island…and even then there may be rights of other living beings to be considered). Equally rights are non-axiomatic: on this we openly follow Hobbes' logic. What is the point of having elaborate sets of human rights in a society riven by conflicts and insecurity? Human rights are wonderful and we hold them in high esteem but they presuppose an already peaceful respectful and tolerant community living in peace and security with a decent stan-

[11] For an up to date insight on the situation as between the US government and access to big tech's applications, see *Wired* 21st March 2025, "How to avoid US based digital services and why you might want to", available at https://www.wired.com/story/trump-era-digital-expat/. Accessed 9 June 2025.

[12] Whomsoever pays the highest fee gets to be first on the list of search results; and who pays highest often already has a dominant market position. It's all about marketing, silly.

[13] See Kant (1795) op. cit; and on the link between Kant's principle and cosmopolitanism, see Wallace Brown G (2014) The European Union and Kant's Idea of Cosmopolitan Right, *European Journal of International Relations* 20(3) 671–693.

dard of living for all; not many rights are being respected in violent war zones. In short, human rights are for civilised inclusive communities where the use of violence and the war of all against all has been definitively renounced.[14] Until this has been achieved there is not a great deal of point in declaring universal human rights. Indeed one of the greatest tragedies of the UN is that despite its admirable Universal Declaration of Human Rights many of these rights are systematically flouted by various member states in almost entire impunity for the by now familiar reason: the UN's lack of enforcement powers. What we are in effect suggesting is that if we really do want to initiate a world in which human rights are universal and guaranteed we need a supranational World Authority with real enforcement powers such as we have described in the previous chapter to replace the UN and to put an end to the effective war of all against all that still prevails in the international arena…and which leads (in war zones) to by far the most egregious violations of the human rights of individual citizens in the world today.

It is also true that the comprehensive blockade that we advocate involves a kind of fortress mentality that will troublesome. Again we say yes: this is indeed a fortress mentality. But given that we do not want in any way to engage in military force to bring new members on board for the supranational World Authority what other realistic options of suasion have we? If people outside of our supranational structures witness the peaceful and civilised way of life that is possible inside the new order they may begin to put pressure on their recalcitrant governments to seek to join the new "club"; and it goes without saying that the new supranational club would welcome with open arms any new members who agree to its laws and structures. That is the real meaning of Kant's Hospitality Principle in this context.[15] Hospitality was never about opening the door to just anyone who presents and allowing them to do as they please. Hospitality implies a respect and reciprocity whereby we open our doors without question to

[14] This point will be elaborated in a little more detail in Chap. 7.

[15] In the Third Definitive Article of his essay on Perpetual Peace, Kant speaks not only of hospitality as a right of temporary visit for foreign citizens (immigration he sees as requiring a separate and explicit contract of permanent residence for a foreigner): he is also adamant that the hospitality should be extended only on a basis of mutual respect. He says, "Hospitality means the right of a stranger not to be treated as an enemy when he arrives in the land of another. One may refuse to receive him when this can be done without causing his destruction, but so long as he peacefully occupies his place one may not treat him with hostility" (Kant, 1795 op. cit; Nisbet H 1991 translation: Ch 4 p. 105).

those who will in turn respect the basic rules and laws of our civilised community.[16] Mutual tolerance and respect are of the essence of hospitality.

A nice question which can fairly be posed at this stage is how long the kind of blockade stalemate that we have just described between a nascent World Authority and recalcitrant "great" powers and other nationalist hangers-on might last? To that question we have, let us be frank, no answer. All we can say is that the logic of the Hobbesian (and Kantian) argument points very clearly in the direction of an all-inclusive supranational world authority which would make war among states "unthinkable ever again"; and that surely is a worthwhile goal for the whole of humanity given the ugliness, the barbarism, the privations and the tragic disruption of so many individual lives that warfare implies. Only those who uphold some kind of superiority complex whereby they are somehow better than others can logically defend the war of all against all precisely because they think that they can easily win that war and either exterminate or somehow enslave their inferiors while arrogating to themselves enjoyment of the material wealth of the world. This sort of belief has unfortunately been regularly recrudescent in the history of the world, and it reached its apogee in eighteenth- and nineteenth-century slavery and colonialism. Nonetheless, it has to be said that no claim to superiority has ever stood up philosophically and most have ended eventually in disastrous humiliation for those with supremacist pretensions. The most obvious example is Nazism, but readers will on reflection be able no doubt to recognise a variety of other supremacist pretensions that have bitten the dust in the history of humanity.[17]

Hence, we would argue that while it is difficult to put a time scale on how soon a supranational geopolitical order once initiated would be transformed into an all-inclusive entity embracing all of the world's states, rational argument decidedly points in that direction. One could equally

[16] This point has been obfuscated and even abused in the debates on immigration policy in Europe and elsewhere. We are not making out here a blanket anti-migration argument. We are certainly not against migratory flow within established civilised communities and as already noted in our supranational world geopolitical entity there would be freedom of internal migration as well as freedom of capital movements and freedom of trade. But for those who do not respect such rules there would be no such freedoms. That being said from the moment that outsiders propose to respect the laws of our civilised community, they can be admitted. Is this not what we do with criminals today; and is this not what happens when terrorist organisations lay down their arms and propose to negotiate?

[17] The sporting world is replete with parables of this kind.

ask how long before the first steps of putting in place even a partial supranational order may take: however, the awareness of the need to pass beyond the contemporary geopolitical order based on the UN and international law as we know it is already present among scholars and at least for some politicians (Emmanuel Macron and Volodymyr Zelensky,[18] for example). Where Reason leads practice will eventually follow, kicking and screaming no doubt and with many temporary setbacks, but it will follow since we are rational beings. The gradual abolition of slavery and the gradual emancipation of women to take just two examples testify to the power of rational argument in human history. This was the insight at the heart of Hegel's much misunderstood philosophy of history when he declared "*World history is governed by an ultimate design, that it is a rational process... this is a proposition whose truth we must assume; its proof lies in the study of world history itself, which is the image and enactment of reason*".[19]

It goes without saying of course that humanity today is also facing other major challenges besides widespread violent conflicts. Among the most immediate is the need to counteract the protectionist disarray into which trading patterns have been thrown as the result of just one powerful sovereign state unilaterally trying to bully almost all of the other states in the world by threats of swingeing tariffs and outright protectionism, a process in which there is not even the pretence of considering anything other than the (supposed) interests of the USA. Given the failures of the essentially intergovernmental WTO to counter this despite its noble aims, the world's trading system is manifestly in need of the institution of a supranational authority with real powers of enforcement such as we have been describing in this book to oversee the world's trading arrangements in a way in which the necessarily intertwined interests of all of the world's states and peoples are recognised and respected. There are of course many other challenges that require a common collaborative response and while we have focused on the fundamental need for gradualist institutional reforms we would not want to discount or minimise such other challenges to the survival of humanity as are posed by the despoliation of the natural

[18] See, for example, Zelensky's scathing critique of the Security Council in his address to that body on 05 April 2022. A report on the speech can be found at https://www.france24.com/en/europe/20220407-act-or-dissolve-zelensky-challenges-un-but-ukraine-atrocities-already-pile-pressure-on-russia. Accessed 12 September 2025.

[19] Hegel G (1975) *Lectures on the Philosophy of History* first published in German (1837) translated to English with an introduction by Nisbet H, Cambridge University Press Cambridge.

environment, social inclusivity and equity in the enjoyment of resources: in short the challenges of sustainable development. Some idea of the scope of these ulterior challenges can be gleaned from the work of Edgar Morin who has written extensively about the imposing array of social, political and economic problems and even flash-points that are leading to social conflicts, economic crises ecological disasters and political polarisation and breakdown.[20] We would certainly not want to gloss over these contemporary challenges and we would be inclined to follow Morin in suggesting the need for serious efforts at rethinking and reform on a variety of fronts simultaneously in face of what he sees as a *polycrisis*.[21] In particular, what is urgently needed is to pass beyond simplistic short-term would be fixes that are blinkered to the interdependence of people's lives in today's world. Sustainable development implies a concern for the planet which future generations will inherit from those alive and active today and an economic system that is capable of guaranteeing a fair share in wealth for all in a stable economic environment (not riven by repeated financial crises).

For Morin, achieving progress on these multiple fronts is at least in part a matter for better more enlightened government across the world, and on that point, there is a significant convergence with what we have been arguing in this book. We believe that the institutional reforms we are proposing in the form of a supranational World Authority are in fact an indispensable first step towards a better world governance which in turn might lead to truly effective policies that might meet the shared challenges of the polycrisis. Our proposals are not intended as a panacea that if put in place will solve all of the world's contemporary social, economic and political challenges. Rather we see them as an indispensable first step towards a truly effective attempt to solve the many interrelated challenges we face. It is in fact interesting to note that while there has been a considerable amount of effort devoted to looking at technological innovations which might help to address various aspects of the polycrisis (renewable energies, greener transport modes, recycling and circular economy practices, various uses of artificial intelligence in the medical field and in plastic waste recycling), what has been notoriously absent is any kind of serious political

[20] See Morin E (2012) *La Voie pour l'avenir de l'humanité*, Hachette Paris.

[21] Polycrisis is a term introduced in effect by Morin to describe how a series of crises interact with and may reinforce each another in a complex interdependent world. See Morin E (1993) *Terre-Patrie*, Seuil, Paris: translated as Morin E (1999) *Homeland Earth: a manifesto for the New Millennium*, Hampton Press, University of Michigan, Ann Arbor.

and governance innovation. We are stuck with the same international order based on sovereign nation states, "great" powers and their supposed "zones of influence" and an international law that is honoured more in the breach than the observance…for at least the past 250 years. Our thesis is that it is high time for serious efforts at **political institutional innovation**. We believe that our proposals are a first step in that direction and as framed they transcend most of the great ideological divides of the past and would upon critical reflection be something on which left, centre and even many right wing thinkers could easily and rationally agree. Only the most die-hard nationalist supremacists might ultimately disagree.

Bibliography

Allison, G. (2020). The new spheres of influence: Sharing the globe with other great powers. *Foreign Affairs,* March/April 2020.

Esty, D. (2006). Good governance at the supranational scale. *The Yale Law Journal, 115*, 1490–1562.

Hegel, G. (1975). *Lectures on the philosophy of history* first published in German (1837) translated to English with an introduction by Nisbet H, Cambridge University Press.

Kant, I. (1795). *Zum Ewigen Frieden*, Nicolovius, Königsberg. Available in English in Kant I (1991) *Political Writings* 2nd ed, translated by Nisbet H Cambridge University Press.

Macron's speech in The Guardian (03 March 2022). Accessed September 12, 2025, from https://www.theguardian.com/world/2022/mar/03/europe-must-become-more-independent-shore-up-defence-emmanuel-macron

Morin, E. (1993). *Terre-Patrie.* Seuil, Paris: Translated as Morin E (1999) *Homeland Earth: A manifesto for the new millennium.* Hampton Press, University of Michigan.

Morin, E. (2012). *La Voie pour l'avenir de l'humanité.* Hachette Paris.

Schumacher, E. (1973). *Small is beautiful: A study of economics as if people mattered.* Blond & Briggs.

Wallace Brown, G. (2014). The European Union and Kant's idea of cosmopolitan right. *European Journal of International Relations, 20*(3), 671–693.

Wired 21st March 2025. How to avoid US based digital services and why you might want to. Accessed September 9, 2025, from https://www.wired.com/story/trump-era-digital-expat/

Zelensky's scathing critique of the Security Council 05 April 2022. Accessed September 12, 2025, from https://www.france24.com/en/europe/20220407-act-or-dissolve-zelensky-challenges-un-but-ukraine-atrocities-already-pile-pressure-on-russia

CHAPTER 7

Reflections on Some Corollary Questions for a Supranational World Order

Abstract The project of creating a supranational world order centred on a World Authority with real enforcement powers would represent a huge upheaval in relation to the contemporary order based on sovereign nation states, and so naturally, a number of corollary issues will naturally be raised, and in this chapter, we seek to deal with some of these. Perhaps, an issue which will cause considerable unease is that of the cultural, religious and ethical diversity which would be present in such a World Authority; and since in effect within the sphere of the new entity, there would be complete freedom of trade and factor movement, hence entirely free migration how can we hope to cope with the possible tensions to which this may give rise (given the explosive nature of these questions in many states around the world today). Part of our tentative response is to suggest that if the world can indeed be broken down into about 1000 cantons and city states, there would be the possibility for like-minded groups to coalesce into the communities they find most congenial to their values and culture. There would be a place for everyone. A second part of our response would be to ensure through a generous welfare state (or "welfare world") that there would be a real equality of economic opportunity throughout the sphere of the World Authority as such would greatly reduce the incentive to economic migration. Finally, we address the question of human rights in the proposed World Authority. On this question, we rather follow Hobbes, arguing that no human right is ever absolute since it can only be exercised

P. O'Sullivan et al., *Overcoming Gangsterism and Geo-Political Anarchy*, https://doi.org/10.1007/978-3-032-22438-5_7

in a manner consistent with the rights of others and so that all rights (individual and of component states) must in the first instance be vested in the supranational World Authority which will then accord rights to all in accordance with mutual respect by all of the rights of all. In short, the primordial *fons et origo* of all rights will be the supranational World Authority.

Keywords Supranational authority • Single market • Freedom of movement • Immigration • Cultural diversity • Human rights • Responsibility to respect rights (of others) • Moral origins of sovereignty

We have reflected in the previous chapter on some of the practical challenges which would be involved in moving to a supranational world order under the Hobbesian logic and the focus was on how those states who might insist on remaining outside of the new order might be persuaded to join. In this chapter, we turn our attention to some of the further difficult issues that might arise within and between the members of the new supranational order.

Perhaps, one of the most obvious internal challenges for the supranational order centres on cultural and religious diversity: how can we get various peoples of widely different cultural background and religious beliefs to come together and collaborate in a supranational World Authority with strong enforcement powers for promotion of peace and an end to warfare? Part of the answer already lies in the goal of peace itself: whatever may be the cultural and religious diversity of the world virtually all people prefer to live in peace and security. That is a goal which transcends cultural and religious differences; and since in the first instance the transfer of sovereignty to the supranational World Authority would be restricted to matters regarding keeping the peace and avoiding warfare, it should therefore be possible relatively easily to get agreement despite the diversity. It is worth noting that at the level of individual people as opposed to at state/governmental level virtually every human individual appreciates peace and living their lives in tranquil harmonious societies as opposed to being in war zones or involved directly in warfare. Wars are waged by governments or by gangs, not by individuals as such and they are built up on various forms of groupthink induced by propaganda and today fake news on social media that promote supposed gang interests but which in reality are just the interests of a very few individuals. People at an individual level will rarely favour the mass systematic violence of warfare…and it is pertinent to note that wars are rarely if ever declared on the basis of referenda.

Hence, we can take it that for the bulk of humanity at a personal level to live in peace, harmony and tranquillity is a highly desirable goal. There may be residual groups with supremacist pretensions that do not value peace but rather aspire to the use of violence and military force to assert their supremacy while eliminating or subjugating those whom they see as inferior or as infidels, but as noted in the previous chapter, such supremacist claims are not only obnoxious, human history suggests that those who push them eventually face humiliation. In the previous chapter, we were referring to this phenomenon in "great" powers which would disdain any kind of participation in a supranational order but the same problem could in principle arise even within the new supranational order based on certain cultural or religious views sympathetic to supremacism. This is actually one of the reasons why we have suggested that eventually the bigger nation states need to be broken up and that below the World Authority we should have political units small enough to be governable and to practise direct democracy: the lesser the size of the political unit, the less the chances of supremacist pretensions. Also as noted in Chap. 5, if we have such small political units, there would be up to 1000 states in the world order, and people of like mind, of particular religions or cultures, could easily coalesce into their own small states where they can be as different as they please without threatening any others of different cultural views or religious beliefs.[1] We are not necessarily suggesting that this would be an optimal solution since one might ultimately prefer states to manifest a sufficient tolerance and respect to be multi-cultural and to embrace religious and other forms of diversity; but the small states with the possibility of "doing their own thing" could offer a safety valve against cultural and religious tensions in particular if the World Authority acts on a strict Principle of Subsidiarity as discussed in Chap. 5.

[1] Such ideas of separate facilities solutions tailored to the specific tastes of certain social groups have been proposed in Economics by E J Mishan, not without controversy. See Mishan E J (1969) *Growth: the Price we Pay* Staples Press, London. See also the critical comments in *Commentary* September 1970 available at https://www.commentary.org/articles/lawrence-malkin/technology-and-growth-the-price-we-pay-by-e-j-mishan-21-popular-economic-fallacies-by-e-j-mishan/. Accessed 13 September 2025.

Thinking through the challenges of religious and cultural diversity does throw up two difficult corollary political issues for our supranational order on which we will now comment: migration and human rights. Implicit in the idea just mentioned of what would in effect be a "separate facilities" solution to cultural and religious diversity in small states is the presumption that people would be free to move around the nascent world state as they pleased and in particular that they should be free to migrate and settle where they see best fit. But is the world yet ready for such a universal free migration of people? In one way, the answer is patently no as the tensions caused by large-scale migration from Africa to Europe or from South America to the USA testify. But the migration is happening anyway, whatever may be the tensions and whatever may be the privations suffered by the migrants at their eventual destinations. Hence, whether we embark on a supranational path or not, the developed world is facing a challenge that is just not going to go away.[2] It can almost certainly be said that much if not the vast majority of such migration is economically motivated; people in poorer parts of the world where there is severe poverty and pressure of population on exiguous infrastructures have little to lose and (for them) much to gain by taking their chances on migrating illegally to developed economies to do menial jobs often initially in an underground economy. Those advanced countries in turn often have significant shortages of unskilled labour and so supply meets demand. When seen in this economic perspective, it becomes clear not only that the ultimate root of the large-scale illegal migrations we are seeing today is a huge gap in economic opportunities as between the poorer and the more developed countries, it is also clear that the problem is not going to go away until that economic gap is closed at least to a level which will dramatically reduce the incentive to migrate. We do not claim any originality for this insight which is quite widely shared by scholars[3] and even by some European politicians regarding the challenges of illegal migration. Indeed as early as 1959 the great Swedish economist Gunnar Myrdal had already warned us of the impending challenges if the European nations, then busily constructing their nascent welfare states, did not pay attention simultaneously to

[2] It may even be mentioned that climate change will if anything only increase migratory flows as certain geographical regions become less habitable.

[3] See, for example, Donato K & Massey D (2016) Twenty-first century Globalisation and Illegal Migration in *Annals of American Academy of Political and Social Sciences*, 666: 7–26. See also on the policy side Frontex (2009) *The Impact of the global economic crisis on illegal migration to the EU*, Frontex, Warszawa.

constructing what he described as a "welfare world". Put very bluntly paraphrasing Myrdal, he was saying: Fine to construct the European welfare states but don't forget to help the poorer countries to construct similar structures of their own: otherwise, the inequalities in economic opportunity will in the long run become explosive in their implications.[4]

Relating this now to our proposal for a supranational World Authority and to the question of freedom of migration within its domain the first key point to reiterate is that whether or not we proceed with the supranational project the world's advanced countries are going to have to face the challenge of large-scale illegal migration in any case; and the only policies that can effectively and sustainably reduce the migratory flows are those which can reduce the gaping economic gap that has opened up as between the advanced economies and poorer areas of the world, especially those experiencing violent conflicts of various kinds. Nation states may seek to erect various kinds of frontier barriers and enforce these by strong policing and military means but while these may have a short-term effect, in the medium to long term, they just displace the point of entry of illegal migrants since the economic incentive to migrate remains and the advanced countries have very long frontiers not all of which can practicably be patrolled. The ingenuity of illegal migrants seeking to get to Europe testifies not only to the incredible risks that illegal migrants are prepared to take to reach the "promised land" but also to the futility of this whole fortress approach. The key to addressing illegal migratory flows lies rather in addressing the economic inequalities of opportunity: in short we need to build up Myrdal's welfare world.

Once this point sinks in together with the much higher degree of solidarity and willingness to share wealth throughout the world that it implies, we can actually say that the construction of a supranational World Authority for peace-keeping purposes could in fact help towards creating the necessary sense of solidarity for a welfare world. The experience of intimate interdependence of all of the world's states and citizens that underpins the Hobbesian transfer of peace-keeping powers to a world sovereign can as we noted earlier be extended to other policy areas where there is patent interdependence and need for collaborative action among all states for policies to be effective (e.g. climate change); and for all such areas of policy a transfer of competence to the World Authority can be envisaged. In particular, therefore, once it is recognised that the immigration question

[4] See Myrdal G (1960) *Beyond the Welfare State*, Duckworth, London.

cannot be solved unilaterally by a fortress approach but rather requires a strongly collaborative effort across states to construct a welfare world, then if we were to transfer the policy competence of constructing that welfare world to the supranational World Authority the policy would have a significantly increased effectiveness by comparison with nation states seeking to go it alone. Put simply: far from the supranational World Authority exacerbating problems of illegal migration, if it takes on the task of creating a welfare world this can make a very effective contribution to reducing permanently the problems of illegal migration.

In the period (which could span decades or more) before the World Authority can become inclusive of the whole of humanity, there would remain the challenge of immigration from the other side of the iron curtain that we proposed in Chap. 6. No iron curtain on earth can ever be completely impermeable. However, as mentioned in Chap. 6, what we are envisaging is that there would among other things be no possibility of granting asylum under any circumstance to people from states outside the new supranational initiative. Illegal migrants would therefore in all cases be unceremoniously dropped back on the opposite side of the iron curtain. If this policy, however harsh it may seem, were systematically applied then illegal migrants would soon give up their attempts and concentrate their attentions on pressing their national governments to join the new supranational order together with its welfare world state as outlined above. Once inside the new supranational entity they would of course be free to migrate internally as they wished. Moreover, given that the World Authority would be built on foundations of Kantian hospitality, we could allow that in certain exceptional cases where people outside of the World Authority's sphere are being subject to manifest persecution because of their desires to be within the new supranational order rather than outside of it, a channel of entry by legal asylum could be opened. But in view of the fact that "great" powers would probably be doing their utmost to undermine the new order such asylum would have to be subject to the strictest of controls against possible subversion and entrants would be required to renounce completely and for ever their citizenship of the states from which they come. It should be noted in any case that the countries most likely to remain outside of the new supranational governing entity are not the poorer countries of Africa and elsewhere but rather the "great" powers and from the latter potential migratory inflows would probably be limited. Especially in the light of what has just been said about a welfare world, the world's poorer states from which illegal economic migrants mainly come would probably demonstrate a certain enthusiasm for joining the new supranational entity from the start.

Rumbling behind the question of free migration in the domain of our proposed supranational World Authority is the wider question of human rights: what rights are to be guaranteed to citizens and how are they to be enforced? In the contemporary geopolitical order, every member state of the United Nations is in principle committed to uphold the UN Universal Declaration of Human Rights.[5] Hopefully, we do not need to labour the point (as already mentioned briefly in Chap. 6)[6] that while this is an admirable declaration, it is honoured more in the breach than in the observance in many parts of the world;[7] and it is hamstrung above all by the lack of any serious power of enforcement: the International Court of Justice (ICJ) in Den Haag as we saw in Chap. 2 has no powers to enforce its decisions. It should however be noted that since the Lisbon Treaty of 2009 the European Union has adopted a Charter of Fundamental Rights[8] which reproduces most of the UN Declaration but goes beyond that declaration in certain aspects: and this Charter being now an integral part of the binding supranational law of the EU, its provisions can be adjudicated at *and enforced* by the supranational European Court of Justice (ECJ).

The above point suggests that if we want to ensure the respect of human rights in an effective manner they need to be guaranteed by an authority with power of enforcement and where rights which cross national boundaries in any way are concerned, that authority needs to be supranational in character. But how extensive are these rights to be and what is to happen if they enter into conflict with each other? This question (to which passing reference has already been made in Chap. 6) is necessarily thrown up by the Hobbesian argument in defence of a supranational authority that we have here deployed and the question raises wider questions that go right to the heart of human rights theory. In the Hobbesian argument as made out for individuals in a pre-political state of nature amid the anarchic war of all against all, Hobbes clearly envisaged that all natural rights should be

[5] Available at https://www.un.org/en/about-us/universal-declaration-of-human-rights. Accessed 13 September 2025.

[6] See Chap. 6, p. 78.

[7] Consider article 4: No one shall be held in slavery or servitude; or Article 5: "No one shall be subjected to torture or to cruel inhuman or degrading treatment or punishment". Respected everywhere today???

[8] Full text available at https://www.europarl.europa.eu/charter/pdf/text_en.pdf. Accessed 13 September 2025.

transferred by individuals to the sovereign precisely because if any rights are held back by individuals to exercise as they see fit there will be the danger of violent conflict breaking out again when people disagree and clash in the exercise of the rights they have reserved to themselves. What this in turn means is that for Hobbes all rights are vested in the sovereign rather than in individual human beings; and it is the sovereign which then decides what rights can be safely transferred back to citizens to exercise freely as they see fit but always with the proviso that the sovereign can intervene to resolve disputes regarding rights and enforce those resolutions. In Hobbes thought, therefore, human rights are not absolute and vested in individuals: they are rather a political privilege accorded to citizens by the sovereign to be exercised in a manner that is consistent with the exercise of their rights by all other citizens, thereby maintaining a peaceful harmonious community.[9] The practical significance of this Hobbesian perspective on human rights has been thrown up in sharp relief in European states in recent years. For example, is freedom of speech an absolute right or is it a right which may be curtailed by the sovereign with a view to preservation of peace and harmony? The outlawing of any kind of "hate" speech on the internet (or elsewhere) as has happened in many countries has been challenged to a greater or lesser extent by those who would defend an absolute individual right to free speech; but in fact such prohibitions clearly take the Hobbesian approach to rights seen not as absolute but as a privilege to be accorded by the sovereign in pursuit of an ordered harmonious society. Exactly the same tension between upholders of absolute human rights and the Hobbesian approach can be found in the surprisingly heated debates that occurred in many European countries regarding the wearing of face masks during the Covid-19 pandemic.

In this work, we have drawn heavily on the compelling logic of the Hobbesian argument, and not surprisingly, therefore, we would tend to agree with his perspective on human rights seen not as absolutes in themselves but as privileges accorded by the sovereign; and actually, that in practice is the most common position over almost all of the world's states today, however authoritarian or democratic they may be. Of course in

[9] In this respect, Hobbes social contract is significantly different from that proposed later by John Locke. In Locke, individuals in a state of nature form the state to protect certain inalienable rights that they never transfer to the sovereign, most notably the right to private property. See Locke J (1988) *Two Treatises of Government*, Cambridge University Press, Cambridge, Second Treatise.

authoritarian states the degree of personal rights and freedoms accorded to citizens is less than in the typical European democracies but the differences on this question are not differences of principle regarding rights as between authoritarian states and democracies but rather differences of degree (in respect of the liberties to be allowed as the example of freedom of expression most clearly shows).

We have of course been applying the Hobbesian argumentation not at the level of individuals forming states in a state of nature by a hypothetical social contract but rather to the war of all against all among already formed nation states that characterises the contemporary geopolitical order. Hence, we now need to reflect on the question of transfers of rights as between states and the supranational World Authority that we have proposed. The first point to make is that for reasons both of practicability and of principle we have not suggested a total transfer of all state rights to the supranational World Authority. In practice, as the EU experience readily demonstrates, nation states as we know them today are very far from being ready to transfer all of their sovereignty to a supranational authority even in Europe. In any case, as we noted earlier in view of the massive democratic deficit that would be present in a single world state, it would be vital that a significant range of (perhaps even most) policy competences should be retained ideally at the level of local cantons capable of functioning as direct democracies; or if that is not immediately possible, at the level of the existing nation states (the Principle of Subsidiarity as mentioned above). Hence, we do not believe that the surrender of sovereign policy competences (one might say state's "rights") to the World Authority should be total as in the original Hobbesian argument for individuals in a state of nature; in effect we agree with Kant's suggestion in his essay *Perpetual Peace: a philosophical sketch* that the transfer of sovereignty should be partial and at least sufficient to keep the peace.[10] Hobbes after all did not consider or face practical questions of democratic deficit such as our proposal given its scale and the world in which we live must consider. Hence, the transfer of sovereign policy competences to the supranational World Authority should be strictly limited. But where we would still follow the Hobbesian approach is in arguing that the sovereign powers to be transferred should not be a matter for choice by each state in pursuit of what

[10] Kant I (1795) op. cit. Where Kant worried about the danger of tyranny in a World Sovereign with extensive powers, we are casting the argument more in terms of democratic deficit, but the concern is similar. See also Chap. 3, p. gg.

suits its own interests: the competences to be transferred should be decided by considerations of the common good of the whole of humanity rather than by narrow national interests. Put in more concrete terms it should be for the World Authority once constituted to propose the policy competences that need to be made into a supranational matter; and for the World Council of Ministers (or World Parliament) to legislate by qualified majority vote for these competences to become supranational in character. Moreover, there would be no question of nation states being able to revoke these transfers; any revocation of sovereign powers to reallocate them to nation states or to the cantons (as we have ideally proposed for the long term) would be decided at supranational level by qualified majority vote of the World Council of Ministers or World Parliament in the common interest rather than just to suit the narrow or transitory national interests of nation states or other lower level political units. In effect, the *fons et origo* morally and ideally also legally of rights allocated to any political community would not be the arbitrary claims of nation states to an absolute sovereignty (based on might is right as we have at present) but rather sovereignty would be vested originally in the world sovereign which would then delegate wide ranges of powers to lower level units through the subsidiarity principle on the basis of majority decisions taken at the supranational level in the common interest of humanity. Just as we saw above that individual human rights in Hobbes *Leviathan* are not absolute but rather exercised at the pleasure of the sovereign, so also the rights of political communities would in effect be exercised at the pleasure of the world sovereign.

In the array of powers to be exercised by the world sovereign, the most fundamental would of course be that of maintaining and enforcing peace in the world to replace the war of all against all; but as noted in earlier chapters there would be other candidates for policy competences that could be transferred to the supranational level precisely for the common good of the whole of humanity, trade policy, financial stability and climate change being perhaps the clearest and most pressing examples; and it would be up to the World Authority and World Council/Parliament to take the decisions of principle on which other policy competences beside peace-keeping should become supranational; or as just argued above, which competences are to be left with nation states or cantons; or which might in the light of evolving circumstances be transferred back to lower level political units.[11]

We believe that in the above we have dealt with some of the more sensitive corollary issues that a drive towards a supranational geopolitical order would imply. It would be all too easy to say it will never happen because of this or that vested interest or ideological blind spot. Our aim has been to show that in the face of some of the more obvious potential blockages the supranational arrangements can readily face up to these and in many cases actually offer from a global perspective an even more effective solution as, for example, with the enforcement of rights. There is a final point to make in this chapter of which hitherto we have only given the briefest of hints when discussing above the question of reallocating certain policy competences to nations or other lower units through the Principle of Subsidiarity...but always as we argued through a supranational decision of the world sovereign rather than unilaterally say by nation states. As already hinted in Chap. 6, the transfer of rights from contemporary nation states (or later from direct democracy cantons) would be irrevocable in the sense that there would be no possibility whatever for states at some point to leave the supranational arrangements. The reason for this is readily seen from the logic of the Hobbesian argumentation. If states reserve the right for themselves to leave the supranational world order put in place to promote the common good of humanity over areas that require collaboration for policies to be effective then there would be the immediate danger of a relapse into violent conflicts among states and the war of all against all once more. In respect of shared policy competences such as climate change mitigation, it would mean the frustration of the effectiveness of common policies which can only breed resentment. Where the destinies of human beings are inextricably intertwined in an interdependent world there should no longer be any room for a blinkered pursuit of national interests at the expense of the rest of humanity in the formulation of policies in such areas of interdependence. We have illustrated this in particular with regard to economic policies when looking at the obsolescence of the nation state as an economic policy-making entity in Chap. 2.

To formalise the irrevocability of the transfers of sovereignty it would be advisable as in most of the world's federal states today to have a legally

[11] In this respect, our suggestions depart significantly from current EU practice. At present, for a policy competence to be transferred from nation states to the supranational EU institutions, new treaties between the member states are in effect needed.

drafted Constitutional document for the World Authority which most basically would set out the institutional structures with their checks and balances for the innovative institutional project. But because any political set-up or project requires ultimately an explicit ethical foundation to secure commitment and "buy-in" from the citizens concerned, such a Constitutional charter could also set out the moral foundations of the whole project as being inspired by the goal of instituting peace, harmony and prosperity among all human (and even all living) beings as a fundamental shared value for all; and by a will and shared commitment to address effectively such problems as are common to humanity as a whole and which because of interdependence require a supranational response if they are to be effective.

Therefore, the transformation we are proposing is not yet another intergovernmental treaty among nation states which retain their absolute sovereignty (as with almost all treaties and pacts as we know them in international law today). What we are proposing is a radical legal and political act whereby nation states irrevocably and completely surrender their sovereignty over the defined areas of competence in the rational pursuit of the common good of humanity as a whole. Nation states and national sovereignty would no longer be the unquestioned cornerstones of international law; rather the supranational World Authority and related institutions (World Council of Ministers or World Parliament) would be the *fons et origo*, the foundation stones and first premises of the world's legal and political order.[12]

As just remarked above, this new world order would need to be enshrined in a constitutional framework whose central principles would be the promotion of peace for all, the promotion of universal global cooperation and the allocation both of individual human rights and the political rights and responsibilities of the cantons in a manner compatible with the common good of all. But such a constitutional charter would not be dreamt up by some type of intergovernmental conference. If we follow the

[12] Seen in this perspective Article 50 of the Lisbon Treaty of the European Union (2009) which allows any state to withdraw from the EU at its own discretion was arguably a major political mistake since it means that in a deliberately supranational arrangement such as the EU nation states are still seen as sovereign. This is a political contradiction: and it had the predictable consequence of leading Britain to leave the EU (Brexit). Not surprisingly, the main protagonists for getting this provision written into the Lisbon Treaty were the British. Prior to the Lisbon Treaty, there was no provision of any kind for states to withdraw even if the supranational commitment was not explicitly stated to be irrevocable.

Hobbesian logic the first act would be a complete surrender of all areas of sovereignty by the participating states to the World Authority; and it would then be for the legislative organs of that Authority (World Council of Ministers or World Parliament) to draft the further details of the new overarching constitutional framework. This is the real and in Hobbesian terms indispensable significance of the World Authority becoming the *fons et origo* of all law and government in replacement of the contemporary legal order based on sovereignty of nation states.

Bibliography

Commentary September 1970. Accessed September 13, 2025, from https://www.commentary.org/articles/lawrence-malkin/technology-and-growth-the-price-we-pay-by-e-j-mishan-21-popular-economic-fallacies-by-e-j-mishan/

Donato, K., & Massey, D. (2016). Twenty-first century globalisation and illegal migration. *Annals of the American Academy of Political and Social Science, 666*, 7–26.

European Union EU. *Charter of Fundamental Rights of the European Union.* Accessed September 13, 2025., from https://www.europarl.europa.eu/charter/pdf/text_en.pdf

Frontex. (2009). *The impact of the global economic crisis on illegal migration to the EU.* Frontex.

Kant, I. (1795). *Zum Ewigen Frieden.* Nicolovius, Königsberg. Available in English in Kant I (1991) *Political Writings*, 2nd ed, translated by Nisbet H Cambridge University Press.

Locke, J. (1988). *Two treatises of government.* Cambridge University Press (Second Treatise).

Mishan, E. J. (1969). *Growth: The Price we pay.* Staples Press.

Myrdal, G. (1960). *Beyond the welfare state.* Duckworth.

United Nations UN. *Universal Declaration of Human Rights.* Accessed September 13, 2025., from https://www.un.org/en/about-us/universal-declaration-of-human-rights

CHAPTER 8

Avoiding the Dangers of Corruption of Absolute Power

Abstract One corollary question that would arise in implementing our proposals for a supranational World Authority which deserves special attention is the danger of the absolute powers of that Authority (in its defined area of policy competences) becoming a source of absolute corruption (as in Acton's famous dictum).We are speaking here of the dangers of political corruption, of "the abuse of entrusted public office for private gain" (Kurer, *Routledge handbook of political corruption*. Routledge, 2015), and a first point to make is that such corruption is already rampant in many nation states including in representative democracies and so is not a problem specific to the World Authority. Nonetheless, because of the distance and aloofness of such an Authority from most people's everyday lives, securing its legitimacy against corrosive populist cynicism makes it all the more important that the World Authority should be manifestly free from corruption and publicly accountable and transparent in this respect. Some detailed suggestions are made as to how exactly this can be achieved drawing in part on the remarkable achievements of Singapore in virtually eliminating corruption. A carrot and stick approach is proposed with severe and enforced penalties for corrupt actions both for corrupter and corrupted, while at the same time having handsome salary and benefits packages for World Authority public servants comparable with those of the private sector. At the same time beyond a certain age or points in their careers, a strict separation of careers between public servants and private

P. O'Sullivan et al., *Overcoming Gangsterism and Geo-Political Anarchy*, https://doi.org/10.1007/978-3-032-22438-5_8

business people could be applied to mitigate state capture. Lobbying of all kinds whether at local or at supranational level, we also identify as a form of corruption (seeking to divert public policy from pursuit of the common good to private gain for the interest groups lobbying), and we argue that this too needs to be very strictly regulated and rendered transparent and open to all irrespective of their financial means.

Keywords Supranational authority • Corruption and political power • Perceived legitimacy (of government) • Lobbying as corruption • Measures to combat political corruption • Separation of careers • Singaporean example

> *Power tends to corrupt and absolute power corrupts absolutely. Great men are almost always bad men, even when they exercise influence and not authority.*
> Lord Acton (1887)[1]

For many who recall the famous dictum of Lord Acton (above), the prospect of a supranational World Authority with significant powers of enforcement even if limited to certain defined supranational competences will generate a frisson of foreboding: with such a concentration of absolute power is there not a danger of high level abuses of that power, "absolute corruption"? Being indeed adherents to Acton's maxim this is a matter that we need to address specifically in our outline of a new supranational world order. We could of course dismiss the whole theme of abuse of power as peripheral to our purpose since corruption of all kinds is in any case pervasive among large numbers of today's nation states and so is not a problem specific to a supranational order: we face it anyway. But the sting in the tail of Lord Acton's quotation suggesting that "*absolute power corrupts absolutely*" means that given the powers we are proposing for the World Authority, it would be advisable to address these issues.

We believe that there are distinct types of issue that arise with the concentration of certain policy competences in a supranational World Authority which we have proposed in previous chapters of this work. The

[1] From an 1887 letter of Lord Acton to Bishop Creighton in Figgis J & Laurence R eds (1907) *Historical Essays and Studies*, Macmillan, London.

first type of issue is the one highlighted by Lord Acton, namely that the functionaries of the supranational institutions could be tempted into abuses of power that would have consequences for the whole of humanity. We have used the European Union as a template of inspiration for our supranational World Authority in its legislative, executive and judicial functions and the record of the EU's institutions in this respect is not at all edifying. The entire EU Commission of Jacques Santer had to resign *en bloc* (1999) to avoid impeachment over matters of corruption while recent years have seen the exposure of serious corruption of members of the European Parliament in vote buying scandals.[2] These examples underline very clearly the need for us to address the abuse of power question for the World Authority we are proposing.

The second type of issue that arises from such a concentration of power in the World Authority is the so-called democratic deficit problem. This is not a type of corruption but refers rather to the fact that decisions would be made in institutions and places that are very far removed literally, virtually and metaphorically from the millions of people who would be affected. This would generate sentiments of frustrated impotence and incomprehension for many people with a resultant tendency to defiance and questioning of the political legitimacy of the World Authority. Simplistic nationalist and identitarian populisms as described in Chap. 3 would merrily exploit this sense of democratic deficit. However, we have already made some proposals to address this problem in Chap. 5 above. We have proposed that in respect of policy-making the Principle of Subsidiarity should be strictly applied with the central world authority institutions making decisions and executing policies (a) only in those areas of clearly defined supranational policy competence as stipulated by the foundational charter of the World Authority and (b) wherever possible delegating policy responsibility to lower level political authorities to the greatest extent that would be practicable. Moreover, we have also argued in Chap. 5 that the next level of political authority below the World Authority should ideally be small states with a maximum population of 10 million which would practise direct democracy; that is to say all citizens voting by referendum

[2] There were reports in a variety of reliable news outlets in December 2022 of vote buying by Qatar at the European Parliament as well as an investigation by Belgian police. See, for example, Pop V et al. European Parliament shaken by Qatar Corruption Scandal, *Financial Times*, London 11 December 2022 available at https://www.ft.com/content/1023d8aa-1fa4-4e6f-abbb-68ef101ccb72. Accessed 26 August 2025.

on all policy questions within the competence of the states after application of the subsidiarity principle. We believe that these two aspects of our proposals, direct democracy combined with the subsidiarity principle would go a long way towards addressing the concerns of democratic deficit in our proposed new geopolitical order.

There remains the danger of absolute power potentially corrupting absolutely. One difficulty that arises in any discussion around topics of corruption is the precise meaning of the term. But since we are talking here of the potential pitfalls of a supranational geopolitical order we are concerned specifically with what may be called **political corruption** which in turn has been neatly defined by Oskar Kurer (2015) as "misuse of public office for private gain".[3] Such a definition can encompass a wide range of phenomena or activities all of which have the feature that holders of entrusted powers of public office, when corrupt, carry out their functions in a manner which is geared to their own personal advantage (the gains need not be financial but often are) rather than acting as any public official should in principle act, that is to say in pursuit of the common good for the community which they represent and of which they are functionaries.[4] Hence, political corruption can take the form of outright bribery of politicians by special interest groups or individuals to secure their specific agendas. It can also take the form of nepotism where personal family interests[5] take precedence over the public good when making public appointments or allocations of public contracts (to one's own family enterprises). In any case, whatever definition one adopts, political corruption affects not only

[3] Kurer O (2015) *Definitions of Corruption* in Routledge handbook of Political Corruption, Routledge, London: chapter 2. Kurer is aware that this definition remains rather vague in respect of "misuse" or "abuse", but he argues that it encompasses most of what would be widely recognised as corrupt political practices.

[4] The oath of office for the EU Commissioners is very interesting in this respect: they explicitly swear to act for the common good of the EU as a whole rather than in the national interest of any one country or for personal gain. In the oath, the Commissioner swears that in the conduct of their duties they will "be completely independent in carrying out my responsibilities, in the general interest of the Union; in the performance of my tasks, neither to seek nor to take instructions from any Government or from any other institution, body, office or entity; to refrain from any action incompatible with my duties or the performance of my tasks". Available at https://ec.europa.eu/commission/presscorner/detail/en/ip_10_487. Accessed 22 August 2025.

[5] On the prevalence of individual and family interests over public and community interests, especially in smaller and more backward societies, see Banfield E (1958) *The Moral Basis of a Backward Society*, with Laura Fasano Banfield, The Free Press, Glencoe, Illinois.

collective trust and social capital, it also invariably generates disvalue, that is, a loss of value in narrowly economic terms for the community, for example, when corrupt kickbacks to politicians inflate the costs of public infrastructural or other projects. Some studies have demonstrated the relationship between corruption and such destruction of value, and how it is possible, precisely through a full understanding of the phenomenon of corruption and its effects, to try to rebuild favourable and positive conditions for a region or community. Public managers, politicians and their organisations should be playing a leading role in creating public value in the widest sense, not only by producing—efficiently and effectively—goods and services that can add value to their community, but also by pursuing social and ethical goals. Public servants should surely be the guarantors and the custodians of the public interest, putting its citizens'/users'/customers' welfare before any personal interest.[6]

Crony capitalism wherein public contracts or exclusive and lucrative monopoly positions or licences are handed out to a narrow set of oligarchic interests close to the regime in power and invariably with kickbacks to officials on contracts awarded are manifestly corrupt even if widespread in certain states.[7] They are corrupt simply because the common good is entirely subverted to the personal interests of the oligarchs in question and their public official buddies. Two centuries ago, Adam Smith was already warning us in no uncertain terms of the dangers in effect of crony capitalism even if he did not use those words. Far from being the champion of an anarcho-capitalist ideal, Adam Smith had warned us of the tendencies to concentration of monopoly power under free market capitalism which he roundly condemned as against the public good…and in the same breath he warned us of the dangers of co-option of public officers by the rent-seeking monopolist. In a lesser-known quotation, Smith tells us, "*People of the same trade seldom meet together, even for merriment and diversion, but the conversation ends in a conspiracy against the public, or in some contrivance to raise prices…. But though the law cannot hinder people of the same trade from sometimes assembling together, it ought to do nothing to facilitate*

[6] See Esposito P & Ricci P (2015). How to turn public (dis)value into new public value? Evidence from Italy. *Public Money & Management*, *35*(3), 227–231. https://doi.org/10.1080/09540962.2015.1027499

[7] See, for example, Burgis T (2020) *Kleptopia: how dirty money is conquering the world*, William Collins, London. See also Bullough O (2019) *Moneyland: why thieves and crooks now rule the world and how to take it back*, Profile Books London.

such assemblies, much less to render them necessary".[8] The phenomena of crony capitalism have justly been described in our own day as "state capture"[9] by narrow special interests; and for completeness it should be noted that the special interests seeking to bend politicians and public servants to their own narrow ends could as well as being oligarchs or large corporate business interests equally well be non-governmental organisations (NGOs) or other pressure groups promoting very specific special interests.[10] State capture today goes far beyond oligarchic crony capitalism: it embraces all of the various forms of lobbying and of influence peddling that have become so commonplace especially, dare we say, even in representative democracies. Millions of euros are dispensed by large companies or alliances of smaller sector-specific business interests either in directly lobbying politicians or in employing professional lobbying outfits to seek to persuade legislators to make laws in their favour or to get executive officials to favour them in the everyday application of laws and regulations and in the award of public contracts. Although such lobbying has come to be accepted as a normal part of the political process especially in the USA (but with some reservations in Europe) and is paraded as an expression of freedom of speech and opinion it is always a form of corruption for the simple reason that the lobbying interest groups are in effect seeking a second bite of the democratic cherry. In representative or direct democracies, every citizen has a right to vote and express their opinion in elections: this is the simple principle of one person one vote. But lobbying involves an attempt by various organised special interest groups to have a second opportunity after elections to influence legislators and executive officials; and being special interest groups they are rarely seeking the

[8] Smith A (1776) *An Enquiry into the Nature and Causes of the Wealth of Nations*, Strahan & Cadell, London. Reprinted 2000 by Penguin Books, London (Penguin Classic). The quotation is from Book 4 chapter 8.

[9] The term state capture originated in a World Bank Report in 2000: Hellman J et al. (2000) *Seize the State, Seize the Day: State capture, Corruption and Influence in Transition*, World Bank Policy Research Working paper 2444 available at https://documents1.worldbank.org/curated/en/537461468766474836/pdf/multi-page.pdf. Accessed 22 August 2025. Usage of the term has subsequently widened out to encompass any (successful or partly successful) effort to subordinate the public interest to the agendas of specific special interest groups.

[10] The power exercised by some NIMBY (not in my back yard) consumer groups comes to mind. However, we are not suggesting that all NGOs are promoting only the interests of a narrow few. Many have noble aims dedicated to the good of humanity as a whole such as Red Cross/Red Crescent.

common good of all in doing so. Lobbying can only be fair and compatible with pursuit of free speech and the common good if every single possible special interest group has the possibility to organise and lobby on its behalf ***and with the same financial means.*** Need we say that of course this is very far from being the case.[11] Furthermore, the persuasion of politicians and officials that is pursued especially by "professional" lobbyists today does not just rely on rhetorical sophistry, it is almost invariably accompanied by blandishments of various kinds designed to bend the will of the legislators or officials. Some small (or not so small) free gifts, some sumptuous free lunches or dinners, a few days free on a nice yacht, free touristic visits to far-off discreet exotic locations are all commonplace as well as good old-fashioned suitcases of cash or today practically untraceable deposits of crypto-currency into digital wallets. The persuasion can also take the more sinister form of blackmail by threatening to expose perhaps embarrassing details of the private lives of politicians or officials. All of these latter stratagems as commonly employed by today's lobbyists are we would argue unambiguously and outright corrupt: they seek to bend the legislator or official to the narrow special interests of the lobbying group and away from pursuit of the common good by appealing to the self-interest of said legislators or officials.[12] The latter are led to misuse (in a partisan way) their public office for private personal gain (or in the case of blackmail avoidance of personal loss).

Having catalogued the forms which corruption of political power may take (and we do not claim that the list is exhaustive) there remains the question of how the dangers of such corruption, abuses of entrusted political power for private gain, can be limited in our supranational world authority. We say limited because we are all too aware of human frailty and so we recognise that it would be difficult ever to eradicate all forms of

[11] See, for example, Corporate Europe Observatory website and in particular the 2025 Lobby League Table available at https://corporateeurope.org/en/2025/02/eus-lobby-league-table. Accessed 23 August 2025.

[12] We do not for one moment entertain the argument that maybe lobbying is not so corrupt and even OK when the lobbyists are acting for the common good. There may as noted be some NGOs with very noble goals; but when they engage in lobbying, they are already having a second bite of the democratic cherry after elections…and some may not always have been very ethical in the tactics of their lobbying, for example, the practice of "astroturfing" whereby a false impression of widespread popular support is created by online manipulations and surveys. One of the authors has regularly received incredibly manipulative surveys from more than one NGO whose overall cause may be laudable.

political corruption; and indeed political philosophers have been reflecting on this at least since the time of Plato's *Republic*[13] in ancient Athens. Certainly, given the extent of the various forms of corruption that we have described in the previous paragraphs, in today's world, it is legitimate to raise concerns about the absolute power of the World Authority (over the defined areas of competence) possibly leading to "absolute corruption". We have already noted above that the danger of absolute corruption is hardly an argument against a World Authority for the simple reason that in the contemporary international order there is already rampant political corruption both at the level of nation states and in many intergovernmental organisations.[14] Political corruption is not something that is suddenly going to appear *pari passu* with a supranational order. But what it does mean is that we need to give some attention to the question of how corruption can be restrained in the World Authority especially in virtue of the fact that its policy actions and regulations will affect the whole of humanity. The suggestions we make below would also apply to efforts to restrain corruption at the level of nation states and apart from some of our suggestions regarding lobbying they are not particularly original; but their application and strict enforcement would be a more crucial requirement perhaps than at nation state levels and indispensable to building confidence in the World Authority among the peoples of the world at large. That being said it is also true that a central premise in our Hobbesian argument for a World Sovereign has been the rationality of cooperation in the face of the war of all against all; and when individual subjects or states engage in an explicitly collaborative enterprise to further their common good, narrowly self-centred behaviour to promote mere personal gain (or the narrow interests of specific states or organisations) becomes more difficult to defend. Arguably state capture and corrupt practices of all kinds subverting the common good to narrower personal or national interests

[13] Plato (2007) *The Republic*, Penguin Classic, London. Plato's solution to the danger of corruption of his philosopher rulers was to require that they be allowed no private property of any kind and no children. Hence, there would be no point in their being corrupted or in engaging in nepotism.

[14] See the Transparency International website (2019) at https://www.transparency.org/en/news/25-corruption-scandals. Accessed 22 August 2025. See also the Corruption Perceptions Index league tables of Transparency International compiled annually. The 2024 table can be found at https://www.transparency.org/en/cpi/2024. Accessed 22 August 2025.

are the ultimate resultant of an exaggerated and arguably short-sighted individualism inspired by Ayn Rand's so-called Ethical Egoism.[15]

We believe that political corruption can most effectively be minimised by a carrot and stick approach to eradicating the various manifestations of abuses of entrusted political power for private gain. On the stick side, what is needed is a stringent set of regulations explicitly outlawing all of the various forms of bribery, nepotism, kickbacks on public contracts and so on where these regulations are backed up by **strict and severe penalties which are enforced to the letter**. When one considers that while individual acts of corruption may seem innocuous enough, the real danger with corruption is at macro level when if corruption of all kinds, petty and more grandiose, become endemic in a society, not only is this profoundly inegalitarian (as, e.g. when "public" healthcare requires expensive gifts to medical doctors for speedy access) it also insidiously and gradually erodes the legitimacy of governments whose officials and ministers become ensnared in corruption and so increasingly powerless to curb it. Hence, arguments about the proportionality of punishment to fit the crime should with corruption take into account not just the micro-level individual act but also the macro-level consequences in undermining the legitimacy of government. But as hinted above it is not enough just to have a system of penalties: these need to be enforced both in spirit when there is any ambiguity and to the letter when the legal case is clear-cut. When one considers the effective power of political manipulation wielded by super-rich oligarchs and by the gangster bosses of organised crime, such enforcement is easier said than done. Italy has grappled for decades with trying to eradicate the corruption of public officials by the activities of Mafia, Camorra and 'Ndrangheta, while large areas of Mexico are effectively run by drug cartels against which the Mexican government remains relatively powerless, and there are even areas of cities such as Bruxelles, Marseille and Paris which are the effective fiefs of organised criminality and where the police enter with trepidation if at all.

Economic globalisation and widespread digitalisation have made some corruption phenomena even more difficult to uncover, interpret and address. This tendency has only been accelerated by the phenomenon of crypto-currencies. The latter are much hyped for their lower transactions

[15] On Ethical Egoism as a radical individualism see Rand A (1964) *The Virtue of Selfishness*, New American Library, New York. See also Rand A (1967) *Capitalism: the Unknown Ideal* Signet Books, New York.

costs by comparison with established official banking channels and in the case of bitcoin and other similar cryptos especially for their speculative value. But as the emergence and prevalence of stablecoins linked to established currencies (mainly US$) shows, the real attraction of cryptos is not their speculative value or the relatively trivial saving of transactions costs, it is the secrecy which the underlying blockchain technology offers that is the main attraction. Organised criminality has been quick to digitalise in this and other ways, and this has greatly facilitated what we might call its globalisation. Today, at least in the case of the biggest organised criminal organisations, they can no longer be traced back as in the past to single areas or specific territories, where everything originated. The Mafia itself, for example, has branches and criminal masterminds in Belgium, Netherlands and Germany (for narco-traffic purposes), with control and significant influence over the public interests of port cities and regions.[16] A digitalised crypto-using "mafia", whether Italian, Russian or African, without bombs and machine guns is even more dangerous, being able to simultaneously and negatively affect the well-being of entire communities without them even realising it.

The subordination of political power to the will and agendas of rich oligarchs may be a little less crudely manifested than that of the mafiosi and the drug barons and therefore more difficult to counter with legal and regulatory instruments, but it is nonetheless a very real phenomenon and eventually highly corrosive of the political legitimacy of governments who succumb to it.[17] Indeed, in 2025, one could say that we have been witness to the most brazen abuse of power by rich oligarchs in the activities of Elon Musk at the supposed US Government Department of Government Efficiency (DOGE) whereby he simply closed down government regulatory agencies that impacted certain of his businesses.[18]

What all of this shows is that while it may be reasonably straightforward to draft regulations outlawing a wide variety of corrupt activities it is rather

[16] On this, see Shenaway S & Sbouai S (2025) *Crime gangs exploit EU ports to smuggle record drug loads*, OCCRP, 27 June 2025, available at https://www.occrp.org/en/news/crime-gangs-exploit-eu-ports-to-smuggle-record-drug-loads. Accessed 29 August 2025.

[17] For a good account of this phenomenon, see Bullough (2019) op.cit. and Burgis T (2020) op.cit. They even show how certain oligarchs have effectively used the English legal system to their advantage when seeking to cloak their activities in secrecy.

[18] On this, see Robins-Early N (2025) Elon Musk's Conflicts of Interest in *The Guardian*, 28 April 2025 available at https://www.theguardian.com/technology/2025/apr/28/elon-musk-doge-conflict-of-interest. Accessed 23 August 2025.

more difficult to get these enforced (or in some countries even to get them passed into law by their legislatures). Once again, it therefore becomes indispensable that the World Authority should have strong and effective enforcement powers coupled with the courage and the integrity to use these fearlessly in countering the efforts at manipulative corruption to which it would be subjected. Speaking of courage and integrity of the World Authority's legislators and executive functionaries brings us to mention the carrot element in our approach to eradicate corruption at any level. Certainly many public servants will want to act courageously and with integrity but it will also help if they are suitably rewarded for their high-minded efforts by being paid handsome salaries and enjoying strong social security and pension rights. In the age of post-truth-induced cynicism in which we are living, it is doubtful that we can expect many of those in public service to act solely out of a sense of duty and honour. While these virtues in public service should at all times be extolled and promoted, it will help if our public servants and representatives are paid handsome salaries and benefits and generally enjoy a social prestige commensurate with their central roles in society. It is well known that Singapore has some of the best paid and most efficient public servants in the world and it is no accident that it also is ranked among the least corrupt countries in the world by the Transparency International Corruption Perceptions Index.[19] Moreover, Singapore's legendary Prime Minister Lee Kuan Yew had always insisted on the high payments to Singaporean public servants precisely to keep pace with private sector pay and to discourage corruption by rendering it just not worthwhile (in a kind of echo of Plato's solution for his philosopher rulers).[20] It was also a way to encourage some of the most talented Singaporeans to take on public sector roles and jobs, thereby ensuring a high level of competence and efficiency in its public administration.[21] Hence, we would strongly advocate for our World Authority an approach to the payment to all of its functionaries, legislative,

[19] The 2024 table can be found at https://www.transparency.org/en/cpi/2024. Accessed 22 August 2025. Singapore is ranked third least corrupt country (behind Denmark and Finland).

[20] See, for example, Challenge magazine of Public Service Division of Singapore (2015) *Remembering Lee Kuan Yew*. See especially Pgs 3–5 "On Integrity": available at https://psdchallenge.psd.gov.sg/docs/default-source/challenge/lky-challenge-commemorative-publication.pdf. Accessed 23 August 2025.

[21] See, for example, Amalgamated Union of Public Employees Singapore (2024) *Singaporean Civil Service ranked the world's best in Oxford University study* available at

executive and judicial of salary and benefit packages generous enough to render their corruption simply not worthwhile following the Singaporean example; and if this involves indexing the pay and benefits at least of the top officials of the World Authority on the average pay + benefits of the top three richest private sector CEOs in the world then so be it.

What we have described so far is the approach to limiting or even eradicating the most blatant forms of corruption consisting of bribery and assorted other benefits to politicians and public servants and this must be the spearhead of any effective anti-corruption policy. But we have also noted earlier that the perversion of entrusted public office for private gain can also happen through state capture by oligarchic business interests and by the effects of extensive lobbying. Part of the solution to discourage oligarchic manipulation can come from a strict enforcement of laws against abuse of dominant market position and the World Authority could adopt a set of laws and enforcement practices such as those of the European Union[22] in this respect given that the EU has had a modicum of success in actually enforcing its anti-monopoly laws. More difficult to deal with is the state capture that occurs through what have been called revolving door appointments or in French "*pantouflage*".[23] Here, leading public servants may be drawn from (transferred over from) high level private business positions supposedly for their (business) competences which of course may be very different from the competences required of a public servant expected to act for the common good with integrity. Alternatively leading public officials may move into highly paid positions in private sector companies once they have left office acting then no longer as public servants but as advocates for narrow private business interests while retaining established influential connections with government ministries. All of these practices are contributing to state capture and thereby to the gradual cynical erosion of public trust in governments even in some the most advanced countries of the world today. What comes to mind as a solution to these revolving door practices (and which would be all the more

https://govinsider.asia/intl-en/article/singapores-civil-service-ranked-worlds-best-in-oxford-university-study. Accessed 23 August 2025.

[22] See European Commission website *Competition Policy: Ant-Trust and Cartels*, available at https://competition-policy.ec.europa.eu/antitrust-and-cartels_en. Accessed 23 August 2025.

[23] A wonderful word meaning moving around between public services positions and high level well paid business positions in one's slippers or house shoes (to denote the incestuous intimacy).

necessary at World Authority level to retain its legitimacy given its power and remoteness) is a strict separation of careers. After a certain age or beyond a certain level of managerial responsibility, it should just be prohibited for business executives to enter public service and vice versa. That solution is admittedly radical, but it is not at all original: Plato in his *Republic* was quite clear that those involved in trade and commerce should be entirely debarred from holding public office.[24]

We have also suggested earlier that lobbying activity and influence peddling of all kinds are invariably associated with the perversion of public office for private gain and so strictly speaking a form of political corruption. But while most of the types of corruption for which we have suggested restraints in the previous paragraphs are fairly widely perceived as such, lobbying and influence peddling are rarely thought of as corruption and so are either unregulated or very lightly regulated (as, for example, by requirements for lobbyists to register themselves as such in the EU). Lobbying indeed is regularly perceived a matter of freedom of speech and opinion and as an integral part of the democratic process. Alberto Alemanno writing on this topic in 2017[25] while noting that the lobbying power of large industrial groups or by wealthy firms or even individuals was undermining faith in representative democracy and fuelling populism argued that the only way to deal with this skewing of the democratic process was for everyone in society to become effective citizen lobbyists; and he saw a key role for social media in this. In effect, Alemanno echoes the point we made earlier in this chapter when we asserted that lobbying can be defensible as compatible with representative democracy only if every single citizen or possible special interest group has the possibility to organise and lobby on its behalf ***and with the same financial means***. Where we part company with Alemanno's well-meaning solution is on that final sting in the tail about equal financial means. It is plainly the case that we are very far from every citizen having at their disposal the same financial means for lobbying and there is no prospect of that changing any time in the near future given the concentrations of oligopoly power in many sectors of the economy (e.g. big pharma or the US tech giants) and the growing inequalities in individual personal wealth in many countries including the most

[24] Plato (2007) op. cit.

[25] Alemanno A (2017) *Lobbying for Change*, Icon Books, London.

advanced economies.[26] There is also a touching and forgivable naivety in Alemanno's (2017) idea that social media can be a force for universal citizen lobbying. That was before we became aware of the manipulations and distortions that are constantly being created on various social media platforms through fake news, bots and botnets to create a false impression of support for various viewpoints and so on; and with all of this being further aggravated today by the algorithms that underpin the use of artificial intelligence in these applications.

Consequently, we do not believe that Alemanno's solution is the best way to deal with the corruptive influence of lobbying activity. Rather we would argue that if the principle of one person one vote is to be preserved all lobbying and influence peddling activity should be just banned outright. Perhaps we are stressing the obvious but government policies and regulations should be devised and developed solely with the common good of the relevant community in mind and not on the basis of what cause has the most effective (read usually "richest") lobbyists. Given the huge responsibilities to promote the common good of humanity as a whole which would be incumbent on the supranational World Authority that we have proposed in this work we would certainly recommend that all forms of lobbying of the World Authority should be outright illegal; and that this should be enforced by a strict system of severe penalties (including prison terms in certain cases) both for the lobbyists and for the lobbied politicians. In answer to the immediate challenge that such a policy would in theory prevent politicians from even talking to people with special interests even in a social setting (on golf courses or at parties), we would simply say that we expect of politicians and public officials that they meticulously document in a register any such meetings whether formal or informal;[27] and recuse themselves from any subsequent vote on matters pertaining to the special interests in question. The latter requirement would go a long way simply to discouraging politicians and public officials from having such conversations in the first place.

[26] For comprehensive data on evolution of inequalities, see the World Inequality Database available at https://wid.world/. Accessed 25 August 2025.

[27] Requirement to declare in an official register *all* meetings with potential lobbyists or influencers already exists in many representative democracies. See OECD (2022) Regulating Corporate Political Engagement, OECD Paris: available at https://www.oecd.org/content/dam/oecd/en/publications/reports/2022/03/regulating-corporate-political-engagement_180040f6/8c5615fe-en.pdf. Accessed 25 August 2025. See in particular the table at p. 19 of this work.

But it will be argued with pathetic self-pleading that surely politicians and public officials when faced with policy and regulatory decisions in complex areas that require a degree of scientific expertise that the officials may not readily possess (e.g. aviation safety, intricate medical questions) should welcome the specific professional perspective that can be provided by representatives of special industrial interests. This may well be true but what matters is the way in which such professional advice is sought. We would argue for two key criteria for any such consultation legitimately to occur: (a) the initiative must always come from the governmental side: it is up to governments to govern and so to decide when and from whom they need to seek professional advice (b) where any such consultation does occur it should be in the *simultaneous* presence of all relevant possible stakeholders to the decision.

Furthermore, once policies are adopted there will be a crucial role for public accountability on the part of the World Authority. A strong culture of accountability can ensure follow-up appraisal of public policies with an orientation towards transparency and responsible relations with *all* stakeholders thereby discouraging the hijacking of public policy for private gain by politicians or officials and/or by the narrow vested interests of restricted stakeholder groups (oligarchic interests). Public accountability[28] if used convincingly and constantly by politicians and officials can make a contribution to limiting certain vices of human nature, in particular the acquisitive rent-seeking greed that underpins many forms of corruption and crony capitalism. Periodic thematic meetings with communities and citizens, frequent reports with comprehensible indicators on the social and economic impacts of the Authority, inserted in a context that plans and periodically verifies the state of achievement of the objectives in a democratic and transparent debate, can certainly be part of an adequate response to the corruptive dangers of absolute power in the World Authority.

These then are the safeguards that we believe need to be in place in order to ensure that in our supranational World Authority absolute power does not end up corrupting absolutely. We believe that given the undoubted remoteness and aloofness from most people's daily lives that would perforce be associated with such an authority, the insistence on

[28] See *Accountability* in Global Encyclopedia of Public Administration, Public Policy and Governance, Editor: Ali Farazmand, Springer International Publishing Switzerland, 2016, Print ISBN: 978-3-319-20927-2; Print + eReference ISBN: 978-3-319-20929-6; eReference ISBN: 978-3-319-20928-9; https://doi.org/10.1007/978-3-319-31816-5_2321-1

such high standards of integrity together with a clear and strict enforcement of these would make a key contribution to underpinning the legitimacy of and support for the World Authority.

It may be remarked that the tough solutions that we have advocated for the restraint and eradication of all forms of corruption that we have outlined could all be applied at the level of today's nation states and as we noted *en passant* in some cases these solutions have already been adopted by certain states (e.g. Singapore). Hence, while certainly demanding, they are far from being impossible to apply. Governments, well, need to govern and make it clear that policy-making and regulation are not up for sale; they are not ultimately transactional even if a healthy debate among all stakeholder interests and resultant compromises may be necessary as governments seek to act for the common good of all.

Bibliography

Alemanno, A. (2017). *Lobbying for change*. Icon Books.

Amalgamated Union of Public Employees Singapore. (2024). *Singaporean Civil Service ranked the world's best in Oxford University study*. Accessed August 23, 2025, from https://govinsider.asia/intl-en/article/singapores-civil-service-ranked-worlds-best-in-oxford-university-study

Banfield, E. (1958). *The moral basis of a backward society*, with Laura Fasano Banfield. The Free Press.

Bullough, O. (2019). *Moneyland: Why thieves and crooks now rule the world and how to take it back*. Profile Books.

Burgis, T. (2020). *Kleptopia: How dirty money is conquering the world*. William Collins.

Challenge magazine of Public Service Division of Singapore. (2015). *Remembering Lee Kuan Yew*. See especially Pgs 3–5 "On Integrity". Accessed August 23, 2025, from https://psdchallenge.psd.gov.sg/docs/default-source/challenge/lky-challenge-commemorative-publication.pdf

Corporate Europe Observatory. (2025). *Lobby League Table*. Accessed August 23, 2025, from https://corporateeurope.org/en/2025/02/eus-lobby-league-table

Corruption Perceptions Index league tables of Transparency International compiled annually. The 2024 table can be found at https://www.transparency.org/en/cpi/2024. Accessed 22 August 2025.

Esposito, P., & Ricci, P. (2015). How to turn public (dis)value into new public value? Evidence from Italy. *Public Money & Management, 35*(3), 227–231. https://doi.org/10.1080/09540962.2015.1027499

European Commission. (2010). *European Commission swears Oath to respect EU Treaties.* Accessed August 22, 2025, from https://ec.europa.eu/commission/presscorner/detail/en/ip_10_487

European Commission website *Competition policy: Ant-Trust and Cartels.* Accessed August 23, 2025., from https://competition-policy.ec.europa.eu/antitrust-and-cartels_en

Figgis, J., & Laurence, R. (Eds.). (1907). *Historical essays and studies.* Macmillan.

Global Encyclopaedia of Public Administration, Public Policy and Governance. (2016). *Entry on Accountability.* Springer International Publishing.

Kurer, O. (2015). Definitions of corruption. In *Routledge handbook of political corruption.* Routledge.

OECD. (2022). *Regulating corporate political engagement.* OECD. Accessed August 25, 2025, from https://www.oecd.org/content/dam/oecd/en/publications/reports/2022/03/regulating-corporate-political-engagement_180040f6/8c5615fe-en.pdf

Plato. (2007). *The republic.* Penguin Classic.

Pop, V., et al. (2022). European Parliament shaken by Qatar corruption scandal, *Financial Times*, London 11 December 2022. Accessed August 26, 2025, from https://www.ft.com/content/1023d8aa-1fa4-4e6f-abbb-68ef101ccb72

Rand, A. (1964). *The virtue of selfishness.* New American Library.

Rand, A. (1967). *Capitalism: The unknown ideal.* Signet Books.

Robins-Early, N. (2025). Elon Musk's Conflicts of Interest. *The Guardian*, 28 April 2025. Accessed August 23, 2025, from https://www.theguardian.com/technology/2025/apr/28/elon-musk-doge-conflict-of-interest

Shenaway, S., & Sbouai, S. (2025). *Crime gangs exploit EU ports to smuggle record drug loads*, OCCRP, 27 June 2025. Accessed August 29, 2025, from https://www.occrp.org/en/news/crime-gangs-exploit-eu-ports-to-smuggle-record-drug-loads

Smith, A. (1776). *An enquiry into the nature and causes of the wealth of nations.* Strahan & Cadell. Reprinted 2000 by Penguin Books (Penguin Classic).

Transparency International website. (2019). Accessed August 22, 2025, from https://www.transparency.org/en/news/25-corruption-scandals

Transparency International website. (2025). *Corruption perceptions index.* Accessed August 22, 2025, from https://www.transparency.org/en/cpi/2024

World Bank Report in 2000: Hellman J et al. (2000) *Seize the State, Seize the Day: State capture, Corruption and Influence in Transition*, World Bank Policy Research Working paper 2444. Accessed August 22, 2025, from https://documents1.worldbank.org/curated/en/537461468766474836/pdf/multi-page.pdf

World Inequality Database. Accessed August 25, 2025., from https://wid.world/

CHAPTER 9

A Conclusion Set in the Philosophy of History

Abstract This chapter first of all summarises in 11 succinct points the at-times complex arguments of Part I of the volume. It notes that despite the logical cogency of the arguments and the widespread perception in our day of the clamorous failures of the contemporary geopolitical order based on nation states, there will be strong resistance to the ideas presented by various vested interests that might stand to lose out in such a transition to a supranationally based order with enforcement powers, not least by the so-called great powers of today. But it is argued, drawing on Hegel's philosophy of history as ultimately a rational process, that given the signal failures of the contemporary set-up and the logical cogency of the supranational argument buttressed by the political philosophies of Hobbes and Kant, this is the way that the world must evolve; perhaps not in the very immediate future but over the coming decades. The chapter closes with some further reflections on Hegel's philosophy of history noting that while it has certain clear weaknesses, it contains a spectacular core of truth regarding the centrality of rationality to human endeavour in all fields and in particular in the sciences: for reality to be intelligible, it must be ultimately rational.

P. O'Sullivan et al., *Overcoming Gangsterism and Geo-Political Anarchy*, https://doi.org/10.1007/978-3-032-22438-5_9

Keywords Vested interests • Resistance to political change (in world order) • "Great powers" • Zones of influence • Enforcement power • Rationality in history • Hegel (philosophy of history) • Hobbes Leviathan • Kant (Perpetual Peace)

In this work, we have sought to put forward a logically compelling argument for the instigation of a genuinely supranational geopolitical order with a World Authority charged with keeping the peace among states and capable of enforcing its decisions regarding dispute resolution. In developing the argument, we have drawn significantly and explicitly on the political philosophy of Thomas Hobbes Leviathan and Kant's Essay on Perpetual Peace. In this concluding chapter of Part I, we will seek to summarise the overall argument laying out its basic presumptions and logical structure before situating it in a wider philosophical context relating it to the philosophy of history.

1. In human history and specifically in the contemporary era, it is vital to distinguish between the will and aspirations of people at large (who generally aspire to peace, harmony and prosperity) and that which is desired and pursued by political leaders and powerful vested interests of all stripes. This is most obviously true of monarchic and totalitarian regimes, but it is also patently present in contemporary representative democracies.
2. Partly because of what we might call this hijacking of political decision-making, philosophical critique and reflection continue to have an immense Socratically inspired relevance to political debate and decisions.
3. Despite the existence in principle of a framework of international law to govern the interactions of nation states and governments which increasingly claim an absolute sovereignty, that framework of international law despite being mutually agreed through the United Nations is regularly and systematically ignored by nation states in the pursuit of what they perceive to be their own interests. As repeatedly emphasised in the volume, the major reason for this is lack of enforcement power for the International Court of Justice, World Trade Organisation and other UN bodies.
4. This lack of enforcement power of the ICJ and of other UN bodies is directly attributable to the intergovernmental character and legal

nature of these institutions: that is to say that these institutions of international collaboration are explicitly and at root based on the notion that the nation states remain the ultimate sovereign units of the world order: they remain self-determining and in no way surrender their sovereignty. This is most obviously illustrated by the fact that sovereign nation states can simply and quite legally abrogate and walk away from any intergovernmental treaty as and when they will.

5. In a world where the lives and fates of all peoples are increasingly interdependent both because of hugely increased levels of economic interaction and because of the impact of economic activities on the natural environment and climate, the contemporary world order based as it is on networks of ultimately unenforceable intergovernmental treaties has become hopelessly ineffective. This is most poignantly illustrated by some of the major ongoing wars that have been waged in direct violation of the UN's treaties (and condemned as such), most notably the war in Ukraine; and most recently by Donald Trump's trade wars in complete violation of all WTO principles as well as by his militarist adventurism.
6. Therefore, drawing on the inspiration of Hobbes political philosophy (1651) and Kant's essay *Perpetual Peace: A Philosophical Sketch* (1795),[1] we have made the case for the institution of a supranational World Authority which would be charged at a minimum with keeping the peace, resolving disputes between states and/or regions and with absolute powers of enforcement of those resolutions. We are using the term supranational here in its precise legal sense: in a supranational order nation states are no longer absolutely self-determining completely sovereign entities: rather some aspects of sovereignty are vested in the supranational institution that is created.
7. The ultimate inspiration and reason for moving towards institution of such a supranational geopolitical order is the pursuit of peaceful co-existence among all peoples (and indeed one could argue with

[1] Hobbes T (1651) *Leviathan* reprinted with an introduction by Plamenatz J (1969) 4th edition, Fontana London. Kant I (1795) *Zum Ewigen Frieden*, Nicolovius, Königsberg. Available in English in Kant I (1991) *Political Writings* 2nd ed., translated by Nisbet H, Cambridge University Press, Cambridge. In this work, the essay "*Perpetual Peace: A Philosophical Sketch*" is contained.

all living beings). The first we would submit is an aspiration of virtually all human beings taken as individuals not least because of the economic prosperity which has always accompanied sustained periods of peace but also for pleasantness of lives lived in tranquillity and harmony with others. We have admitted that there have been throughout the ages various groupings of individuals who as a group come to believe themselves to be superior racially, religiously, culturally or whatever and who on the basis of these supremacist premises have sought to assert themselves and their own narrow self-interests by violence, military conquest, enslavement and colonialism. But we would submit that no supremacist premises have ever withstood the test of historical time and are in any case philosophically not only reprehensible but also indefensible.

8. If then peaceful co-existence with all living beings living lives in harmony mutual respect and tranquillity is embraced as the ideal for humanity in our interdependent world then we argue that good and above all effective governance in pursuit of those goals must be supranational in character. The old order of international law and intergovernmental treaties simply has not delivered the goods and arguably never could have been expected to do so precisely because of its overriding Achilles heel: the lack of supranational enforcement powers.
9. Throughout the book, we used the European Union as a practical illustration of many of the institutional suggestions points that we made: not so much because the EU is a perfect institution (it can certainly be improved in many ways) but because it does involve transfer of certain sovereign powers by member nation states to a set of supranational institutions *with enforcement powers*. The EU in other words shows that in practical terms surrender of sovereignty *can* occur in practice, and so our suggestions cannot just be dismissed as Utopian dreaming.
10. Following up on that practicality in the later sections of the book, we sought to discuss some of the institutional detail of how our proposed supranational order would operate and how countries could be enticed to come aboard. It goes without saying that since the ultimate aim would be a "peace-enhancing union" of peoples, countries and regions would have to come aboard of their own volition although once on board the surrender of sovereignty

would be irrevocable and residual disputes would have to be settled at the supranational level.

11. In answer to the legitimate concern of democratic deficit in such a centralised supranational world order, we made the suggestion that there would still of course be levels of governance below the supranational level operating under the principle of subsidiarity but that these should ideally be state units with populations no greater than 10 million and this with a view to facilitating direct democracy in their political decision-making (as Swiss cantons do to this day).

In the course of Chap. 6 when looking at some of the practicalities of putting in place a supranational geopolitical order, we noted that while it is very difficult to estimate any kind of timetable for achieving such a radical reorganisation of the geopolitical order, nonetheless since the logic of the argument is rationally compelling, eventually as rational beings we will be led in this direction. This is especially true in the contemporary context with a significant increase of armed aggression with a view to territorial annexation in various parts of the world including a major war of aggression in Europe in violation of the UN Charter (confirmed by the International Court of Justice in its judgement on the legality of Russia's invasion of Ukraine on 16 March 2022) highlighting for all to see the need to act decisively to put an end to what is really none other than gangland warfare among strutting "great" powers who recognise no authority other than themselves and no order other than that which they choose to impose by force. Of course there are major vested interests that stand in the way of the construction such a radical political institutional innovation as a supranational order as well as supposedly realistic cynics who say that it will never be so or is too good to be true; and these in our own day have tended to paralyse any serious discussion of how the geopolitical order may be reformed or even revolutionised in a manner that can effectively guarantee peace by making "war among nation states unthinkable and materially impossible" in Schuman's memorable phrase. We would not be the first to point out that while Europeans have been unambiguous and generous in the immediate support of Ukraine in its conflict with Russia, rather less clear-cut has been their view of how that conflict might eventually end. While, for example, most European political leaders would like to see a negotiated settlement, if the Russian state acquires any new territory as a result of such settlement, smash and grab military action will have been rewarded and the United Nations Charter which purports to prevent the wars of aggression and territorial aggrandisement, already observed more in the breach than in the observance (including by founder states of the UN) will be definitively dead and buried. It is in the moment of realisation of that sobering point that leaders may begin to recognise that a radical reform of the geopolitical order has become necessary…and that (for the moment) silence then descends.[2]

Similarly disappointing conclusions apply to the widespread protectionism and trade wars which have been unilaterally initiated by the USA under Trump in manifest violation of all of the principles of the WTO and of multilateralism in the organisation of trade. While many countries with their politicians recognise clearly the arbitrary, economically unfounded and destructive nature of these policies and deplore them (how often do we hear the observation that ultimately there are no winners in trade wars), nonetheless the world's political leaders seem to be mesmerised and panicked, at a loss of what to do to counteract so many of Trump's depradations.

We have been arguing that rationality, human beings universally shared ability to engage in reasoning, can lead us out of the unsatisfactory impasse that is the contemporary international order based on the sovereignty of nation states and whose limitations have been cruelly exposed by the war in Ukraine and by Trump's unilateral aggressive protectionism and violent military adventurism. It is that same rationality which through the natural sciences has unleashed waves of innovation that have transformed the lives and health of large swathes of humanity over the past three centuries since the invention of the steam engine. Earlier, we noted what one might call circumstantial if not conclusive evidence for the power of Reason in history seen in the long but eventually successful efforts to abolish slavery and forced labour and to give equal rights and opportunities to women. What we will now attempt is to lay both those dramatic social institutional innovations as well as those future developments for which we have argued in this book on the foundations of a philosophy of history. When this is attempted, the prospects for eventual attainment of a supranational geopolitical order look significantly more promising…even if we may need patience in getting there.

[2] Not entirely since Volodymyr Zelensky has called for radical reform of the UN. See Chap. 4 and Financial Times (2022) "Volodymyr Zelensky ratchets up criticism of UN Security Council", *Financial Times* 06 April 2022.

The philosophy of history has been somewhat of a Cinderella in philosophy taken as a whole as a discipline. No doubt this is because it attempts to answer highly challenging questions: what (if any) is the meaning of the whole panoply of events and actions, good and evil, that characterise human history; and even more daunting, what (if any) is the meaning of the evolving parade of events in the universe as a whole (natural and human)? We are in effect searching for meaning in everything that is and that happens: good and evil, creative and destructive, at micro and at macro system levels both in relation to human actions and interactions and to natural events in the space–time continuum. For a philosophy of history to be convincing and complete, it must be capable of explaining literally everything that happens and why it happens. To that extent, the philosophy of history is probably the most demanding branch of all of the discipline even more so than such notoriously intractable areas as epistemology or cosmology. Given this daunting level of difficulty including the challenge of establishing if there is indeed any meaning at all in history it is perhaps not so surprising that so few philosophers have attempted to elaborate comprehensive philosophies of history. Inevitably, Plato did so in an embryonic way but really only in relation to political philosophy and history in Book 8 of the Republic when he discussed how the various types of political regime would evolve into each other in a systematic and ultimately circular sequence: aristocracy→timocracy→oligarchy→democracy →tyranny→aristocracy→timocracy→ etc.[3] After Plato, it can fairly be said that the next serious sortie in the philosophy of history seen as a theory to explain everything that happens came in the work of the great German idealist, G W F Hegel. There have of course been attempts by various religions to offer all-embracing accounts of the ultimate meaning of life and of everything that happens. These however are not strictly rational accounts and so not philosophies *stricto* sensu; they rely on acceptance of certain articles of faith in the religions in question and in seeking to develop an explanation of every aspect of life in the universe many have struggled with the problem of theodicy (the justice of God). This is particularly true of Judaism, Christianity and Islam: if God is seen as a supremely good and all powerful being who has created the universe and is its source of meaning, then how can a good God permit suffering, disease, rampant violent criminality and natural disasters to happen in this world?

[3] Plato *The Republic*, op. cit. Book 8.

Hegel gamely took up the challenge of developing a comprehensive philosophy of history seeking to explain everything that happens in strictly rational terms, as part of a rational process. His ideas on history are scattered throughout the whole of his philosophical work but the most succinct and explicit statement can be found in his *Lectures on the Philosophy of History*.[4] At the outset of that work, we find Hegel's strong and by his standards very explicit statement as already quoted in Chap. 6: "*World history is governed by an ultimate design, that it is a rational process... this is a proposition whose truth we must assume; its proof lies in the study of world history itself, which is the image and enactment of reason*". Hegel's philosophy of history has been widely criticised and even ridiculed for some of its further details but we will suggest that while there are indeed some bizarre and challengeable idiosyncrasies shall we say in Hegel's elaboration,[5] these should not be allowed to obscure the powerful philosophical insight that underpins the approach.

Hegel's starting point is "a proposition that we must assume", which is that history is a rational process and so has an ultimate design of some kind. But one may ask why must we assume this? The answer lies in a philosophical principle that stretches back before Hegel and has been a centrepiece of all rationalist philosophical thinking at least since Spinoza and especially Leibniz who gave it a name: the Principle of Sufficient Reason. For Leibniz, if we are to be able to understand the world and the events that unfold therein, everything that happens must have a reason of some kind. As he himself put it, "*Our reasonings are based....on the principle of sufficient reason by virtue of which we consider that we can find no true or existent fact, no true assertion, without there being a sufficient reason why it is thus and not otherwise, although most of the time these reasons cannot be known to us*".[6] Essentially, for the world and every aspect of its evolution to be intelligible, its processes must be rational. If not then it is unintelligible and the attempts by philosophers and scientists of all stripes

[4] Hegel G (1975) *Lectures on the Philosophy of History* first published in German (1837) translated to English with an introduction by Nisbet H, Cambridge University Press Cambridge.

[5] Probably one of the better known is his reaction to the arrival of Napoléon in Jena (where Hegel was a professor of philosophy). It was reported that he was very impressed to see the "World Spirit on horseback" entering Jena. See https://www.lichtgedanken.uni-jena.de/ausgabe-09-kalenderblatt-die-weltseele-in-jena. Accessed 13 September 2025.

[6] Leibniz G (1875) *Die Philosophischen Schriften*, edited from Leibniz originals of 1663–1671 by Gerhardt C, Weidmann Berlin. See Volume 6, pg 612.

to understand it are completely futile. In other words, if in science and philosophy we set out to develop an understanding of the world, we are inevitably presuming that reality is a rational process. The primordial moment of wonder and curiosity that is the starting point of all science and philosophy seeks precisely to find a rational explanation of events; and if no such explanations are available then the efforts of scientists and philosophers are entirely in vain. Of course as Leibniz reminds us the explanations may often be recondite and difficult for us to discover; but as scientists and philosophers we must assume that in principle they exist and are waiting to be discovered; otherwise all of our efforts in these disciplines are a complete waste of time. We may note at this point (although it would merit an entirely separate book) a link between Leibniz principle and the great debates regarding the interpretation of quantum states in physics and the idea of randomness in the universe. Effectively Leibniz principle together with its warning about the difficulty of discovery of the reasons for events suggests that there is in fact no randomness in the universe; everything has a rational explanation if only we are able to drill down sufficiently into the details of complex systems. Randomness is not an ontological state but rather an epistemological comment to the effect that there is an aspect of reality that we do not yet fully understand. Erwin Schrödinger's famous cat thought experiment comes to mind as also Einstein's rejection of the Uncertainty principle of Heisenberg and the Copenhagen interpretation of quantum physics immortalised in Einstein's dictum that "*God does not play dice with the universe*".[7]

We will not attempt to take the discussion of the intricacies of quantum physics (or should we say metaphysics) any further here since our aim is only to show how central is the imperative of assuming that reality is a rational process not only for Hegel in the philosophy of history but also for some of the greatest minds in theoretical physics. Applied to human history the principle of sufficient reason would mean that history is not just a chaotic sequence of random events and actions but rather that there is an underlying logic in the way in which it unfolds. Even if human beings are presumed to be freely choosing agents (as in philosophies of free will such as Sartre's Existentialism[8]) their free and so radically creative choices are made not randomly but rather with certain goals in view; and the

[7] For a fascinating discussion of these themes, see Halpern P (2016) *Einstein's Dice and Schrödinger's Cat*, Basic Books Hachette, London.

[8] See Sarte J-P (2007) *Existentialism and Humanism*; Methuen, London.

courses of action chosen reflect the free agent's best guess on current knowledge as to how to reach those goals.[9] The logic in history is to be sought by seeing it as a process of reasoning by which humanity seeks to advance itself towards greater freedom and fulfilment. We are rational beings and so we will seek to reason about our aspirations and the challenges in meeting them. Reasoning is quintessentially a dialectical process: that is to say that when reasoning about any matter where we are seeking to discover truths we will proceed if not literally at least metaphorically (in a dialogue with ourselves) by a process of discussion with proposed conjectures (theses) which are then compared with possible refutations of the theses to test its strength (antithesis) with a view ultimately to reaching tentative conclusions regarding what to do, how best to achieve our goals (synthesis). This process of reasoning through a succession of thesis→anti thesis→synthesis→synthesis as new thesis→antithesis→synthesis→etc. is what Hegel called the dialectical logic (the logic of a rational argument conducted as in a Platonic dialogue or as in a Popperian methodology of science[10]); and as beings who reason about our aspirations, we can therefore expect to be able to detect a dialectical logic in history. This is what Hegel means when he speaks of "*world history itself, which is the image and enactment of reason*".

Of course as human beings, our actions are not entirely motivated by reasoning about our courses of action; people may act blindly on emotional motives or on the basis of obscurantist beliefs and superstitions of various kinds (which we might label as short cuts to knowledge). Hence, it would be a mistake to think of history as an uninterrupted process of ever more rational organisation of societies and smooth attainment of greater fulfilment and freedom. There will be setbacks and even major retrogressions from time to time as the dialectic unfolds in human history. Drawing on Eastern wisdom we can even see a cyclical process in which history constantly repeats itself: for example, periods of peace and

[9] For a detailed discussion of free will and its implications for the understanding of human action, see O'Sullivan P (1987) *Economic Methodology and Freedom to Choose*, Allen & Unwin, London; reprinted as a Routledge Revival (2012): Chapters 4, 12, 13.

[10] Some readers may be surprised to see the parallel drawn with Karl Popper's methodology of science as outlined in Popper K (2002) *Conjectures and Refutations*, Routledge, London since the same Popper has elsewhere been highly critical of Hegel's work, for example, in Popper K (2011) *The Open Society and its Enemies*, Routledge, London. In the latter, Popper is objecting to Hegel's rather conservative political philosophy rather than to the central insight of his philosophy of history.

prosperity alternating with periods of warfare, atrocities and retrogression. But amid this cyclical pattern we can also ask if there may not also be a gradual rational progression whereby certain irrational beliefs or manifestly untenable positions are definitively put behind us through the force of reasoning and the logic of a constructive dialectic. In the examples mentioned earlier, despite the vicissitudes of history and its repeated cyclical retrogressions, certain untenable ideas have definitively been abandoned: slavery and the subjugation of women as somehow second-class beings. But there are countless other examples that today we take for granted but which clearly show humanity's potential for progress through the application of Reason. Consider for example the medical field where so many diseases which in previous centuries were lethal and a cause of great suffering have today been either eradicated or reduced to minor treatable annoyances (most recently Covid-19). Or consider any of the many fields where through the application of science in technology we have been able to enrich human lives, for example, through travel, the improved insulation of buildings... Of course some of the scientific advances have been associated with problematic side-effects (as with carbon emissions effect on the climate) or with sad perversions (nuclear physics being used for weaponry), but these are testimony to the incompleteness of our knowledge (as Socrates and Leibniz had warned us) and to human weaknesses, especially moral weaknesses. To denigrate the rational quest for knowledge in science and philosophy because of these undoubted shortcomings and human waywardness would be gravely to overlook the huge strides in the improvement of human lives that have been made possible by the application of Reason.

This then is the insight that underlies Hegel's much misunderstood conception of history as a rational process, as "*the image and enactment of reason*". It is the ultimate driving force that allows progress in human affairs. It is true that Hegel in the elaboration of this conceptualisation of history put forward some corollary ideas which today may seem bizarre and more challengeable. He spoke of a World Spirit, an Absolute Reason or Absolute Subject as the fundamental first principle of the everything that is; and history as the process whereby Absolute Reason comes to know itself. He thinks of those political leaders who manage to bring dramatic rationally based improvements in human affairs (social progress we might say) as embodiments of the World Spirit, leading the way in the rational dialectic of history. Thus, as already mentioned, Hegel thought of Napoleon Bonaparte as an embodiment of the World Spirit in his own times in view of the Napoleonic wars which sought to extend the ideals of the French Revolution throughout Europe. Given the reality of Napoleon's activities that was a rather strained interpretation as also were some of Hegel's interpretations of earlier historical epochs. But the limitations and idiosyncrasies of the ways in which Hegel sought to apply his insight of history as a rational dialectical process should not be a reason for throwing out the fundamental insight he had achieved, an insight which we have seen is not just an option but rather a logical imperative if the whole gamut of science and philosophy are to make any sense at all. The pursuit of truth in science and philosophy must presume intelligibility of the objects we are studying; and only processes which in some sense are rational can be intelligible.

In conclusion, we are suggesting that the Hobbesian-inspired argument that we have been developing can be inscribed and understood as the direction in which in our own day Reason in the dialectical logic of history is pointing. Just as in Hobbes day in an England beset by constant civil wars between rival gangs degenerating into a war of all against all he was led to make the eminently rational logical case for the surrender of individual rights to a sovereign authority which would keep the peace, so in our day as the international order based on unenforceable international law and a toothless intergovernmental organisation that is the United Nations shows itself incapable of keeping the peace, the dialectical logic of history is pointing inexorably towards the need for a major political institutional innovation, the institution of a supranational geopolitical order based on a World Authority with sovereign powers of enforcement in the areas of policy competence assigned to it (and which at a minimum will include peace-keeping). The logic of history we have endeavoured to show is clearly on the side of the supranational argument for the geopolitical order. Hence, however much the cynics may wring their hands and the gangland barons of the supposedly "great" powers may seek to strut their stuff on the world stage, we believe that the era of the supranational geopolitical order has arrived. It may not be for tomorrow or even for some decades yet but manifestly its time in the greater sweep of human history has come and as rational beings that is the order in which we must aim to be and to live. This book has been an attempt to nudge in a small way the nascent discussions regarding the geopolitical order in that direction.[11]

[11] We certainly would not want to depict ourselves as Hegel rashly depicted Napoléon, as the "World Spirit on horseback". See above reference in this chapter, p. zz and footnote 5.

Bibliography

Financial Times. (2022). Volodymyr Zelensky ratchets up criticism of UN Security council. *Financial Times*, 06 April 2022.

Halpern, P. (2016). *Einstein's Dice and Schrödinger's Cat.* Basic Books Hachette.

Hegel, G. (1975). *Lectures on the philosophy of history* first published in German (1837) translated to English with an introduction by Nisbet H, Cambridge University Press.

Hobbes, T. (1651). *Leviathan* reprinted with an introduction by Plamenatz J (1969) 4th edition, Fontana.

Kant, I. (1795). *Zum Ewigen Frieden.* Nicolovius, Königsberg. Available in English in Kant I (1991) *Political writings* 2nd ed, translated by Nisbet H, Cambridge University Press.

Leibniz, G. (1875). *Die Philosophischen Schriften*, edited from Leibniz originals of 1663–1671 by Gerhardt C, Weidmann Berlin.

O'Sullivan, P. (1987). *Economic methodology and freedom to choose.* Allen & Unwin; reprinted as a Routledge Revival (2012).

Plato. (2007). *The republic.* Penguin Classic.

Popper, K. (2002). *Conjectures and refutations.* Routledge.

Popper, K. (2011). *The open society and its enemies.* Routledge.

Sarte, J.-P. (2007). *Existentialism and humanism.* Methuen.

Univresität Jena *Lichtgedanken.* Accessed September 13, 2025., from https://www.lichtgedanken.uni-jena.de/946/kalenderblatt

PART II

Putting the Arguments in the Context of Complexity: Independent Reflections from a Variety of Specialist Perspectives

CHAPTER 10

Norms in Governance Design and the Path to Supranationality in Asia

Francis D. Kim

Abstract This chapter contributed by Francis Kim brings to the book some insights regarding an Asian perspective on the themes of supranationality. It is argued that supranationality in Asia, though for the moment unlikely, is increasingly necessary amid rising geopolitical tensions. The 2025 Xi–Putin–Kim summit underscores the return of bloc politics, while structural inequalities fuel nationalism and strain voluntary cooperation. Drawing on DeLong and Piketty, the chapter links political economy and social grievances to cycles of nationalistic populism and interstate hostility. The receding role of US hegemony, from the "America First" isolationism after the Great Depression to the "MAGA" in the Trump era, signals that a new international order is inevitable, whether welcomed or not, compelling Asia to rethink its institutional architecture. ASEAN's Bangkok Declaration illustrates a useful precedent in Southeast Asia for how norms of cooperation and consultation helped preserve stability, but arguably, it is no longer sufficient for today's challenges being hamstrung by a unanimity requirement for collective decisions and a widening political and economic diversity among its members. The chapter calls for innovations in governance design, including flexible coalitions to pioneer closer integration, and frames crises as potential catalysts for reform.

P. O'Sullivan et al., *Overcoming Gangsterism and Geo-Political Anarchy*, https://doi.org/10.1007/978-3-032-22438-5_10

Keywords ASEAN • Unanimity principle • Bloc politics • 1930s and MAGA • Institutional innovation • Strongman leaders • Societal fractures • Cultural memory and identity • Caste (India) • Scale and scope in integration

A quarter way into the twenty-first century, Asia is turning into a geopolitical hotbed zone. The meeting of Xi Jinping, Vladimir Putin and Kim Jong Un in 2025, the first time the three leaders have been seen together, was rich in symbolism and bodes ominously with consequence. Together, they climbed to the top of the Gate of Heavenly Peace to watch a grand military parade, the same place where Mao Zedong proclaimed the founding of the People's Republic of China in 1949 and where he hosted Kim Il-sung and Nikita Khrushchev in 1959 at the dawn of the Cold War. The message was unmistakable: the era of Chinese passivity is over, and Beijing now holds the reins in this triangular relationship.

The display was breath-taking in both scale and intent. A gun salute thundered 80 times, marking the anniversary of victory over Japan, as 50,000 spectators sat in reverent silence. Choirs sang, fists raised, that "without the Communist Party, there is no modern China". Xi inspected the troops as tanks, hypersonic missiles, nuclear-capable systems and laser weapons rolled by. Drones, underwater, airborne and even "robot wolves", underscored that this was no mere ceremony but a show of power aimed at Washington, its allies and even the two men standing beside Xi.[1] Kim, whose impoverished but nuclear-armed country relies on Chinese aid, has been sending troops to Russia in exchange for cash and technology, bolstering Putin's war in Ukraine over Eastern Europe. Now Xi's public alignment with both men signals a sharpening of bloc, or turf, politics. India, meanwhile, still grappling with the aftermath of clashes with Pakistan and its own uneasy border tensions with China, is considering new diplomatic openings with Beijing to avoid being cornered as the US–China tariff war deepens.

The meeting also had a surreal, almost grim edge. Reporters overheard Xi and Putin joking about organ transplants and the possibility of living to

[1] BBC News (2025) *China's Xi steals the limelight in a defiant push against US-led world order.* 3 September. Available at: https://www.bbc.com/news/articles/cn0rllxld8go. Accessed 5 September 2025.

150.[2] While delivered with smiles, the conversation captured the foreboding tone of leaders who see themselves as shapers of history, even masters over life and death, while displaying the weaponry that could decide the fate of many other nations. This is the world Asia faces: nuclear brinkmanship, coercive economic statecraft and a growing sense of ideological confrontation. Left unchecked, these dynamics risk locking the region into cycles of confrontation that no single nation can escape. Supranationality is a long shot in Asia, but more urgent than ever and anywhere.

Gangsters Are Not the Great Men, but the Structural Conditions

In order to grasp why today's geopolitical tensions resonate so deeply, however, one must step back, go beyond the Great Man Theory and examine the politico-economic foundations of the past century.[3] Brad DeLong, in *Slouching Towards Utopia*, calls the period 1870–2010 the "extraordinary century", marked by a historic leap in productive capacity, health and technological reach.[4] Breakthroughs such as electricity, mass production, antibiotics and digital computation transformed life expectancy and living standards worldwide. Yet, as DeLong cautions, the arduous process was no utopia: progress was "punctuated by depressions, wars, and repeated crises" and distributed unevenly across nations and social classes. Technological advance, in his telling, did not guarantee justice.

When growth's benefits are narrowly shared, DeLong argues, social grievances accumulate, among those left behind, those excluded and those who watch elites prosper while their own prospects stagnate. Such disillusionment fuels populism and, in extreme cases, what he terms "force-and-fraud exploitation" and the impulse to "join a gang … running a domination game on the rest of humanity".[5] In this framing, gangster-style politics is less a matter of individual villainy and more a structural

[2] BBC News (2025) *Xi and Putin discuss organ transplants and living 'indefinitely'*. 4 September 2025. Available at: https://www.bbc.com/news/videos/c059jl0323po. Accessed 5 September 2025.

[3] Carlyle T (1841) *On Heroes, Hero-Worship, and the Heroic in History*. London: James Fraser.

[4] DeLong J B (2022) *Slouching Towards Utopia: An Economic History of the Twentieth Century*. New York: Basic Books.

[5] DeLong, J B (2023) "*Slouching Towards Utopia, with Brad DeLong*." Vital Center Podcast, hosted by Geoff Kabaservice & Brink Lindsey. Niskanen Center.

response to the breakdown of faith in democratic bargaining and peaceful redistribution.

DeLong's perspective is thus systemic rather than biographical. Gangsters, strongmen or demagogues, are symptoms of deeper fractures: slowing growth, rising inequality, failing legitimacy and institutional inertia. Leaders like Xi, Putin or others matter, but they ride larger waves of discontent created by an economy that no longer seems to deliver broadly shared prosperity. The true danger, DeLong suggests, lies not merely in the men who exploit the crisis, but in the structural conditions that make their appeal possible.

Emmanuel Todd adds a geopolitical dimension to this structural view. In *After the Empire: The Breakdown of the American Order*, Todd argues that the declining capacity of the USA to act as global hegemon makes the emergence of a new international order inevitable, "whether we like it or not".[6] The waning of American predominance does not merely redistribute power but compels other regions to shoulder greater responsibility for maintaining stability. In this sense, Todd's analysis reinforces the argument that the drivers of today's turbulence are systemic: the world must renegotiate its institutional architecture in response to the shifting balance of power, just as it must respond to deepening inequalities. And a quarter century has passed since his argument, making the call for institutional renewal more pressing than ever.

The receding role of US hegemony, from the "America First" isolationism that followed the Great Depression to the Trump era's "Make America Great Again" turn, underscores this systemic shift. Each episode signalled a step back from global stewardship, whether through neutrality acts in the 1930s or the withdrawal from multilateral frameworks such as the Paris Agreement and the Trans-Pacific Partnership nearly a century later. For the past eight decades, we have lived through what Joseph Nye famously called "the American Century", a period of unrivalled political, economic and military power, during which the USA shaped the global order and underwrote much of its stability.[7] These retreats communicate to allies and rivals alike that the USA will no longer guarantee the same degree of international order, leaving regions such as Asia to assume greater responsibility for maintaining stability. This evolving context

[6] Todd E (2003) *After the Empire: The Breakdown of the American Order.* Columbia University Press, New York.

[7] Nye, Joseph. S. Jr. (2024) *A Life in the American Century.* Cambridge, UK: Polity Press.

strengthens the case that a new institutional architecture is not optional but inevitable, and that Asia must proactively design mechanisms capable of managing conflict and cooperation in a less US-centric world.

A Déjà Vu of Globalisation's Fallout and Populism's Rise in a Century

To see where this is going, it is crucial to look back at history. The current structural condition of the world economy bears an unsettling resemblance to the years preceding the First World War, when the first great wave of globalisation reached its zenith and then abruptly fractured. As Piketty documents, the late nineteenth and early twentieth centuries were marked by an extraordinary concentration of wealth: the top decile of the population owned 90% or more of all private capital in many European countries, and inherited wealth accounted for the majority of fortunes.[8] The return on capital systematically outpaced the growth of income, allowing the "patrimonial" elite to tighten its grip on economic and political life. Global trade, capital flows and migration expanded rapidly under the gold standard, yet this very integration intensified tensions, as mass migration depressed wages in receiving countries and fuelled backlash, while free trade provoked fears of foreign domination and hollowed-out local industries.[9]

These structural stresses collided with geopolitical crises. The First World War shattered the liberal economic order and destroyed a substantial share of European private wealth, but the postwar settlement failed to stabilise the system. Reparations, competitive devaluations and hyperinflation in Germany further eroded middle-class savings and intensified distributional conflict, producing a fragile recovery that by 1924 had barely restored political or economic equilibrium.[10] As noted in Chap. 11, Eichengreen suggests that these pressures opened the door to the

[8] Piketty, T (2014) *Capital in the Twenty-First Century* Belknap Harvard University Press Cambridge, MA.

[9] O'Rourke K & Williamson, J (1999) *Globalization and History: The Evolution of a Nineteenth-Century Atlantic Economy*. MIT Press Cambridge, MA.

[10] Eichengreen B (1996) *Golden Fetters: The Gold Standard and the Great Depression, 1919–1939*. Oxford University Press, Oxford.

"populist temptation": a wave of mass politics and charismatic figures who promised to avenge the grievances of ordinary citizens.[11]

Piketty interprets these developments as the political consequence of unchecked inequality: when liberal regimes failed to respond to widening gaps in wealth and power, societies lurched towards radical solutions. The Bolshevik Revolution of 1917 represented a "monstrous but comprehensible" attempt to abolish private property and reset the social order.[12] The lesson, he warns, is that failure to reform capitalism in the face of inequality can produce either nationalist authoritarianism or revolutionary upheaval. Today, as inequality again approaches Belle Époque levels, populist-nationalist leaders exploit similar resentments, raising the spectre of a repeat cycle unless institutions find ways to distribute the gains of globalisation more broadly. That is, the driving force behind these geopolitical shifts is not simply ideology or personality but the underlying economic structures that set the stage on which politics unfolds. And historical precedents suggest that, when economies become less interdependent, it becomes far easier for nations to slip into a Hobbesian struggle, where rivalry and confrontation seem preferable to compromise and cooperation.

Prevailing Norms and Ongoing Brutalities in Asia

If structural forces as discussed in the global context above are the underlying conditions that fracture integration, then shared norms are the counterweights that hold it together. Before we examine the scale–scope tradeoffs, and how to push its possibilities frontier upward, it is worth asking what "cohesive factor" could hold supranationality together. Unlike Europe, Asia lacks region-wide shared norms, such as medieval Christianity, the Enlightenment or liberal democracy, that historically bound Europe's members together. Yet, certain historical events suggest that moments of cohesion have arisen in Asia too when elites articulated common values or faced common threats.

The Bangkok Declaration of 1967 was one such moment. Signed by the foreign ministers of Indonesia, Malaysia the Philippines, Singapore and Thailand, the declaration established ASEAN on principles of mutual

[11] Eichengreen B (2018) *The Populist Temptation: Economic Grievance and Political Reaction in the Modern Era*. Oxford University Press, Oxford.

[12] Piketty T (2019) *Capital and Ideology* Harvard University Press, Cambridge, MA.

respect, equality and non-interference.[13] It called for collaboration across economic, social, cultural and technical fields, signalling a collective determination to maintain regional autonomy amid Cold War turbulence. Thailand's Foreign Minister Thanat Khoman played a pivotal role by reconciling Indonesia, Malaysia and the Philippines after the Konfrontasi period and then convening them, alongside Singapore, to formalise the agreement. Singapore's Foreign Minister S. Rajaratnam and then-Prime Minister Lee Kuan Yew strongly supported the initiative, viewing ASEAN as a way to prevent great-power manipulation, anti-communism in particular, and to secure peace through dialogue rather than confrontation.

From its inception, ASEAN's strength lay not in coercion but in cultivating norms. Non-interference, consensus-based decision-making and voluntary cooperation became the organisation's informal constitution. These "habits of consultation" provided a stabilising function, allowing members to resolve disputes quietly and to gradually deepen economic and functional cooperation. In this sense, ASEAN's early cohesion was built as much on trust and political will as on formal treaties, a lesson that remains crucial for any future attempt at Asian supranationality.

In today's increasingly uncertain world, the maintenance of shared norms is a necessity for stability. Danny Quah argues that as multilateralism retreats, Asia ought to strengthen its own rules-based systems to preserve order and credibility, warning that the region cannot rely indefinitely on a global order shaped by others.[14] Norms function as the cohesive factor that holds diverse states together, preventing fragmentation even when interests diverge. Thomas Schelling's bargaining logic reinforces this view: credibility and reputation are strategic assets, and violating implicit codes of conduct undermines the ability to deter or persuade in future negotiations.[15] Together, institutions like ASEAN and other regional frameworks must protect their reputational capital, using consultation and consensus not as mere rituals but as investments in collective security and economic resilience at a time when trust is under severe global strain.

Unlike ASEAN in Southeast Asia, which was anchored by a shared anti-communist norm in the Cold War and a desire to avoid great-power

[13] ASEAN Secretariat (1967) *The ASEAN Declaration (Bangkok Declaration)*. ASEAN Legal Instruments.

[14] Quah D (2024) "ASEAN's Challenges in an Increasingly Fragmented World." *Lee Kuan Yew School of Public Policy Global-is-asian*; available at https://lkyspp.nus.edu.sg/gia/article/asean-s-challenges-in-an-increasingly-fragmented-world. Accessed 18 September 2025.

[15] Schelling, T C (2006) *The Strategy of Conflict*. Harvard University Press, Cambridge, MA.

manipulation, East Asia's attempts at cohesion among China, Japan and Korea have been far more turbulent. Historical memory remains the chief obstacle to deeper integration. Disputes over issues such as the "comfort women" and territorial claims continue to shape both elite and public sentiment, ensuring that diplomatic friction persists even when economic cooperation would be mutually advantageous.[16] In Europe, Germany's wartime aggression was confronted through explicit contrition, reparations and integration into multilateral institutions, allowing France and Germany to reconcile and anchor the European project.

In East Asia, Japan's colonial legacy in China and Korea remains unresolved. Although Tokyo has issued treaties and apologies, these have often been perceived as insufficient or undermined by symbolic acts like visits to Yasukuni Shrine.[17] China and South Korea have kept wartime memory central to national identity, reinforcing grievances through education and commemorations. Historical memory remains central to China's political narrative. Upon the aforementioned 80th anniversary of victory in the War of Resistance in this chapter, China has launched a wave of films and documentaries about Japanese wartime atrocities such as human experiments, underscoring how the past remain part of active cultural memory.[18] This has created a cycle of rapprochement and renewed tension: economic cooperation expands, but political trust remains brittle in East Asia. Without a shared "never again" narrative or a multilateral integrator like the European Economic Community (later to evolve into the EU) NATO or the Marshall Plan, East Asia never consolidated a collective security or reconciliation framework. As a result, trilateral cooperation has been episodic, with summits pausing whenever bilateral disputes flare up, a stark contrast to the steady deepening of European integration.

South Asia has experienced repeated cycles of turmoil since the postwar era, but it is now entering a serious period of acute instability in which domestic crises rapidly spill across borders into geopolitical risks. In 2025,

[16] Chatham House (2019) *Governance, Leadership and Legitimacy in East Asia.* Chatham House, London.

[17] Reuters (2024) "South Korea Protests Japanese Leaders' Offerings to Yasukuni Shrine." *Reuters, 21 April 2024.* Available at https://www.reuters.com/world/asia-pacific/south-korea-protests-japanese-leaders-offerings-yasukuni-shrine-2024-04-21/. Accessed 18 September 2025.

[18] BBC Monitoring (2025) "Briefing: China Media Blitz Spotlights Japan's Wartime Past." *BBC Monitoring 07 August 2025.* Available at https://monitoring.bbc.co.uk/product/b0004dvo. Accessed 18 September 2025

India launched Operation Sindoor, striking militant camps in Pakistan-administered Kashmir after a deadly terror attack.[19] The action prompted retaliatory fire and raised fears of full-scale war before a ceasefire was finally brokered. Even within the more democratic of the two rivals, India, populism has deepened internal divisions that weaken regional trust. Amartya Sen observes that Indian populism fuses nationalism with caste and communal fault lines in the world's largest democratic nation: "We have integrated populism with our divisions of caste… The Indian combination of animosity that goes with division in terms of caste and tribe has given populism a further shade that European populism does not have".[20] Such politics turns social tensions into interstate risks, heightening India–Pakistan hostility. Sen further warns that sedition should mean "violently destroying a state and not just disagreeing with the government", yet "entire institutions are able to do sedition in India" when they suppress dissent.

This pattern is mirrored across the region. In Nepal, youth-led protests over corruption and unemployment have escalated into deadly clashes, forcing the prime minister's resignation and triggering fresh elections.[21] The intensity of these demonstrations can be read through Piketty's framework: rising inequality, elite capture of economic gains and slow social mobility create the conditions for mass mobilisation and demands for redistribution. Such domestic unrest does not remain contained, and disruptions to cross-border trade and migrant labour flows spill over into neighbouring economies, adding a layer of regional tension. Together, these crises underscore South Asia's structural fragility: entrenched corruption, elite dominance and rising popular anger reminiscent of Piketty's description of "patrimonial" societies.

Unlike the supranational European Union, which can override nationalist decisions through binding law and qualified majority voting, the South Asian Association for Regional Cooperation (SAARC) remains a purely intergovernmental forum. Established in 1985, SAARC is a regional organisation that promotes economic, social and cultural cooperation

[19] Drury F (2025) "What we know about India's strikes on Pakistan and Pakistan-administered Kashmir." *BBC News*, 8 May 2025.

[20] Mint (2019) "Amartya Sen Draws Line between Populism in West, India." *Mint*, 28 February 2019. Available at https://www.livemint.com/news/india/amartya-sen-draws-line-between-populism-in-west-india-1551296377737.html. Accessed 18 September 2025.

[21] Economist (2025) "Huge demonstrations bring down Nepal's government." *The Economist*, 09 September 2025.

among its eight members: Afghanistan, Bangladesh, Bhutan, India, Maldives, Nepal, Pakistan and Sri Lanka. Decisions are made by consensus, and the association has no supranational authority to enforce compliance, leaving national sovereignty intact. Its unanimity rule all but guarantees paralysis, leaving it poorly equipped to deliver timely or meaningful resolutions. ASEAN has better managed to produce momentous acts, thanks to its formal practice of consultation and consensus-seeking, but it remains fundamentally intergovernmental. East Asia lacks any comparable supranational organisation either, relying instead on loose, dialogue-based forums with no binding legal authority. Supranationality thus remains essentially a distant dream, a longshot in Asia, but more urgent than ever and anywhere.

The ongoing Asian geopolitical conflicts and structural fragilities show the limits of Asia's current intergovernmental system. As conflicts spill across borders and domestic crises erode trust, voluntary cooperation alone is proving inadequate to maintain order. This reality invites us to consider whether Asia must go beyond consultation and consensus, building stronger forms of collective governance. It is from this sense of necessity that we now turn to the question of a possible supranationalism for Asia.

Moving Towards Supranationality

Supranationality is not only desirable but morally imperative if humanity is to move beyond the rivalry of nation-states. How has humanity achieved supranationality to some extent in the past? As discussed earlier in this chapter, moral imperatives acting as cohesive factors have repeatedly proven pivotal in guiding the creation of roadmaps for building durable institutions. The European Union's reliance on the Copenhagen Criteria and ASEAN's principle of consensus and the anti-communist norm are key examples of how shared norms can generate trust and sustain cooperation despite diversity. Recalling this point here underscores the central question that follows: whether Asia today can draw on similarly powerful normative anchors to push the region towards a higher frontier of supranational cooperation. The real question is what kind of supranational order can be both inclusive and effective. Historical experience suggests that regional bodies either can become paralysed by diversity or be too weak to matter. The task is to design a path to establish supranationality in the real world.

A helpful way to think about this task is to understand the tradeoff between scale and scope. Scale refers to the number of member states in an organisation. Scope refers to the range of policy areas that members can agree to integrate, from trade and security to human rights and climate regulation. Expanding membership size increases reach and legitimacy, but it also introduces more heterogeneity of history, regime type and national interest, which makes agreement harder. Smaller, more cohesive groups can often pursue broader and more ambitious agendas, while larger groups must settle for narrower, lowest common denominator outcomes. This is why the scale–scope relationship tends to slope downward as organisations grow in size. The concave shape of the curve suggests that the last members to join are often the more difficult to integrate, and their entry is more likely to slow or even halt the ability to reach resolutions.

From Intergovernmental Tradeoffs to Supranational Governance

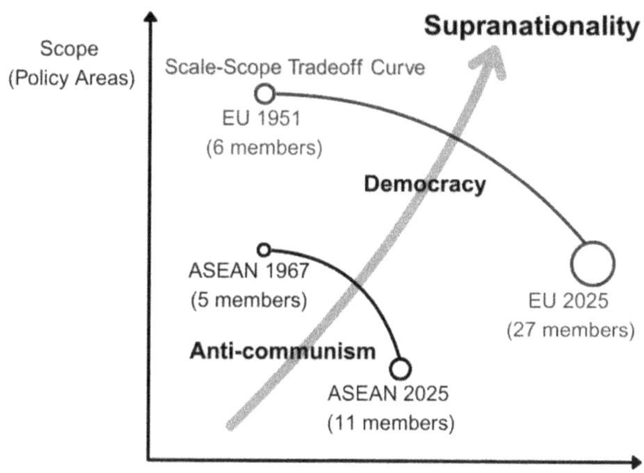

Source: Author's own presentation

Research by Diana Panke clarifies that when larger, groups can successfully take on more tasks rather than fewer. In a study of 76 regional organisations, she found that large groups only expand their activities when three conditions hold: members are economically strong, decisions can be taken by majority vote rather than unanimity, and regional courts or secretariats exist to enforce agreements.[22] Her work also shows that when states belong to several overlapping organisations, cooperation can stall unless rules and norms prevent duplication and conflict. The lesson is that size alone does not achieve supranationality. The UN is one such obvious case. To ride on the scale and to include the great postwar powers, the UN was created as an intergovernmental organisation, not as a body standing above states. Nation-states remain the ultimate sovereign units of world order as explained in Chap. 2. They voluntarily agree to the UN Charter but retain the right to withdraw or ignore obligations if they choose. Supranationality is by definition lost in that tradeoff.

ASEAN's historical development path illustrates the point about shared values/goals to achieve supranationality. The collapse of communism ironically weakened ASEAN's original shared values, anti-communism, reducing its resolution capacity and slowing decision-making. Its early cohesion came less from legal rules and more from shared threat perception, especially fear of communism. This political philosophical alignment supported security cooperation but also entrenched non-interference as a principle, which limited ASEAN's ability to act on contentious political issues. In the post–Cold War era, Lee Kuan Yew warned that admitting former communist states too quickly would dilute ASEAN's identity. He worried that the inclusion of Myanmar, Cambodia, Laos and Vietnam would complicate decision-making, and events since the 1990s have largely borne out this concern.

Lee saw Cambodia's admission to ASEAN in 1999 as one of the cases where the original values of ASEAN, among older members, were diluted. He suggested that Cambodia's behaviour, including how its government was organised around Hun Sen, did not align with the older members' expectations of governance norms, regime type or administrative style. And he was right. In 2012, ASEAN failed for the first time in its history to issue a joint communiqué because Cambodia blocked any mention of the South China Sea disputes, rejecting language on Scarborough Shoal and Vietnam's EEZ claims.[23] More recently, after the 2021 military coup, ASEAN adopted a "Five-Point Consensus" on Myanmar, but as violence

[22] Panke D & Starkmann C. (2021) Trajectories of Regional Cooperation: A Comparative Analysis *Comparative European Politics* 19: 1–25. Oxford University Press, Oxford.

[23] Bower E Z (2012) "*China Reveals Its Hand on ASEAN in Phnom Penh*," CSIS Commentary, 20 July 2012 available at https://www.csis.org/analysis/china-reveals-its-hand-asean-phnom-penh. Accessed 18 September 2025.

escalated, the junta ignored those commitments.[24] In 2025, Cambodia's renewed border aggression against Thailand (spurred on by the retired Hun Sen's son) once again exposed ASEAN's inability to act, as the bloc failed to produce a binding resolution or deter escalation.[25] ASEAN's paralysis to enforce the agreement or prevent further brutalities among all member states confirms that expansion without stronger institutions weakens collective capacity.

The central challenge for Asia is to design a configuration in which cooperation yields benefits that clearly outweigh the sovereignty costs of participation. If integration is too shallow, members risk drifting apart, treating the institution as a talk shop rather than a framework for joint action. Conversely, if the scope of integration expands too quickly without preparing members' institutions or public opinion, backlash becomes likely, as the Brexit experience demonstrated (at least for Britain). A viable way forward may be to form flexible, issue-specific coalitions, sometimes called "coalitions of the willing", that allow interested states to advance more quickly on targeted areas such as supply chain integration, digital standards, climate adaptation financing or even limited security guarantees. These coalitions can co-exist under a broader regional umbrella, gradually pushing the governance frontier upward and strengthening collective capacity without overburdening members that are not ready or willing to move as fast. This is in fact the core of the EU's Enhanced Cooperation Principle and has facilitated such major transfers of national to supranational competence as the adoption of a common currency (the Euro) by 21 EU member states.[26]

Importantly, this governance frontier, the line between what is politically feasible and what is seen as too costly, is not fixed. It is shaped by mechanisms of cohesion such as shared norms, legal conditionality and the perception of common threats. When these mechanisms align, they shift expectations and make deeper commitments possible. The European

[24] Human Rights Watch (2022) *"Myanmar: ASEAN's Failed 5-Point Consensus a Year On"* available at https://www.hrw.org/news/2022/04/22/myanmar-aseans-failed-5-point-consensus-year. Accessed 18 September 2025.

[25] Rattanasevee P (2025) "Asean must act for peace in Thai-Cambodian clash or risk irrelevance," *South China Morning Post*, 25 July 2025.

[26] See European Union EU-Lex *Enhanced Cooperation* available at https://eur-lex.europa.eu/EN/legal-content/glossary/enhanced-cooperation.html. Accessed 17 September 2025. Excerpt from the Lisbon Treaty on European Union.

Union illustrates this dynamic. Its Copenhagen Criteria[27] and strict accession process established a foundation of trust by requiring that new members meet standards on democracy, rule of law, human rights and functioning market economies. This sequencing allowed the EU to integrate an ever larger and more diverse membership while preserving the integrity of its institutions.

Ukraine's trajectory is a striking example. For years after the Orange Revolution, which set the stage for its later democratic move, Ukraine was not considered a realistic candidate for EU membership, not because of geographic location but because its institutions suffered from chronic corruption, weak rule of law and state capture by oligarchic interests. These deficiencies meant Ukraine did not meet the Copenhagen Criteria, and Brussels had little appetite to risk diluting the *acquis communautaire* or the EU's credibility. The war fundamentally changed this calculus. Russia's invasion in 2022 galvanised European public opinion, reframed Ukraine as a frontline defender of the European security order and indeed of certain very basic European values/freedoms and created strong political incentives for the EU to offer a credible membership perspective. Simultaneously, wartime reforms accelerated Kyiv's efforts to strengthen judicial independence, combat corruption and align its laws with EU standards. As a result, Ukraine's candidacy became not only geopolitically urgent but institutionally more plausible.[28]

This sequence underscores two lessons relevant to a possible supranationality in Asia. First, geopolitics can act as an accelerant, bringing previously stalled integration projects back to the agenda when security or normative stakes rise. Second, credibility remains essential. Even under crisis conditions, admission to deeper cooperation frameworks depends on whether a candidate can uphold shared rules and values. For Asia, this means that crises such as pandemics, climate shocks or security threats can open windows of opportunity for greater regionalism, but only if institutional readiness and trust are cultivated in advance.

[27] See European Union EU-Lex Accession criteria (Copenhagen Criteria) available at https://eur-lex.europa.eu/EN/legal-content/glossary/accession-criteria-copenhagen-criteria.html. Accessed 17 September 2025. Excerpt from the Lisbon Treaty on European Union.

[28] See European Council (2023) *Press release: European Council conclusions on Ukraine, enlargement and reforms*. 14 December 2023. European Council/Council of the European Union.

An East Side Story

The argument of this chapter has been that supranationality in Asia is at once improbable and indispensable. As the American Century wanes, and the USA signals through repeated turns towards isolationism that it will no longer underwrite global order to the same degree, Asia must increasingly shoulder the burden of maintaining stability. The region's present trajectory, marked by coercive economic statecraft, historical grievances and mounting domestic unrest, demonstrates that voluntary cooperation and "habits of consultation" alone are no longer enough to bind commitment to a central authority above the national level. Following Danny Quah, we affirm that a rules-based order is not a luxury but a necessity if Asia is to prevent rivalry from hardening into permanent fracture.[29] But where Quah stresses rules, this chapter adds a further point: rules must be accompanied by supranational qualities and institutions capable of enforcing them and mechanisms capable of renewing trust when shocks occur.

The path forward is unlikely to come in a single leap towards a European-style supranational union unless some catalytic event or external threat provides a unifying push. More realistically, Asia's integration will unfold through a sequence of carefully designed steps that approach what Thomas Schelling called a tipping point moment.[30] Flexible and issue-specific coalitions of the willing could pioneer integration where demand is highest, including digital standards, supply-chain security and climate adaptation, without compelling reluctant members to move prematurely. When these narrower arrangements succeed, they can gradually shift expectations about what is politically possible, lower the perceived cost of integration and move the region towards a higher supranational frontier.

Crises, far from being merely sources of danger, can serve as accelerants for reform, as Ukraine's trajectory towards the European Union illustrates. Institutional preparation meant that crisis-driven deepening was credible rather than chaotic. Asia may find its own moment of collective resolve, perhaps in response to a pandemic, a climate emergency or a security flashpoint that makes fragmented responses obviously inadequate. In

[29] Quah D (2024) *Economic Principles for a New World Order of Multipolarity, Multilateralism*. Lee Kuan Yew School of Public Policy, Singapore; available at https://dannyquah.github.io/Storage/2024.03-Danny.Quah-New-World-Order-Multipolarity-Multilateralism.pdf. Accessed 18 September 2025.

[30] Schelling T C (1971) Dynamic Models of Segregation *Journal of Mathematical Sociology*, 1(2), 143–186.

such a moment, philosophical resources may prove as crucial as institutional ones. The Buddhist Middle Way, with its emphasis on balance, compromise and the avoidance of extremes, could serve as a culturally resonant starting point for shared norms, especially when paired with Confucian ideals of harmony. Korea's foundational governance ethic, *Hongik Ingan*, which calls for "broadly benefiting humankind", adds an a-religious layer, reminding the region that integration should aim not only at peace but at advancing collective human flourishing. Together these traditions suggest that moderation, dialogue and equilibrium can form the moral foundation for an Asian model of supranationality.

Speculatively, one can imagine an Asia that does not merely follow Europe's path but joins it in shaping a truly global order. In the very long term, enhanced cooperation between an increasingly cohesive Asian bloc and the European Union could become a stepping stone towards an embryonic supranational world authority, a body that respects cultural diversity yet coordinates collective action on existential global challenges. This may sound utopian, but imaginative exercises of this kind have historically inspired practical institution building. Contemplating this horizon reminds us that supranationality is not merely a technical or legal design problem but a moral and civilisational question about how humanity chooses to govern itself in the inevitably interdependent world.

Bibliography

BBC Monitoring. (2025). Briefing: China media blitz spotlights Japan's wartime past. *BBC Monitoring* 07 August 2025. Accessed September 18, 2025, from https://monitoring.bbc.co.uk/product/b0004dvo

BBC News. (2025a). *China's Xi steals the limelight in a defiant push against US-led world order.* 3 September. Accessed September 5, 2025, from https://www.bbc.com/news/articles/cn0rllxld8go

BBC News. (2025b). *Xi and Putin discuss organ transplants and living 'indefinitely'.* 4 September 2025. Accessed September 5, 2025, from https://www.bbc.com/news/videos/c059jl0323po

Bower, E. Z. (2012). *China reveals its hand on ASEAN in Phnom Penh.* CSIS Commentary, 20 July 2012. Accessed September 18, 2025, from https://www.csis.org/analysis/china-reveals-its-hand-asean-phnom-penh

Carlyle, T. (1841). *On heroes, hero-worship, and the heroic in history.* James Fraser.

Chatham House. (2019). *Governance, leadership and legitimacy in East Asia.* Chatham House.

DeLong, J. B. (2022). *Slouching towards utopia: An economic history of the twentieth century*. Basic Books.

DeLong, J. B. (2023). *Slouching towards Utopia, with Brad DeLong*. Vital Center Podcast, hosted by Geoff Kabaservice & Brink Lindsey. Niskanen Center.

Drury, F. (2025). What we know about India's strikes on Pakistan and Pakistan-administered Kashmir. *BBC News*, 8 May 2025.

Economist. (2025). Huge demonstrations bring down Nepal's government. *The Economist*, 09 September 2025.

Eichengreen, B. (1996). *Golden fetters: The gold standard and the great depression, 1919–1939*. Oxford University Press.

Eichengreen, B. (2018). *The populist temptation: Economic grievance and political reaction in the modern era*. Oxford University Press.

European Council. (2023). Press release: European council conclusions on Ukraine, enlargement and reforms, 14 December 2023.

European Union EU-Lex. *Enhanced Cooperation*. Accessed September 17, 2025., from https://eur-lex.europa.eu/EN/legal-content/glossary/enhanced-cooperation.html

European Union EU-Lex Accession criteria (Copenhagen Criteria). Accessed September 17, 2025., from https://eur-lex.europa.eu/EN/legal-content/glossary/accession-criteria-copenhagen-criteria.html

Human Rights Watch. (2022). *Myanmar: ASEAN's Failed 5-Point Consensus a Year On*. Accessed September 18, 2025, from https://www.hrw.org/news/2022/04/22/myanmar-aseans-failed-5-point-consensus-year

Mint. (2019). Amartya Sen draws line between populism in West, India. *Mint*, 28 February 2019. Accessed September 18, 2025, from https://www.livemint.com/news/india/amartya-sen-draws-line-between-populism-in-west-india-1551296377737.html

Nye, J. S. (2024). *A life in the American century*. Polity Press.

O'Rourke, K., & Williamson, J. (1999). *Globalization and history: The evolution of a nineteenth-century Atlantic economy*. MIT Press Cambridge.

Panke, D., & Starkmann, C. (2021). Trajectories of regional cooperation: A comparative analysis *Comparative European Politics 19*, 1–25.

Piketty, T. (2014). *Capital in the twenty-first century*. Belknap Harvard University Press.

Piketty, T. (2019). *Capital and ideology*. Harvard University Press.

Quah, D. (2024a). *ASEAN's challenges in an increasingly fragmented world*. Lee Kuan Yew School of Public Policy Global-is-asian. Accessed September 18, 2025, from https://lkyspp.nus.edu.sg/gia/article/asean-s-challenges-in-an-increasingly-fragmented-world

Quah, D. (2024b). *Economic principles for a new world order of multipolarity, multilateralism*. Lee Kuan Yew School of Public Policy, Singapore. Accessed September 18, 2025, from https://dannyquah.github.io/Storage/2024.03-Danny.Quah-New-World-Order-Multipolarity-Multilateralism.pdf

Rattanasevee, P. (2025). Asean must act for peace in Thai-Cambodian clash or risk irrelevance. *South China Morning Post*, 25 July 2025.
Reuters. (2024). South Korea protests Japanese leaders' offerings to Yasukuni Shrine. *Reuters,* 21 April 2024. Accessed September 18, 2025, from https://www.reuters.com/world/asia-pacific/south-korea-protests-japanese-leaders-offerings-yasukuni-shrine-2024-04-21/
Schelling, T. C. (1971). Dynamic models of segregation. *Journal of Mathematical Sociology, 1*(2), 143–186.
Schelling, T. C. (2006). *The strategy of conflict*. Harvard University Press.
Todd, E. (2003). *After the empire: The breakdown of the American order*. Columbia University Press.

CHAPTER 11

The Economic Imponderables of Supranational Global Governance: An Economist's Perspective

Alojzy Nowak

Abstract This chapter written by Prof. Alojzy Nowak brings to the book the perspective of a trained economist in relation to the proposals of this book for a radical reform of the contemporary geopolitical order by institution of a supranational World authority with enforcement powers. It is shown how the dramatic globalisation of all aspects of economic affairs in the past 25 years has occurred within the premises of the market fundamentalism of the Washington Consensus which has promoted a largely unregulated form of globalisation of trade and international flows of funds. The "casino capitalism" which this encouraged exploded with drastic consequences for the whole of the world economy in the Financial Crisis of 2008. But in the absence of any truly effective global regulation to curb the kinds of excesses that led to the Financial Crisis, the vacuum has been filled by nationalist populisms and assorted protectionism of which Trump's trade policies are an egregious example. Given the relative impotence of the nation state as an economic policy maker in a globalised world economy (as already argued in Chap. 2), this is an unfortunate and retrograde step economically speaking. The globalisation of the world economy has brought great benefits albeit unevenly, and what is now needed rather than manifold

P. O'Sullivan et al., *Overcoming Gangsterism and Geo-Political Anarchy*, https://doi.org/10.1007/978-3-032-22438-5_11

nationalist protectionisms is an effective supranational approach to regulation of the world economy which can only come about through a supranational World Authority such as has been argued for in this book.

Keywords Economics of globalisation • Unequal distribution of benefits (of globalisation) • Interdependence of economic policy challenges • Washington Consensus • Market fundamentalism • Financial Crisis 2008 • Economic nationalism (protectionism) • Supranational policies for trans-national challenges

The ongoing conflict in Ukraine, initiated by Russia's war of aggression against the country, has further exacerbated the difficulties facing the world as a whole as a result of the ongoing global energy and food crisis, global supply disruptions in the coronavirus pandemic and its consequences market shortages, all now further aggravated by Donald Trump's disruptive trade policies if not trade wars and invasion of Iran.

Russia's brutal assault on Ukraine heightens concerns about the stability of the security system and international cooperation based on the United Nations Charter. Therefore, the effort to give radically critical answers to the challenges posed by this war, in particular, to the question of how to avoid definitively the use of violence by nation states with the aim to annex territories from each other, is a matter deserving of attention. Responding to this challenge, the heart of the deliberations in this book is the radical idea of creating a supranational world order which would replace the current system based on the sovereignty of nation states. Certainly, such a guiding idea in the book makes a contribution to geopolitical theory and it is based on inspiration drawn from the political philosophies of Thomas Hobbes and Immanuel Kant, and on the political thought of Jean Monnet and Robert Schumann, the architects of the European Union. If European countries with their rivalries were able to build a supranational union, why shouldn't the world do so one day?

However, this inspiring and dominant message in the book also calls for reflection, not only inspired by the thought of great philosophers or eminent politicians. All the more so as there appears a thesis which to many political economists would seem challengeable suggesting that, from an economic point of view, the nation state is an increasingly impotent anachronism. Thus, it will be interesting to add reflections and analyses from an economist's point of view to those of a more political philosophical nature on a new global order. So let us look at the problem of sovereignty and the role of the nation state precisely through the eyes of a professor of economics within the current state of global economic governance, shaped to a decisive extent by globalisation processes.

Firstly, it is worth looking at the role of transnational corporations (multinational enterprises), and at the importance of capital ownership in the current international division of labour. The latter is becoming a fundamental influence that is difficult to overestimate. Precisely, the ownership of capital, and therefore the power which belongs to the shareholders and the subordinate managers who run the corporation, even if the latter are recruited from among local residents, determines the nature, quality and development prospects of enterprises and thus, to a large extent, of the economies of individual countries. As we know quite well, capital does not have a homeland, whereas shareholders do. In practice, therefore, the processes of globalisation, in which also the role of transnational corporations is very large, deepen the divide between beneficiaries and outsiders of the modern economy.

Until recently, the development paradigm of many countries was based on the so-called Washington Consensus.[1] It grew out of not only scientific research but also real trends occurring in the process of change taking place in world markets and in economic policies after the failure and fall of communism in the USSR and is in effect an essentially ideological statement of principle for Market Fundamentalism. The dominance of the Consensus explains such megatrends in the global economy as: deregulation, liberalisation, privatisation, fully free trade and freedom of movement of loanable funds (open capital markets) and more controversially, rising migration in search of economic opportunity. However, a watershed moment rather falsifying the consensus principles came with the global financial crisis of 2007–2009+, which was unexpected in scale and magnitude. Certain theoretical assumptions of economic theories based on the belief in the self-correcting mechanisms of the free market failed.[2] Moreover, the world economy, deprived of suitable regulatory mechanisms, has started to "produce" all sorts of degenerations. Some of these are particularly acute and have adversely affected the daily lives of ordinary citizens. The financialisation of the global economy, which is still largely

[1] WILLIAMSON J (1990) "What Washington means by Policy Reform" in WILLIAMSON J (ed) *Latin American Adjustment: how much has happened,* Chapter 2, Institute for International Economics, Washington DC.

[2] Krugman, P (2009) *The Return of Depression Economics and the Crisis of 2008,* W. W. Norton & Company, New York, London.

the result of markets that are not sufficiently controlled, contributed, among other things, to questioning an economic model operating without proper regulatory and control support from government(s). The model of contemporary globalism, which is still based on the neo-liberal market fundamentalist principles, can be also criticised due to its corollary consequences in terms of social frustrations, rising inequalities, environmental damage and pollution risks. A growing number of sociological studies confirm that even in highly industrialised countries, the conception of advanced consumerist societies as built on three main pillars, that is, intensive work—higher savings rate—sustainable capital accumulation, is increasingly implausible and out of touch with realities.[3] It is through this ethos that the foundations of highly developed capitalist states, some with high levels of welfare and social protection, were built. In many developed countries today, the work ethic is no longer an absolute priority. One destructive factor in this is a growing perception that there is less and less connection between the sense of extra effort and the appropriate financial reward for it. Extremely damaging effects on the public's perception of ethics and morality in business and especially in financial markets have had, and continue to have, a highly corrosive effect; corruption is seen as pervasive and the financial markets as having degenerated into little more than a speculative casino that hardly serves either society or even the economy.[4] There is a growing perception that income from work is not in the least comparable to stock market returns, or to gains from various types of speculative behaviour. Associated with these developments is a sense of lawlessness in business and financial market activities which in turn is creating a dangerous crisis of authority, governance and of law in many countries, including those of Western civilisation.[5]

We shall not take a solely critical approach with reference to reflections and real disputes on the socio-economic development impact of contemporary globalism Foreign direct investment in many countries has contributed significantly to the growth of employment and labour productivity, better organisation of production processes, or better equipping the

[3] See, for example, Tsang J et al. (2014) "Why are materialists less happy?" in *Personality and Individual Differences* 64 July 2014 pp. 62–66; or Senik C (2014) "Wealth and Happiness" in *Oxford Review of Economic Policy* 30(1) pp. 92–108.

[4] The classic reference here is Strange S (2015) *Casino Capitalism*, Manchester University Press, Manchester.

[5] Nowak A.Z (2020), *Polskie dylematy rozwojowe. W poszukiwaniu konkurencyjności strukturalnej*. Wydawnictwo Naukowe Wydziału Zarzadzania Uniwersytetu Warszawskiego: 98.

factors of production with capital and knowledge and to that extent they have contributed overall to a significant degree of modernisation of the economies concerned. For many emerging economies, the participation in the global pool of knowledge and technology has brought a dramatic improvement in the standard of living of their citizens and a degree of poverty reduction. Moreover, the rapid development of many countries has changed and continues to change the global balance of economic power, leading to the formation of a multipolar or at least tri-polar world. While in terms of current GDP per capita expressed in US dollars, the European Union and the USA are still ahead of China, a tri-polar world is already a reality in terms of absolute size of total GDP (USA $25 trillion, EU €17 trillion so $20 trillion, and China $14 trillion in 2024).[6]

However, it must not be overlooked that all the phenomena mentioned above, to varying degrees, encourage unfortunately the emergence of economic nationalisms, and foster the conviction that, given the frailty and collateral damages of past trends in unrestrained globalisation, some form of protectionism, restrictions on free trade, should be introduced, even if this potentially risks triggering trade conflicts. But what is particularly important in the context of the considerations of this book; is that associated with this recrudescent nationalism we face the challenge of a resurgence of aggressive attitudes, views and policies which had seemed to have died out once and for all after the terrible experiences of the two world wars. Thus, in a global competition of an economic nature, the impact of foreign policy on economics is returning in the form of policies which are motivated by chauvinistic ideology rather than economics. Military policy, cyber violence, as well as premeditatedly designed aggressive, imperial manipulative elements, have (re)appeared as essential ingredients supposedly effective in protecting and enhancing the national interest. Russia is a prime example of states appealing to such an interest but so also to an extent are China and the USA.

That said, Putin's war in Ukraine cannot be justified solely by the economic and social consequences of globalisation of the economy as just described and its real weaknesses. Putin may have seen these weaknesses as a possible pretext to invade Ukraine but to try to turn back the clock on

[6] Statistics available at World Bank website https://data.worldbank.org/indicator/NY.GDP.MKTP.CD?locations=1W. Accessed 13 September 2025 and at Eurostat https://ec.europa.eu/eurostat/databrowser/view/tec00001/default/table?lang=en. Accessed 13 September 2025.

globalisation would be a huge strategic mistake for Russia and for the entire world. In any case, one has only to pay attention to Putin's many speeches and even writings on the topic of the USSR and greater Russia (*Russki Mir*) to realise that Putin is primarily waging a war of imperial conquest in Ukraine. This is Russia's war for dominance, for territory, for restoration of empire with the immediate aim of the physical annihilation of the Ukrainian people. So this is not a local war, a neighbourly dispute between Russia and Ukraine, but a war for global order, of democracy against tyranny and one could even say (given the by now extensive civilian casualties and even of war crimes), a war of good against evil.

As has been argued in Chap. 2 of this book, these globalisation trends have significantly reduced the ability of nation state governments to influence and control the activities of footloose multinational companies when their initiatives generate negative consequences in global markets. This in turn can fuel the growth of tensions and policy contradictions in relations between states, regions or even continents. Prof. Harald Sander[7] states in his research that so-called digital markets, for example, are characterised by strong global level network effects, which, in the absence of effective competition, translate into exceptionally high supernormal profits and various abuses of dominant position. Superstar companies, as Prof. Sander calls them, can also be a strong driver of the decline in the share of labour in product manufacture. The big superstar companies strive and will continue to strive to secure higher profit margins through extensive cost-cutting drives and increasing deployment of artificial intelligence, ultimately resulting in a lower share of labour in adding value in the production process. In other words, the increasing share of superstar companies in the national value-added pool shifts income away from labour towards capital. For our purposes here, the core issue is the question of the extent to which the sources of the explosion of nationalist populism, including in rich countries, can be causally linked to the economic upheavals of which globalisation is the source or transmitter, which is often perceived and realised through the instability and economic insecurity of millions of people worldwide.

[7] Sander H. (2018) "Europe in the new global economy" in: Lin J & Nowak A (eds.), *New Structural Economics and Less Advanced Countries.* Scientific Publishing House of the Faculty of Management, University of Warsaw: 85–96.

In his book *The Populist Temptation*,[8] Barry Eichengreen argues that populism is often triggered by a combination of economic uncertainty, a threat to national identity and what is believed to be an insensitive political system, but can be suppressed by economic and political reforms that attempt to allay the fears of the discontented. These reforms, or not infrequently pseudo reforms, take on anti-elitist, authoritarian and nativist (anti-immigration) tendencies. In this way, both left-wing populism, in which the anti-elitist element dominates, as well as right-wing populism, inclined to blame "outsiders" for all difficulties and problems, manifest themselves. As Eichengreen sees it, a cultural revolt against globalisation, against traditional policies and institutions, as well as against immigration and automation, cannot just be an exogenous phenomenon, but is driven by economically motivated discontent and anxiety.

In fact in discussions about the latest wave of populism, two intellectual camps can be distinguished, taking different but emphatic views about the various sources and reasons for this movement. One camp of which Eichengreen is a clear exponent focuses precisely on the increase in economic uncertainty brought by globalisation, particularly in the period following the global financial crisis of 2008, while the second camp focuses more on cultural reaction and contestation especially in relation to migratory flows or (more vaguely) to cultural invasion and cultural imperialism.[9] Quite virulent expressions of identitarian politics have emerged in both poorer and more developed countries in response to the cultural impacts of globalisation trends.

In this context, it is worth noting how far the dominant development paradigm in economic theory has recently been changing in a manner that reflects this reaction to globalisation megatrends. It is eloquently demonstrated by the 2019 Nobel Prize in Economics, which the Swedish Academy awarded to three people: Abhijit Banerjee, Esther Duflo and Michael Kremer who were rewarded for their experimental approach to tackling poverty. All three academics focus on the economics of development by analysing, explaining and showing why countries develop at different rates, why some societies are more productive than others, and why

[8] Eichengreen, B. (2018). *The populist temptation: Economic grievance and political reaction in the modern era*. Oxford University Press: Oxford.

[9] See, for example, Noury A & Roland G (2020) Identity Politics and Populism in Europe, *Annual Reviews* (23): 421–439. See also Samers M & Rydgren J (2024) *Migration and Nationalism*, Edward Elgar, Cheltenham: chapter 1.

income inequality is increasing in some and decreasing in others. The 2019 Nobel laureates, for example, say that financial assistance from institutions such as the World Bank should be aimed at solving specific problems in developing countries, and catching up with the most developed countries, but in a manner carefully tailored to the culture, customs and laws of the host country. The Swedish Academy noted that the work of the Nobel laureates showed how poverty can be tackled, by asking more precise questions about, for example, education and health care. It is therefore important that governments in these countries play an active role in identifying and wisely supporting individualised social needs in context. While it may often be true that the governments of many developing countries do not have adequate expertise, leading to a waste of foreign funds and even increasing income inequality, this does not mean that the role of governments can be marginalised in lifting people out of poverty. It is rather the opposite.

From the point of view of a supranational world order for which this book has argued and which may even be seen to be in its birth pangs and which would replace the current system based on the sovereignty of nation states, the consequences for this order that have arisen as a result of the coronavirus pandemic are also significant.[10] The global pandemic forced reflection and debate on the role and importance of state institutions in modern economies. Until the recent financial crisis 2007–2009+, the greater role of the state and its institutions was strongly questioned, although, as mentioned earlier, various forms of government or central bank interventionism were not ruled out and in some cases implemented. However, when the extent of this interventionism became greater, soon enough calls for it to be reduced began to be heard, for, as it has been argued, withdrawing the state from the economic sphere can only make it more dynamic, more competitive and innovative.[11] Furthermore, the reduction in state activity was often justified by the need to reduce the state's debts. On the other hand, the announcements of a "more frugal state" and a "less bureaucratic and sluggish state" have been welcomed in

[10] Nowak A.Z (2020), *Polskie dylematy rozwojowe. W poszukiwaniu konkurencyjności strukturalnej*. Wydawnictwo Naukowe Wydziału Zarzadzania Uniwersytetu Warszawskiego: 42–43.

[11] One may mention, for example, the reversal of post-2008 financial market regulation in the USA under Trump and similar reversals of financial market regulation in the UK during 2022. The ideological drive seemingly to eliminate almost entirely the state's regulatory role underpins the Trump 2.0 presidency in the USA as seen in the Department of Government Efficiency DOGE's activities.

many political quarters including in some cases by social democratic as well as by liberal or conservative parties. In short, it is not uncommon to see the state cast primarily as a major force of inertia and at best as an institution that reactively corrects the errors and distortions of the free market.

Meanwhile the coronavirus pandemic has forced governments to rethink the previous foundations of socio-economic policy. In this situation, even central bank chiefs have been inclined to convince governments about the benefits of using budgets more boldly to protect the well-being of society and the necessary stimulation of growth. Christine Lagarde began her term as President of the European Central Bank with a call to introduce pro-growth fiscal incentives in governments' economic policies. She argued that Eurozone countries should focus more on strengthening their internal markets, and on investment in the public sector and redressing social inequalities (inclusive policies) to meet the challenges of the globalised economy. She called for strengthening the European internal market by completing the digital single market, a capital markets union and a single market in services, which she said are "the building blocks of the European economy of the future", in addition to the need to complete economic and monetary union.[12]

Increasing the regulatory and stimulative role of governments in the economy is thus seen as a necessary response to reduce adverse processes in the global market; in the face of threats such as wars or pandemics and financial crises. But as Lagarde has in effect argued that does not mean choosing to limit integration and global trade, or attempts to replace market competitiveness through policies of protectionism and economic nationalism. For all its shortcomings, integration and the free movement of technology, capital and labour is one of the strongest development impulses on a national, regional and global scale. A bureaucratised omnipotent state is as unacceptable as a total free market.[13] What is at stake, therefore, is not an omnipotent state, but an efficient one, in which a democratically elected government can pursue autonomous industrial and structural macroeconomic policies. In the reality of many countries,

[12] Lagarde C. (2019) *President of the European Central Bank (ECB) addresses the 29th Frankfurt European Banking Congress in Frankfurt, Germany*, Nov. 22. Available at https://www.ecb.europa.eu/press/key/date/2019/html/ecb.sp191122~0c1f115db0.en.html. Accessed 13 September 2025.

[13] Nowak A.Z. (2013). *Współczesny świat w erze turbulencji.* In: J. Bogdanienko, W. Piotrowski (ed.), Zarządzanie: tradycja i nowoczesność. Warszawa: Państwowe Wydawnictwo Ekonomiczne: 46.

particularly those belonging to the European Union, this industrial and structural policy is not a purely sovereign prerogative of the nation states, since it is constrained by the rules and principles of the Single Market or by the Eurozone convergence criteria and the policy activities of the European Central Bank; but as argued earlier in this book, for many economic policies these are actually more effective to the extent that they are supranationally determined.

It is worth mentioning here a paradox of globalisation, the so-called Rodrik trilemma,[14] that consists of the conflict between democracy, unrestricted economic globalisation and autonomy or sovereignty of nation states in terms of social and economic policy. Dani Rodrik (2011) argues that it is impossible for these three policy goals to coexist at the nation state level. According to him, at most two of the above-mentioned political objectives can be combined and this is a hitherto largely unacknowledged problem in the globalisation discourse. In an argument that closely parallels certain of the economic policy arguments of this book, Rodrik demonstrates that hyper-globalisation is only possible either with the creation of some form of world government (global federalism), or following the abandonment of democracy in favour of the control of individual states by technocratic elites adapting their policies to the demands of the global market (and not to the expectations of citizens). Because he considers the first option unrealistic and the second unacceptable on moral grounds, what remains is the abandonment of hyper-globalisation in favour of a system modelled on the Bretton Woods system. As Rodrik argues, such a system would enable sovereign, democratic states to enjoy the benefits of the global marketplace, within the constraints defined in its international rules of operation.

At the very least, the considerations above in effect highlight an issue worthy of serious debate, namely the economic role of the nation state, its advantages and disadvantages. Certainly, the claim that, from an economic point of view, the nation state is an increasingly impotent anachronism raises difficult questions of a political nature regarding globalisation and democratic deficit as highlighted by Rodrik. However, Rodrik's discussion continues with the axiomatic presumption of the nation state as the basic unit of the world's political order and fails to see that the democratic deficit challenge could be met in other ways, some of which are outlined in

[14] Rodrik D (2011) *The Globalization Paradox: Democracy and the Future of the World Economy*, W. W. Norton & Company, New York, London. ISBN 978-0-393-07161-0.

other chapters of this book. Moreover, the critical philosophical analysis of the foundations of nation state sovereignty and of the contemporary world order as resembling an anarchic war of all against all such as Hobbes described in *Leviathan* (referring to the civil wars in England in the seventeenth century) still stands. Indeed Bretton Woods is not the happiest example for Rodrik since it collapsed after just 25 years arguably for two leading reasons: its absence of enforcement powers in respect of common economic policies and its unreconstructed great power logic inherent in the central role of the US dollar as reference currency in the system. By contrast, the new supranational order exemplified by European integration which in this book is seen as the exemplar of the best way forward geopolitically is being established by a consensus rather than either military might or any "great" power dictate. If European states with their age-old rivalries were able to build a supranational union, why shouldn't the world do so one day. This is not just an intellectual challenge. One motivation for working on such a project is the violent challenge to peaceful coexistence in Europe that the Russian invasion of Ukraine has posed to the world.

Bibliography

Eichengreen, B. (2018). *The populist temptation: Economic grievance and political reaction in the modern era*. Oxford University Press.

Eurostat. Accessed September 13, 2025., from https://ec.europa.eu/eurostat/databrowser/view/tec00001/default/table?lang=en

Krugman, P. (2009). *The return of depression economics and the crisis of 2008*. W. W. Norton & Company.

Lagarde, C. (2019). *President of the European Central Bank (ECB) addresses the 29th Frankfurt European Banking Congress in Frankfurt, Germany*, 22 November 2022. Accessed September 13, 2025, from https://www.ecb.europa.eu/press/key/date/2019/html/ecb.sp191122~0c1f115db0.en.html

Noury, A., & Roland, G. (2020). Identity politics and populism in Europe. *Annual Reviews, 23*, 421–439.

Nowak, A. Z. (2020a). Polskie dylematy rozwojowe. W poszukiwaniu konkurencyjności strukturalnej. *Wydawnictwo Naukowe Wydziału Zarzadzania Uniwersytetu Warszawskiego, 98.*

Nowak, A. Z. (2020b). Polskie dylematy rozwojowe. W poszukiwaniu konkurencyjności strukturalnej. *Wydawnictwo Naukowe Wydziału Zarzadzania Uniwersytetu Warszawskiego, 42–43.*

Nowak, A. Z. (2013). Współczesny świat w erze turbulencji. In J. Bogdanienko & W. Piotrowski (Eds.), *Zarządzanie: tradycja i nowoczesność* (p. 46). Państwowe Wydawnictwo Ekonomiczne.

Rodrik, D. (2011). *The globalization paradox: Democracy and the future of the world economy*. W. W. Norton & Company.

Samers, M., & Rydgren, J. (2024). *Migration and nationalism*. Edward Elgar.

Sander, H. (2018). Europe in the new global economy. In J. Lin & A. Nowak (Eds.), *New structural economics and less advanced countries* (pp. 85–96). Scientific Publishing House of the Faculty of Management, University of Warsaw.

Senik, C. (2014). Wealth and happiness. *Oxford Review of Economic Policy, 30*(1).

Strange, S. (2015). *Casino Capitalism*. Manchester University Press.

Tsang, J., et al. (2014). Why are materialists less happy? *Personality and Individual Differences* 64 July 2014.

Williamson, J. (1990). What Washington means by policy reform. In J. Williamson (Ed.), *Latin American adjustment: How much has happened* (Chapter 2). Institute for International Economics.

CHAPTER 12

Making the Leap from an Agreement-Based World to Supranational Legality: Towards a Global Rule of Law

Alexandru Zgardan

Abstract This chapter contributed by Alexandru Zgardan brings the perspective of trained jurist to bear on the ideas outlined in the book. Echoing the points made in a number of earlier chapters regarding enforcement, it is noted that the International Court of Justice (ICJ), far from having real enforcement powers, can only adjudicate in international disputes when the states and other parties concerned agree to accept its jurisdiction; and if that is agreed, then the eventual of the court relies for their application on moral suasion. The UN Security Council which has in theory some powers of enforcement has never exercised these when it really matters because of the veto powers allocated to the five permanent members of said Council (USA, UK, France, Russia, China). If this points to the need for a fundamental rethinking of the nature and functioning of international law in the face of the increasingly transnational problems of the twenty-first century, it is argued that we are not starting from a tabula rasa in respect of such reform. We already have at least four entities which seek to determine legality above the level of the nation state: the ICJ, the International Criminal Court, the World Trade Organisation's (WTO) Appellate Body (for dispute resolution) and in Europe the European Court of Human Rights as well of course as the European Court of Justice

P. O'Sullivan et al., *Overcoming Gangsterism and Geo-Political Anarchy*, https://doi.org/10.1007/978-3-032-22438-5_12

for the EU member states. The ECJ already has of course full-blown enforcement powers as noted in earlier chapters; for all of the others, one could imagine a path of gradual evolution towards real enforcement powers culminating in a fully supranational World Court of Justice capable of responding to the legal challenges of a complex and highly interdependent globalised digitally interconnected world.

Keywords International Court of Justice (ICJ) • Enforcement power • UN Charter • Security Council (UN) • WTO Appellate Body • European Court of Justice • A new World Court of Justice • Legal basis of sovereignty

The modern world order, shaped since the end of the Second World War in its current form, rests on the doctrine of sovereignty of internationally recognised states (hereinafter referred to as "States"). During the process of decolonisation, sovereignty became something to fight for and came to mean independence, the fight for equality between states and non-interference in internal affairs. States, through their agents (legislative, executive and judicial), under the present system hold an almost absolute monopoly within their borders to enforce the rules they deem necessary, ideally for the well-being of the people living on their territories. The evolution of national law was a long one, but historically, it followed a clear path from power held by a monarch-sovereign authority imposing its will on the people ruled by it, without any need for a moral foundation or at best a pseudo-foundation such as the supposed divine right of kings and queens. Only ancient Athens' direct democracy and the Roman pre-imperial Republic represented significant exceptions to the absolute power of assorted monarchies.

The last 100 years have seen an erosion of the concept of sovereignty through the rise of international organisations, human rights law, and economic interdependence. The issues that threaten humanity most severely—climate change, pandemics, nuclear proliferation, global financial instability, cyberspace influence and artificial intelligence—know no borders. National sovereignty, conceived as an irreplaceable concept for the progress of a people, is no longer able to provide for the solutions sought by humanity.

International Law, on the other hand, has taken a somewhat different path, with states being bound only insofar as they consent to the rules that are negotiated. The vast majority of international obligations of states arise from various international treaties to which they consent directly on an intergovernmental basis, for example, in cases of bilateral agreements, or indirectly when international organisations are created that can draft rules based on their constitutive documents, as, for example, the UN Charter. For centuries, the main idea for the functioning of international law, which allowed a degree of stability, was the goodwill of the party states to keep their promises in order to foster order and avoid chaos in international relations, a principle known as *pacta sunt servanda*, which is enshrined in the 1969 Vienna Convention on the Law of Treaties.[1] However, the enforcement of these promises ultimately relies on the self-interest of states in maintaining their legitimacy and cooperating with other states. This enforcement mechanism (if such it can be called), is based almost entirely on incentives and not on coercion, this being most obviously true of states that wield a lot of power in any form—military, economic or political. Its lack of effectiveness (as mentioned in Chap. 2) has been seen multiple times since the end of the Second World War, with the UN failing to deter states from violating the main international law principles found in the UN Charter signed and agreed by all internationally recognised states. Today, at the end of 2025, as is clear for all to see from the impotence of International Law to stop the violent conflicts currently occurring that transgress a wide array of human rights, the incentives based approach has shown that is tragically unfit for purpose. It is moreover ill-equipped to address the truly global crises of our time that transcend borders: climate change, pandemics, cyberwarfare, international trade regulation, mass migration and other challenges that are in their incipient form, such as AI or bionics. Furthermore, the attempted annexation through the use of military force of Ukrainian territory by the Russian Federation, a permanent member of the Security Council that signed and ratified the UN Charter, is most clearly proving the need for a redesign of how international law functions. The international law system created under the umbrella of the UN in 1945, which was good enough then, is no longer able to provide for the rules needed for us to go forward.[2]

[1] Article 26 of the 1969 Vienna Convention on the Law of Treaties (signed in Vienna, Austria, on 23 May 1969 and entered into force on 27 January 1980). Available at https://legal.un.org/ilc/texts/instruments/english/conventions/1_1_1969.pdf. Accessed 9 September 2025.

[2] As noted in Chap. 2, the International Court of Justice (ICJ) of the UN already pronounced unambiguously in March 2022 (one month after Russia's invasion of Ukraine) that

The question now is whether international law—often criticised as being in effect merely a law of at best aspiration coordination and infinite pointless discussions rather than being a true legal system—can evolve as this book has argued into a supranational rule of law binding on all states and reinvent itself in order to guarantee at least the enforcement of its main principles. The goal of rules that are defined as "international law" can no longer be just aspirationally to urge states to cooperate and respect each other, but rather to manage serious global challenges within a supranational framework of enforceable law.

International law remains ineffective because of its reliance on state consent which results in impunity when the promises confirmed by treaties are violated. As codified in Article 38 of the ICJ Statute, binding sources of law are treaties, custom and general principles accepted by states.[3] The ICJ's jurisprudence illustrates this ineffectiveness. In *Aegean Sea Continental Shelf (Greece v Turkey)* (1978),[4] the Court declined jurisdiction because Turkey had not consented. In the *Lockerbie* cases (*Libya v UK* and *Libya v US*, 1992), the Court issued provisional measures, but Security Council resolutions superseded them.[5] Enforcement mechanisms exist only in relation to weak states: the International Court of Justice cannot compel compliance when powerful states refuse, as, for example, in *Military and Paramilitary Activities in and against Nicaragua* (*Nicaragua v United States*) (1986).[6]

The UN Security Council was originally designated as the enforcement arm of the global peacekeeping system with its "primary responsibility for the maintenance of international peace and security".[7] The UN Security Council, although designed to safeguard peace, is all too often rendered totally ineffective by the veto power of its permanent members under

said invasion was in direct violation of international law. See https://www.icj-cij.org/node/106135. Accessed 6 September 2025.

[3] Art. 38 of the Statute of the International Court of Justice. The Statute is available at https://www.icj-cij.org/statute. Accessed 9 September 2025.

[4] *Aegean Sea Continental Shelf (Greece v Turkey)* [1978] ICJ Rep 3.

[5] Questions of Interpretation and Application of the 1971 Montreal Convention arising from the Aerial Incident at Lockerbie (Libya v United Kingdom; Libya v United States) [1992] ICJ Rep 3.

[6] *Military and Paramilitary Activities in and against Nicaragua: Nicaragua v. United States of America* [1986] ICJ Reports available at https://www.icj-cij.org/case/70. Accessed 21 September 2025.

[7] Art. 24 of the UN Charter: the full charter is available online at https://treaties.un.org/doc/publication/ctc/uncharter.pdf. Accessed 9 September 2025.

Article 27 of the UN Charter,[8] permanent members who in many cases have represented the main threats to peace. The UN impotence over Syria, where Russia and China repeatedly blocked pertinent resolutions, or over Ukraine, where Russia vetoed action against itself multiple times, exemplifies the problem. Similar dynamics occur in climate governance, where heads of state sign treaties with the goal of merely looking nice to the world or appeasing their voters, and later on ignore the commitments they have taken; or in human rights law, where compliance is selective due to endless divergent interpretations of the legal terms used in international human rights treaties.

In practice, international law is ignored too often whenever the promises made no longer fit the interests of the states, partly because political power is transitioning to different actors within the sovereign states. This fragility of the international legal system contributes to what in this book has been called "geopolitical anarchy": a world where people in charge of ruling great powers can flout international norms with limited or no consequences for themselves. It is rather obvious that international obligations are seen by many not as legal obligations, but as a means to present themselves as active members of the international community and can be discarded in cases when self-interest dictates otherwise. The result is an international legal order which Martti Koskenniemi has described as an oscillation between *apology* (politics disguised as law) and *utopia* (law without teeth).[9] Without a supranational framework, international law will always remain both too weak and too abstract to even be defined as "law". Indeed, the great nineteenth-century English jurist J. L. Austin, consistently with his well-known definition of law as a system of commands backed by threats, regarded international law for that reason not as true law at all but simply as "positive morality".[10]

We now turn to review briefly certain attempts—some successful and some less so—which though fragmented, prove that supranational legality is already present to a limited extent within the international legal system. Also, the reasons for the lack of effectiveness of some of these will serve as

[8] Art. 27 of the UN Charter, op. cit.

[9] Koskenniemi M (2005), *From Apology to Utopia: The Structure of International Legal Argument* Cambridge University Press, Cambridge.

[10] Austin J L (1832) *The Province of Jurisprudence Determined*, John Murray, London. See Vol. 1, pp. 188–189.

an extra piece of evidence for the argument that has been developed in this work.

The European Union remains the most advanced precedent in the supranational application of law. In *Van Gend en Loos v Nederlandse Administratie der Belastingen* (1963),[11] the European Court of Justice declared that EU law creates rights enforceable by individuals directly within national courts thereby enforcing direct applicability of rules adopted outside the national jurisdiction. A year later, in *Costa v ENEL* (1964),[12] the ECJ affirmed the supremacy of EU law over conflicting national legislation, thereby enshrining the principle of the superiority of EU law in matters falling under EU competence. For the first time in history, a supranational legal order was established in which states gave up their sovereign powers in specific areas of regulation. It is important to understand that the EU member states decided a priori on the areas they are ready to give away or on which to split responsibility with the supranational entity they formed, and it was done for the benefit of the citizens living under their jurisdiction. So, the decision makers 69 years ago clearly started a process that is still ongoing of thinking about the common good to the detriment of the pursuit of narrowly nationalistic interests.

Besides the explicitly supranational EU, there are also some examples of international bodies based on intergovernmental treaties which have arguably transferred some sovereign competences to overarching international institutions. The following are examples but all still manifest serious limitations in terms of enforcement in contrast to the explicitly supranational EU.

- In relation to international trade regulation, the World Trade Organisation's Dispute Settlement Understanding (1995) provides for binding adjudication with the possibility of sanctions against the parties in violation of the obligations within the WTO framework. In theory, every WTO member should comply, because non-compliance carries material costs through authorised trade retaliation,[13] but in

[11] *Van Gend en Loos v Nederlandse Administratie der Belastingen* [1963] ECJ 001 Case 26/62 document 61962CJ0026.

[12] *Flaminio Costa v ENEL* [1964] ECJ 585 Case 6/64 document 61964CJ0006.

[13] WTO, Understanding on Rules and Procedures Governing the Settlement of Disputes (15 April 1994) available at https://www.wto.org/english/docs_e/legal_e/dsu_e.htm. Accessed 9 September 2025. See also Marrakesh Agreement Establishing the WTO, Annex 2, 1869 UNTS 401 available at https://jusmundi.com/en/document/treaty/en-under-

practice, the differences between the sizes of the economies of the member states, has meant that the WTO lacks real enforcement power against larger states as manifest, for example, with the USA under the Trump administration trade policies. Trump's protectionist policies are in flagrant violation of WTO principles and rules but that has not in the slightest deterred Trump; and in any case since 2018, the USA has refused to nominate judges to the WTO dispute arbitration Appellate Body (court if you like); and in the absence of appointed judges from a key member of WTO, the Appellate Body has not been quorate when it meets and therefore has not been able to pass any valid judgments let alone enforce them.[14] It is interesting in the context of this book to note that the ultimate reason for this abandonment of the WTO Appellate Body by the USA has been US national sovereignty.[15] In any event, law is backed by enforceable consequences if and when all parties fulfil their obligations, showing that supranational enforcement is still possible when the will of the contracting parties is present. The mechanism of accepting supranational jurisdiction for access to the WTO club is functioning as long as all members are on board with the obligations to which they consented. Some WTO states went even further, accepting the direct applicability of the WTO treaties by national courts.[16]

- Probably one of the oldest known cases of supranational jurisdiction is the European Court of Human Rights, operating under the European Convention on Human Rights (1950), deciding on human rights violations cases and issuing binding judgments on individual petitions that may be in conflict with the decisions of the national authorities of the member states. In theory, nation states

standing-on-rules-and-procedures-governing-the-settlement-of-disputes-1994-dispute-settlement-understanding-dsu-1994-friday-15th-april-1994. Accessed 9 September 2025.

[14] For a good concise account of this episode, see https://www.csis.org/programs/economics-program-and-scholl-chair-international-business/world-trade-organization. Accessed 7 September 2025.

[15] On this point regarding sovereignty, see the detailed commentary available at International Institute for Sustainable Development website https://www.iisd.org/articles/policy-analysis/wto-dispute-settlement-without-appellate-body. Accessed 07/09/2025. The US contention that the interpretation of the security clause of the WTO Treaty is entirely a matter for national sovereignty sounds suspiciously like the UK's (wilfully mistaken) Brexit arguments regarding the jurisdiction of the ECJ...

[16] *Amministrazione Finanze dello Stato c. SPA Manifattura Lane Marzotto,* [1973] Corte di Cassazione Italia, Sez 1, Case No. 1455, 21 maggio 1973, 77 ILR 551.

have no option but to comply if they want to keep their membership status. The enforcement mechanism is monitored by the Council of Europe's Committee of Ministers.[17] The hope was and still is that states accept this bargain to give up some of their sovereign power in exchange for the image of a human rights-abiding nation state, so as not to become a pariah state. However, certain states have deliberately rejected rulings of the ECHR without being expelled from the Council of Europe, the intergovernmental body of which the ECHR is the court.[18]

- Another relevant example in line with the trend of giving away a bit of sovereignty with the objective of building a better world was the establishment of the International Criminal Court (ICC) under the Rome Statute (1998). The idea that individuals, including heads of state, may be prosecuted for genocide, crimes against humanity, and war crimes[19] was a breakthrough at the time, although enforcement remains problematic with Brazil, China, India, Israel, Saudi Arabia, Turkey and the USA among others opting out of it and with the Russian Federation withdrawing in 2016.[20] In a sad illustration of the enduring appeal of the cynical maxim that "*might is right*", the principle that nothing can shield perpetrators of serious international crimes from justice appears to be applicable only against those states who do not have large armies, but as mentioned above, it is better than nothing.

All these initiatives, even though imperfect, provide good case precedents for the path to the creation of supranational organisations. Some of them have functioned reasonably well for many years, and some are struggling, but our task in today's world is to consolidate and expand these

[17] Convention for the Protection of Human Rights and Fundamental Freedoms (European Convention on Human Rights, as amended) (ECHR), 4 November 1950, ETS 5.

[18] One of the most well-known cases is that of UK prisoners' voting rights in general elections. For a detailed account from the UK point of view, see https://commonslibrary.parliament.uk/research-briefings/cbp-7461/. Accessed 9 September 2025.

[19] Rome Statute of the International Criminal Court (adopted 17 July 1998, entered into force 1 July 2002) 2187 UNTS 90. Available at https://www.icc-cpi.int/sites/default/files/2024-05/Rome-Statute-eng.pdf. Accessed 9 September 2025.

[20] The ICC currently has 125 member states. See https://asp.icc-cpi.int/states-parties. Accessed 6 September 2025.

precedents. In order to achieve these goals, one could propose a number of reforms:

1. **Compulsory jurisdiction**—International tribunals, first of all the ICJ, should move away from the existing optional jurisdiction to compulsory jurisdiction. This means accession to the supranational entity will automatically mean the acceptance of the ICJ or similar court for all cases that fall under their competence, with no possibility to refuse the jurisdiction of the international court. Basing ourselves on the EU case, in the beginning, the jurisdiction should be limited to specific matters that have a clear global impact, such as climate change concerns, usage of oceans and water resources in general, outer space regulation, cyberspace and new emerging technologies. We already have existing models in maritime issues under the 1982 United Nations Convention on the Law of the Sea.[21] The Paris Climate Accords, similarly, need a Global Environmental Court that should adjudicate state failures to meet climate obligations and decide on damages, especially since the international legal precedent for those already exists,[22] it just has to be extended over to individuals and states on the European Court of Human Rights model. Compulsory jurisdiction is a "fundamental element of a legal system",[23] and the lack thereof leaves any international court's judgements dependent on state consent and reputation.
2. **Universalise criminal accountability for aggression and mass atrocities**—All states must be brought to accept ICC jurisdiction over genocide, war crimes, crimes against humanity and aggression without the possibility of opting out.
3. **Enable World Parliament enforcement**—An automatic intervention by the World Parliament (constituted as proposed in previous chapters) in cases where other institutions are too slow or paralysed by bureaucratic or procedural steps. Under the supervision of the World Parliament, a permanent, quick reaction peace force

[21] United Nations Convention on the Law of the Sea (UNCLOS), 10 December 1982, Part XV. UNCLOS full text available at https://www.un.org/depts/los/convention_agreements/texts/unclos/unclos_e.pdf. Accessed 9 September 2025.

[22] *Trail Smelter Arbitration (United States v. Canada),* [16 April 1938] 3 UNRIAA 1911 & *Trail Smelter Arbitration (United States v. Canada)* [11 March 1941], 3 UNRIAA 1938.

[23] Kelsen, H. (1997) *Law and Peace in International Relations* (first published 1942), William S. Hein & Co, Buffalo New York.

contingent should be formed in order to enforce efficiently the World Parliament or the International Courts' decisions.

4. **Automatic incorporation**—Using the EU law application model, supranational regulations should be automatically incorporated in the legal hierarchy of regulations and be directly applicable within national legal systems, binding for everyone and applicable in national courts. This change would remove the enforcement gap by leaping over the issue of state discretion. The only choice for the member States should be on the method of applicability in order to allow flexibility due to the differences in the legal systems around the world.
5. **Efficient enforcement**—Supranational institutions must have credible enforcement mechanisms; otherwise, the rules become mere recommendations. The Financial Action Task Force (FATF) shows how blacklists can coerce compliance by threatening exclusion from financial markets.[24] Similar mechanisms could apply to any areas regulated by the supranational entities. The mechanism of enforcement must be automatic and without any need for political decision, thus eliminating the possibility of vetoes. A finding from an international court should automatically trigger a number of collective measures such as: arms and other goods embargoes, asset freezes, peace support missions with host consent.
6. **Hard-law concerning the prohibition of "zones of influence"**—An amendment to the UN Charter or a new treaty declaring null and void any claims to "zones of influence" that affect sovereign equality, territorial integrity, or free choice of alliances.
7. **Trade wars prohibition**—Unilateral tariffs or other coercive trade measures used against another state during an identified crisis must be presumed as unlawful and trade disputes judgments should have direct and immediate effect initially through the existing WTO mechanisms and eventually through the World Authority as described in earlier chapters.
8. **Subsidiarity**—In order to prevent overreach, the principle of subsidiarity—found in Article 5 of the Treaty on European Union and

[24] Financial Action Task Force (2025), *International Standards on Combating Money Laundering and the Financing of Terrorism & Proliferation* (2012, updated 2025) FATF, Paris. Available at https://www.fatf-gafi.org/en/publications/Fatfrecommendations/Fatf-recommendations.html. Accessed 9 September 2025.

as outlined in Chap. 5 of this book—should guide the allocation of supranational competence.[25] Only matters requiring collective action should be centralised, the rest should be treated as local affairs and remain within the jurisdiction of the states or sub-state units, preferably.

Sovereignty has provided something that emerging nations have strived for and the first step for the creation of a nation is to ensure sovereignty, but in a century when everyone and everything is interconnected, we have to make the second step and go beyond. This century, with its new challenges, demands a new paradigm: a supranational rule of law that has in mind universal peace, protection of rights and sustainability. Philosophically, this vision is completely in line with Kant[26] and Habermas[27] ideas. The systems of national laws have gone through a long evolution during thousands of years—the transition from duels to courts and from tyranny to democracy took a lot of time and effort. International law, being relatively young in comparison, must also undergo the necessary transformations to answer and be able to cope with the issues we face and the new ones that will require more cooperation and collective effort.

The main catalyst for the creation of rules is so that reason can prevail over violence. In today's world within sovereign states, even if we cannot classify existing laws as universally good, as individual citizens, we have clarity as to what the rules are and what to expect when we happen to go against them, regardless of who we are. This principle of following rationally devised rules governing the lives of individual citizens in an equal manner needs to be applied at the global level to the relations among states and international law. A transformation of international law into real (because enforceable) "law" is both necessary and possible. This is not Utopia, and a number of successful regional and sectoral initiatives already exist and can prove the point. The European Union shows that states guided by a common objective can share power to secure peace and the prosperity of their citizens. With courage, imagination and commitment,

[25] Treaty on European Union (Consolidated Version) [2012] OJ C326/13, art 5. Available at https://eur-lex.europa.eu/resource.html?uri=cellar:2bf140bf-a3f8-4ab2-b506-fd71826e6da6.0023.02/DOC_1&format=PDF. Accessed 9 September 2025.

[26] Kant I (1795) *Zum Ewigen Frieden*, Nicolovius, Königsberg. Available in English in Kant I (1991) *Political Writings* 2nd ed., translated by Nisbet H, Cambridge University Press, Cambridge.

[27] Habermas J (2001), *The Postnational Constellation*, Polity Press, Cambridge.

the world can transcend the gangsterism and anarchy of the current order and build a legal architecture worthy of humanity's aspirations.

One of the biggest resets of international institutions and international regulations since the 1815 Congress of Vienna occurred in the aftermath of the Second World War with the formation of the UN, WTO, WHO, IMF, World Bank and a whole range of other intergovernmental institutions. We should not wait for another massive global crisis or a Third World War in order to start a similar process. There is no need to wait for a total failure of the UN institutions (as happened to the League of Nations) in order to draft the new global world order. Sovereignty does not mean absolute power, but a redefined collective trusteeship over humanity's common goods.

Bibliography

Aegean Sea Continental Shelf (Greece v Turkey) [1978] ICJ Reports 3.

Amministrazione Finanze dello Stato c. SPA Manifattura Lane Marzotto, [1973] Corte di Cassazione Italia, Sez 1, Case No. 1455, 21 maggio 1973, 77 ILR 551.

Austin, J. L. (1832). *The province of jurisprudence determined.* John Murray.

Finance Ministry v. Manifattura Lane Marzotto, SPA [1988] Corte di Cassazione Italia (Joint Session), Case No. 1455, 77 ILR 551.

Financial Action Task Force. (2025). *International Standards on Combating Money Laundering and the Financing of Terrorism & Proliferation* (2012, updated 2025) FATF. Accessed September 9, 2025, from https://www.fatf-gafi.org/en/publications/Fatfrecommendations/Fatf-recommendations.html

Flaminio Costa v ENEL [1964] ECJ 585 Case 6/64 document 61964CJ0006.

Habermas, J. (2001). *The postnational constellation.* Polity Press.

International Court of Justice. (2022). Accessed September 6, 2025, from https://www.icj-cij.org/node/106135

International Court of Justice Statute The Statute. Accessed September 9, 2025., from https://www.icj-cij.org/statute

International Criminal Court (ICC) *Member States.* Accessed September 6, 2025., from https://asp.icc-cpi.int/states-parties

International Criminal Court (ICC) *Rome Statute* (adopted 17 July 1998, entered into force 1 July 2002) 2187 UNTS 90. Accessed September 9, 2025, from https://www.icc-cpi.int/sites/default/files/2024-05/Rome-Statute-eng.pdf

International Institute for Sustainable Development website. Accessed September 7, 2025., from https://www.iisd.org/articles/policy-analysis/wto-dispute-settlement-without-appellate-body

Kant, I. (1795). *Zum Ewigen Frieden.* Nicolovius, Königsberg. Available in English in Kant I (1991) *Political writings* 2nd ed, translated by Nisbet H, Cambridge University Press.

Kelsen, H. (1942). *Law and peace in international relations.* Harvard University Press. Reprinted 1997 William S. Hein & Co, Buffalo New York.

Koskenniemi, M. (2005). *From apology to utopia: The structure of international legal argument.* Cambridge University Press.

Military and Paramilitary Activities in and against Nicaragua: Nicaragua v. United States of America [1986] ICJ Reports. Accessed September 21, 2025, from https://www.icj-cij.org/case/70

Trail Smelter Arbitration (United States v. Canada), [16 April 1938] 3 UNRIAA 1911.

Trail Smelter Arbitration (United States v. Canada) [11 March 1941], 3 UNRIAA 1938.

Treaty on European Union (Consolidated Version) [2012] OJ C326/13, art 5. Accessed September 9, 2025, from https://eur-lex.europa.eu/resource.html?uri=cellar:2bf140bf-a3f8-4ab2-b506-fd71826e6da6.0023.02/DOC_1&format=PDF

United Nations Convention on the Law of the Sea (UNCLOS): full text. Accessed September 9, 2025., from h:ttps://www.un.org/depts/los/convention_agreements/texts/unclos/unclos_e.pdf

United Nations UN Charter. Accessed September 9, 2025., from https://treaties.un.org/doc/publication/ctc/uncharter.pdf

Van Gend en Loos v Nederlandse Administratie der Belastingen [1963] ECJ Case 26/62.

Vienna Convention on the Law of Treaties (signed in Vienna, Austria on 23 May 1969 and entered into force on 27 January 1980). Accessed September 9, 2025., from https://legal.un.org/ilc/texts/instruments/english/conventions/1_1_1969.pdf

World Trade Organisation WTO, Understanding on Rules and Procedures Governing the Settlement of Disputes (15 April 1994). Accessed September 9, 2025, from https://www.wto.org/english/docs_e/legal_e/dsu_e.htm

World Trade Organisation Marrakesh Agreement Establishing the WTO, Annex 2, 1869 UNTS 401. Accessed September 9, 2025, from https://jusmundi.com/en/document/treaty/en-understanding-on-rules-and-procedures-governing-the-settlement-of-disputes-1994-dispute-settlement-understanding-dsu-1994-friday-15th-april-1994

CHAPTER 13

Going Beyond the Rhetoric of War: Giving Peace a Chance

Daniela Russo

Abstract This chapter contributed by Daniela Russo invites us to consider the rhetoric of war and peace, a theme which is of crucial importance to any attempt to construct a "peace-enhancing union" among the peoples of the world as this book has advocated and sketched out in practical terms. If we consider the fields of literature and of historical narrative, it has for centuries been replete with various tales of heroism in warfare, whereas the case for peace and the outline of its immense benefits in terms of prosperity and human well-being achieved through peaceful tolerant co-existence has been overshadowed and marginalised to the extent that in the history of mankind warfare has been the default state of affairs, with the constant warring being punctuated by exceptional short interludes, one might say parentheses, of peace. Moreover, on a closer examination of the relative peace that has characterised the latter part of the twentieth century, this was a peace based on the fear of mutually assured destruction that would result from a nuclear war. Such a situation is inherently unstable, in particular when volatile authoritarian leaders hold the reins of power in certain supposedly "great" power states. Against this background, the case for patient construction of a supranational world authority with real supranational enforcement powers to resolve disputes based on a rational impulse to cooperate for a truly sustainable Kantian-inspired

P. O'Sullivan et al., *Overcoming Gangsterism and Geo-Political Anarchy*, https://doi.org/10.1007/978-3-032-22438-5_13

peace founded on goodwill and mutual trust rather than on fear is compelling. This book makes an important contribution to outlining the institutional innovations which such a transition will require.

Keywords War and peace • Rhetoric of war • Historical parentheses (of peace) • Peace and prosperity • Kant's robust pacificism • Courage and strength of peacemakers • Political institutional innovation for peace

Throughout history, war has been one of the most enduring elements of the human condition, almost a recurring archetype in the narrative of humanity. From the founding myths of civilisations to modern political theory, it has been celebrated as the midwife of history, the engine of progress and the ultimate expression of the will to power, understood as the driving force behind assertion of power to transform the world. It is therefore striking how little attention the concept of peace has received, traditionally relegated to a secondary, ancillary condition: defined only in relation to war and never truly placed at the centre of political or philosophical thought. While war has long been associated with a wide range of positive attributes—glory, sacrifice, virtue, honour, power—peace has largely been conceived as a negative category, defined in effect as the mere absence or suspension of conflict and deprived of conceptual and symbolic autonomy.

This is clearly emphasised by Hobbes in a seminal passage from *De Cive*, where he states: "For what is war, but that same time in which the will of contesting by force is fully declared, either by words, or deeds? The time remaining, is termed peace".[1] Peace, then, is what remains when war falls silent, not a constructive condition but a mere interruption of conflict. This semantic and conceptual imbalance has hindered a genuine cultural and philosophical elaboration of peace, which, in most cases, has been understood simply as a truce, a temporary suspension of violence—a *negative peace*, as John Galtung[2] would say.

[1] Hobbes T (1949). *De Cive; or, The Citizen*. Edited with an introduction by Sterling P. Lamprecht. New York: Appleton-Century-Crofts, p. 29.

[2] Galtung, J. (1996). *Peace by peaceful means: Peace and conflict, development and civilization*, Sage, London.

In contrast to the marginalisation of peace, war has been elevated—not only as a historical force, but even as a tool of moral progress, a crucible for the development of virtues such as courage, the spirit of sacrifice and willpower. This is exemplified by the great idealist philosophy of Hegel, in which war is not understood as mere disorder, but as a necessary moment in the development of the Absolute Spirit. Indeed, in the Hegelian system, the State represents the pinnacle of ethical life (*Sittlichkeit*), the completed form of objective spirit, in which individual freedom is realised through adherence to a rational collective order. And since each State embodies a universal and irreducible ethical principle, relations between States are inevitably marked by tension. Therefore, war takes on a philosophical significance; it becomes the space in which distinct historical ethical orders confront one another, the stage where Spirit both reveals and transcends itself through the clash of civilisations. The conflict between states, then, is not an anomaly but a necessary moment in the unfolding of history—a tragic and irreplaceable phase in humanity's dialectical development.[3] Moreover, in Nietzsche's provocative tones, war is a necessary means to avoid decay and decadence of civilisations through an ultimately debilitating softness. In *Human, All Too Human* (1878), he writes: "Many kinds of such substitutes for war will still be invented, but perhaps through them it will become increasingly clear that a humanity of high culture—and therefore necessarily enfeebled, such as that of present-day Europe—needs not only wars but the greatest and most terrible wars, in order not to lose, by spending the means of culture, both its culture and its very existence".[4]

Anyone who pauses, even briefly, to consider the history of political—and indeed philosophical—thought cannot but acknowledge the fact: there exists a rich and well-developed philosophy of war, conceived as an active and generative phenomenon, whereas a comparably developed philosophy of peace remains, to this day, largely absent. Much of modern political thought—especially with the rise of the sovereign nation state—has in fact taken the form of a continuous reflection on the problem of war and its legitimacy.

[3] Hegel, G. W. F. (1991). *Hegel: Elements of the philosophy of right*. Cambridge University Press, Cambridge.

[4] Nietzsche, F. (1878), *Human, All Too Human: A Book for Free Spirits* published in English (1996) by Cambridge University Press, Cambridge. Published in Italian (1927) Casa Editrice Monanni, Milano: see p. 317.

In this profoundly unbalanced theoretical context, Kant's intervention stands out as an exception of extraordinary significance. He is among the few thinkers to bestow upon peace an autonomous philosophical dignity, extricating it from the realm of utopia or sentiment and instead recontextualising it within a rigorous rational and legal framework. For Kant, peace is not merely a moral aspiration or an unfounded idyllic ideal, but rather a condition that is both historically and normatively possible. The originality of his thought lies in conceiving peace not merely as a suspension of conflict, but as the outcome of a cosmopolitan legal order grounded in practical reason, capable of translating moral ideals into concrete political projects.

However, reasoning within the framework of *Realpolitik*, an attempt to reconcile warlike demands with pacifist principles resulted in the development of the concept of just war—a sort of placebo effect. Conceived as a moral and legal criterion to distinguish the legitimate use of force from the illegitimate, the notion of just war has persisted throughout history, from the religious legitimisation of the Crusades by the medieval Church to its codification in contemporary international law. Indeed, today, according to the United Nations Charter, the sole acceptable justification for the use of force is self-defence against armed aggression. Nonetheless, contemporary warfare strategies increasingly blur the distinction between offensive and defensive wars, particularly since the ambiguous notions of "preventive defence" and "pre-emptive strikes" have gained prominence in political and military practice. While defensive war, in its strict sense, should constitute a proportionate response to an ongoing aggression, in the broader interpretation that has emerged in recent years it ultimately encompasses armed action against a threat that is merely perceived or anticipated, pre-emptively countering a potential attack with the stated intention of preventing it.

This rationale has justified military interventions in recent decades that have sparked significant controversy. For instance, the invasion of Iraq in 2003 was justified by the alleged existence of weapons of mass destruction in the hands of Saddam Hussein's regime, an unverified threat that was used as a pretext for launching a large-scale military operation. A similar narrative was repeated first in 2025 and then again in 2026 to justify th attacks on Iran and its military infrastructures, based on uranium enrichment levels deemed threatening.

The intervention in Afghanistan in 2001 too—though initially aimed at responding to the terrorist attacks of 11 September—soon evolved into a protracted conflict, carried out under the banner of the global war on terror and "preventive security". A more recent example is the 2022 invasion of Ukraine by the Russian Federation. Justified by the Kremlin on the grounds of strategic self-defence and the alleged protection of Russian-speaking populations, it constituted a clear violation of international law, once again demonstrating how the concept of war legitimacy can be manipulated to conceal expansionist ambitions and geopolitical interests.

From the above cases (and no doubt many other examples could be given), what becomes increasingly clear is the fading theoretical and legal substance of the notion of defensive war. The latter, in fact, appears emptied of its original normative rationale as the use of armed force gradually frees itself from the constraint of a response proportionate to an immediate and tangible aggression, instead relying on prognostic constructions and risk hypotheses, often suspended between subjective perception and strategic narrative. Obviously, the nuclear framework further exacerbates this conceptual distortion, embedding the logic of military action in the capacity to initiate pre-emptively destruction in order to avoid suffering it. Thus, a paradoxical rationale emerges, in which the legitimacy of an attack is rooted not in fact but in foresight, and where deterrence transforms into a strategy of domination founded on the asymmetry of time and the anticipation of the possible.

The nuclear strategy, for its part, further exacerbates this dynamic insofar as what matters is the ability to strike first in order to avoid being hit. However, this approach fundamentally undermines the very principle of legitimate self-defence. If a state perceives itself as sufficiently threatened by another to launch a pre-emptive strike, the targeted state may view it as an act of aggression and respond in kind, triggering a devastating escalation that could lead to global suicide.[5] The potential chain of reactions, fuelled by mutual suspicion and amplified by the destructive power of nuclear arsenals, makes the modern world highly unstable. One only needs to consider the incident in 2024 when a Russian missile fell just a few kilometres from the Polish border; had it been interpreted as a deliberate attack, NATO's response could have led to a global conflict. The potential chain reactions have become even more perilous with repeated incursions by Russian drones and fighter aircraft in EU airspace during September

[5] A chilling fictional account of how a war with use of nuclear weapons might pan out can be found in Jacobsen A (2024) *Nuclear War: A Scenario*, Transworld Publishers, London.

2025 on a scale that certainly could not be put down to mere accidents of navigation.

Moreover, the risk of such a scenario intensifies further in a context where the decision-making architecture appears increasingly vulnerable to the actions of individual actors, where the principle of collective responsibility is relinquished in favour of forms of leadership based on charisma, instinct and personal assertion as criteria for political intervention. In this framework, the political and symbolic actions of Donald Trump have played a crucial role in accentuating this international instability. Returning to the presidency with the promise to resolve the Ukrainian crisis in "twenty-four hours", the tycoon, who aims to win the Nobel Peace Prize, exhibited contradictory and impulsive behaviour regarding his pledge to promote global balance. In fact, in an initial phase, he suspended all forms of direct aid to Kyiv, blocking military supplies and financial assistance, only later to authorise a partial restoration that limited support to indirect channels managed by third parties. He has repeatedly blown hot and cold on his assessment of Putin's strategic intentions.

At the same time, the foreign policy of Trump and his allies reinforced the personalisation of decision-making power, particularly through the systematic use of social media. These platforms became instruments for broadcasting announcements that bypassed traditional institutional channels, yet served primarily to fuel global tension. A particularly emblematic episode of this dynamic occurred when, in response to a provocative tweet by the Deputy Secretary of the Russian Security Council, Trump announced—on his personal social media account and without operational details—a supposed deployment of US nuclear submarines near the Russian border. The announcement, shared solely via social media and lacking any official confirmation from military authorities, sparked widespread concern within the international community.

This episode underscores a fundamental challenge of the contemporary world: an international system now confronted with a new mode of strategic communication—informal, aggressive and capable of disrupting traditional diplomacy and indeed the logic of deterrence. What makes this transformation particularly troubling is its intangible and elusive character. Threats no longer take the form of visible missiles approaching national borders, but rather of invisible, instantaneous social media posts—capable of provoking uncontrolled often emotional reactions and sudden crises. This digital volatility makes consequences nearly impossible to predict or contain, generating a pervasive sense of frustration and helplessness for people at large.

As a result, the margin for error in foreign policy decision-making is drastically reduced, intensifying the fragility. Every gesture or utterance—no matter how seemingly trivial—has the potential to ignite tensions beyond the reach of traditional diplomatic mechanisms. As a result, international peace appears increasingly precarious and vulnerable, exposed to threats that transcend conventional categories of security and conflict.

In the face of these developments, the return to the Hobbesian logic advocated in earlier chapters takes on its full significance. As is well known, his philosophy begins with the state of nature, conceived as an original condition of incessant and universal war—and an absolute necessity to escape from it: *pax est quaerenda*. Within this framework, civilised society is conceived as a state of peace, in radical opposition to the state of war—a stark dichotomy in which the former is associated with the highest good, and the latter with absolute evil. This model, besides having shaped much of modern political theory through the concept of social contract, has proven tragically relevant in the age of nuclear and technological warfare; the balance of terror during the Cold War may be seen, in a certain sense, as a return to a globalised Hobbesian state of nature, in which the constant threat of annihilation made the exit from such a condition necessary—though without any real political instruments for achieving it.

And yet, in historical terms, the latter half of the twentieth century witnessed a period in which peace was elevated—not through reconciliation, but through the threat of mutual destruction. The Cold War embodied to perfection the ancient adage *si vis pacem, para bellum*, demonstrating how the balance of terror could freeze conflict without ever truly resolving it. In this scenario, nuclear deterrence took on the traits of a perverse rationality, in which planetary survival depended on the calculated risk of mutual annihilation. It is the logic of *Mutually Assured Destruction* (MAD), a mechanism in which peace was guaranteed not by trust, but by fear.

Peace was no longer an end in itself, but rather a strategic means. It evolved into a functional tool designed to bolster opposing blocs, serving as an ideological narrative that constructed legitimacy and garnered consent. During the Cold War, peace transformed into a form of soft power—essentially a cultural and symbolic weapon used to assert one's political and economic models, while creating enemy categories that influenced public opinion and institutions, all with the aim of winning the war through indirect means. Upon closer examination, peace campaigns, far from defusing conflicts, often ended up polarising them, reinforcing the supremacy of one bloc over the other—this dynamic was also the underlying logic behind NATO's expansion and development. "We will build a better NATO—one that is stronger, fairer, and more lethal—so that we can continue to keep our people safe and our adversaries at bay", stated NATO Secretary-General Mark Rutte during his speech at Chatham House, one of the world's leading think tanks on international affairs.[6] Consequently, peace ultimately loses all authenticity; it ceases to be a genuinely autonomous and shared choice, instead becoming a rhetorical extension of warlike logic.

In this context, the admonition of Pierre-Joseph Proudhon—quoted by Carl Schmitt in 1927—resonates powerfully: "*Wer Menschheit sagt, will betrügen*"—"Whoever speaks of humanity wants to deceive".[7] When a state or coalition positions itself as the spokesperson for all humanity, the war it wages does not automatically become just; on the contrary, it appropriates a universal concept to legitimise its own hegemony and criminalise the enemy. Thus, the very idea of peace is instrumentalised for warlike ends, losing its authenticity. Contrary to the dominant narrative that portrays nuclear deterrence as the guarantor of a prolonged era of peace, historical reality demonstrates that it has not prevented conflicts from breaking out; rather, it has transformed the nature of warfare, making it more fragmented, indirect and covert. The balance of terror between the two superpowers did not pacify the world; instead, it fuelled a climate of permanent tension, resulting in a long series of bloody and destabilising wars. The Korean War (1950), the Vietnam catastrophe (which began in 1962 and stretched for over a decade) and the Soviet invasion of Afghanistan in 1979 are just a few of the most striking manifestations of a global conflict fought by proxy. The superpowers did not confront each other directly but funnelled weapons, resources and ideologies to third nations, turning them into ideological and geopolitical battlegrounds.

This fragile equilibrium of the post-World War II era, which one could accurately describe as an "armed peace", appeared, even then, to be structurally doomed to failure. Grounding global stability in the technical

[6] Rutte M (2025) Speech on Building a Better NATO delivered at Chatham House, London 09 June 2025. Available at https://www.nato.int/cps/en/natohq/opinions_235867.htm. Accessed 5 August 2025.

[7] Schmitt, C (1932) *Der Begriff des Politischen*. München: Duncker & Humbolt: p. 42.

capacity for mutual destruction has meant inhabiting a precarious order fraught with persistent tensions, recurring crises and a strategic silence more akin to paralysis than to genuine pacification. Decades later, this framework has not been transcended: global disarmament remains an unrealised ideal, while the nuclear arsenal not only persists but has also evolved, multiplied and modernised. Indeed, alongside the hegemonic power that emerged victorious from the Cold War—namely, the USA, which continues to regard nuclear technology as a cornerstone of its strategic supremacy—there now exists a geopolitical landscape increasingly populated by regional powers wielding atomic arsenals. China, Russia, Israel, Pakistan, India and, likely, North Korea represent the principal actors within this multipolar scenario, wherein deterrence has expanded well beyond the bipolar axis of the past. Adding further complexity to this picture are two European nations, France and the UK, which stubbornly assert their own autonomous nuclear capabilities, elevating them to instruments of political legitimacy and guaranteeing their influence within the fragmented and unstable geometry of global power.

The nuclear technology continues to be possessed, refined and even experimentally employed, despite concerted efforts by the international community to curb its proliferation. The Comprehensive Nuclear-Test-Ban Treaty (CTBT), adopted in 1996, although symbolically significant, has never formally entered into force due to the persistent reluctance of key states unwilling to relinquish the strategic advantage of testing and upgrading their arsenals. Nuclear tests, although often confined to remote territories and marginalised in the eyes of public opinion, are far from devoid of devastating consequences. They represent one of the most extreme forms of systemic violence inflicted upon the environment and the collective health of humanity. By invoking security and strategic deterrence, a destructive practice is perpetuated that transcends military domains to inscribe itself deeply into the living fabric of the planet, contaminating lands, organisms and entire future generations. The cost of this rationale, cloaked in the rhetoric of geopolitical necessity, falls upon communities deemed expendable, marginalised environments and lives reduced to mere collateral variables.

Several emblematic episodes, extensively documented in the 2008 UNSCEAR Report,[8] reveal the inherent fragility of a technological apparatus that, despite its claims of absolute control, has proven vulnerable to

[8] UNSCEAR 2008 Report Volume I.

disaster since its inception. Criticality accidents—events in which unstable configurations of fissile material trigger unintended chain reactions—offer a stark demonstration of this fragility. Between 1945 and 1946, at the Los Alamos laboratory, two scientists lost their lives during manual experiments involving plutonium cores, victims of direct exposure to radioactive material. Known as the "demon incidents", these events marked the tragic boundary between experimentation and recklessness, between technical knowledge and Promethean hubris.

Along similar lines are the incidents at the Mayak nuclear complex, the beating heart of the Soviet military production programme. During the 1950s and 1960s, numerous technicians were exposed to doses of ionising radiation sufficient to cause amputations, systemic necrosis and immediate fatalities. In one documented case, an operator received a localised dose exceeding 30 Gray[9] to the lower limbs, necessitating surgical amputation; in another, three workers died following exposure estimated between 40 and 50 Gray during a poorly executed drainage operation. The accumulation of these events not only compromised the internal safety of the facilities but also resulted in radioactive releases into the surrounding environment. In 1957, an explosion at Mayak released over 740 petabecquerels of radioactive material into the atmosphere, contaminating more than 20,000 square kilometres and affecting upwards of 250,000 individuals. That same year, in the UK, the Windscale reactor fire emitted iodine-131 and other radionuclides, with effects traceable hundreds of kilometres away—occurring at a time when institutional transparency was virtually non-existent.[10]

This reality of perpetual precariousness and conflict intersects profoundly with Michel Foucault's radical theoretical reinterpretation, articulated in his 1976 lecture series *Il faut défendre la société* at the Collège de France.[11] Foucault overturns Clausewitz's premise: war is no longer merely the continuation of politics by other means; rather, modern politics constitutes the continuation of war by other means. In a world that deludes

[9] The gray (Gy) is the SI unit of absorbed dose of ionising radiation.

[10] All of the above from United Nations Scientific Committee on the Effects of Atomic Radiation. *Sources and Effects of Ionizing Radiation: UNSCEAR 2008 Report. Volume I: Sources. Report to the General Assembly with Scientific Annexes A and B*. New York: United Nations, 2008.

[11] Foucault, Michel. *Il faut défendre la société: Cours au Collège de France (1975–1976)*. Édition établie par Mauro Bertani et Alessandro Fontana sous la direction de François Ewald et Alessandro Fontana. Le Foucault Électronique, 2001. Édition numérique réalisée en 2012.

itself into believing it lives in peace yet co-exists with creeping conflicts and increasingly polarised global tensions, Foucault's reinterpretation of the war-politics relationship proves strikingly relevant. While international chancelleries invoke dialogue and military alliances speak the language of defence, what endures—often beneath the surface of official rhetoric—is a war that has never ceased to be waged but has transformed its form, shifting from the overt dimension of armed confrontation to the realms of power management, trade wars and cyberwarfare.

By inverting Clausewitz's classical notion that "war is the continuation of politics by other means", Foucault reveals how, in modernity, it is rather politics that becomes the continuation of war through sophisticated, invisible, normalised and at times internalised instruments. War, in other words, does not disappear; on the contrary, it institutionalises itself within security apparatuses, the language of emergency, sanction diplomacy, arbitrary applications of tariffs and asymmetric, unequal treaties.

Against the illusion of linear progress proposed by Fukuyama[12]—where liberal democracy is heralded as the "end of history"—the resurgence of conflict and geopolitical fragmentation demonstrate that we remain immersed in a dialectical process, a history that unfolds through contradiction, negation and transcendence. Contemporary geopolitical dynamics offer the clearest illustration of this reality. The wars in Ukraine and Middle East, tensions in the South China Sea and the competition for technological and space dominance all unfold beneath a veneer of pacifying rhetoric, yet respond to profound conflictual logics. The struggle is not merely about weapons or territorial boundaries but concerns competing cultural systems and global orders seeking to assert themselves less through brute force and more through economic, media and digital control.

With the eruption of war in Ukraine, even the leadership of the European Union—emblematically embodied by Ursula von der Leyen—has adopted a new grammar of peace, increasingly distant from the dialogic and cooperative foundations of postwar Europe. The formula "peace through strength",[13] now a hallmark of European political posture,

[12] Fukuyama, F. (1992) *The End of History and the Last Man* Hamish Hamilton, London.

[13] "The European Union maintains its 'peace through strength' approach, which requires Ukraine to be in the strongest possible position, with its own robust military and defence capabilities as an essential component".

Conclusions of the European Council, 20 March 2025, available at https://data.consilium.europa.eu/doc/document/ST-11-2025-INIT/en/pdf. Accessed 13 September 2025.

encapsulates a vision in which geopolitical balance is no longer forged through mediation but through military potential.

The provision of arms to Ukraine, the adoption of the European Defence Industrial Strategy, the widespread increase in defence spending (also responding to NATO's demands) and the initiation of an industrial policy aimed at the continent's re-militarisation are today presented as necessary steps to secure—or more accurately, to conquer—a "just and lasting peace".

This linguistic and strategic transformation reveals a deep symbolic fracture. Peace, which once stood as an ethical horizon and cultural foundation of the European project, now slips into a subordinate condition, bound by the logic of force. It is no longer an alternative to war; rather, it has become a reward for successful armed resistance. In this manner, peace is subverted into its opposite, transforming into an extension of war: it is no longer a substitute for violence but the product of established military superiority.

However, it is well established that those states that speak of a rules-based order are often the ones that hold the interpretive monopoly, while those who invoke law are often among the main authors of its text. Moreover, even today's international institutions, despite their self-presentation as neutral and impartial bodies, frequently operate under deeply entrenched hegemonic power dynamics. Indeed, many of these institutions were created in the post-World War II era under the influence of victorious powers, intending not only to secure peace but also to solidify a specific global order. Consequently, what is framed as multilateral cooperation often takes on the characteristics of negotiated supremacy, a veiled exportation of dominant models legitimised by a normative framework that claims universality. The resounding truth is encapsulated in the ancient maxim, *silent enim leges inter arma*; the rules of law yield to the logic of force, and war does not cease but rather shifts into the mechanisms of diplomacy and administration.[14] Formal peace thus manifests as the elegant façade of a conflict that perpetuates itself through treaties, sanctions and hegemonic manipulation.

This tension between form and substance emerges with particular clarity within the contemporary international structure, which remains

[14] This is precisely what occurs in the conflict between Israel and Palestine, where the rhetoric of dialogue and negotiation has co-existed for decades with the expansion of settlements and the systematic violation of rights.

tethered to the principle of absolute sovereignty, rendering each state the exclusive arbiter of its interests and resistant to any real subordination to a higher authority. The right of veto stands as a striking illustration of this dynamic. Here, philosophical reflection offers a deeper interpretative lens; Hegel observed that the internal order of states is achieved at the expense of external anarchy, as the absence of legitimate power over nations inevitably fosters competition that finds its natural resolution in war. Nonetheless, throughout history, humanity has persistently endeavoured to circumscribe war within defined limits, striving to bind it within a normative framework of rules, conventions and supranational institutions. This endeavour, noble in intention, represented an effort to constrain violence from its blind arbitrariness, subordinating it to the rationality of law. With the advent of post-modernity—characterised by heightened global asymmetries, a crisis of legal universalism and the disintegration of traditional boundaries between war and peace—these fragile bulwarks have progressively weakened, ultimately dissolving and rendering conflict not only more pervasive but also increasingly less recognisable in its canonical forms.

War, having been freed from the classical forms of confrontation between regular armies, has transformed into a pervasive, polymorphic and often invisible phenomenon, operating within the very fabric of society through economic, technological and communicative mechanisms. In this context, there remains a stark choice: either resign oneself to indiscriminate destruction or resolutely embark on the path towards its definitive transcendence. Thus, to speak of disarmament first and foremost entails deconstructing a certain grammar—breaking the symmetry between power and threat, security and domination—and questioning how it might be possible to guarantee international co-existence not through fear but through solidaristic interdependence.

Disarmament, therefore, is not simply the removal of weapons from the hands of states; it is the removal of force as a foundational element of the very idea of order. It is the recognition that a world in which survival depends on the balance of terror is a world perpetually poised on the brink of self-destruction, where peace is always and only the silence of the weaker party.

In other words, if we wish to prevent the future of the world from being constantly suspended on the edge of catastrophe, it is imperative to imagine—and build—a new international system capable of moving beyond diplomacy rooted in contingency. A system in which states do not merely interact according to fleeting interests but commit themselves, through an act of deliberate rationality and political awareness, to a significant and irrevocable cession of sovereignty. As argued in earlier chapters, this cession would aim to confer legitimacy and authority upon an effective supranational body, endowed not only with symbolic authority but with real and binding legislative, executive and juridical power.

This new order cannot be solely founded on the supremacy of a select few, but rather on the shared responsibility of all. Consequently, it must function as an effective guarantor of international law, as a steward of global common (non-rivalrous) goods and as an impartial arbiter in disputes between states. In other words, it must embody what is currently lacking: a recognised and collectively accepted global authority, capable of translating the ideal of peace into a stable and binding institutional framework. Peace is not merely a necessary condition for achieving other objectives, but rather a cornerstone upon which essential values such as justice, freedom and human dignity are built. Absent this foundation, every legal, social and moral principle would become devoid of substance and real purpose.

As Thucydides broadly argues in *The History of the Peloponnesian War*,[15] every present moment is both an inheritance of the past and a foundation for the future. In a world that has consecrated war as the engine of history, to reflect on peace means to restore its conceptual dignity—recognising it not merely as the absence of conflict, but as an active project of justice, co-existence and shared humanity oriented towards the future. For it is only by retracing its often-neglected roots that we can begin to imagine a viable future for peace. Clearly, it is not enough to denounce the shortcomings of the current order; we must commit to building an architecture of peace grounded in memory, responsibility and a shared ethical horizon.

In this context, a Kantian-inspired cosmopolitan pacifism emerges not merely as a utopia but as a systemic necessity, transcending the Hobbesian anthropology of ***homo homini lupus*** in favour of ***homo inter homines custodes***, meaning that the other is no longer an enemy but an active guardian of global co-existence.

[15] Thucydides, (1950) *The History of the Peloponnesian War*. Translated by Richard Crawley, Dent and Sons, Ltd., London.

Bibliography

EU Consilium. (2025). *Conclusions of the European Council, 20 March 2025.* Accessed September 13, 2025, from https://data.consilium.europa.eu/doc/document/ST-11-2025-INIT/en/pdf

Foucault, M. *Il faut défendre la société: Cours au Collège de France (*1975 –1976). Édition établie par Mauro Bertani et Alessandro Fontana sous la direction de François Ewald et Alessandro Fontana. Le Foucault Électronique, 2001. Édition numérique réalisée en 2012.

Fukuyama, F. (1992). *The end of history and the last man.* Hamish Hamilton.

Galtung, J. (1996). *Peace by peaceful means: Peace and conflict, development and civilization.* Sage.

Hegel, G. W. F. (1991). *Hegel: Elements of the philosophy of right.* Cambridge University Press.

Hobbes, T. (1949). *De Cive; or, The Citizen.* Edited with an introduction by Sterling P. Lamprecht. Appleton-Century-Crofts.

Nietzsche, F. (1878). *Human, all too human: A book for free spirits* published in English (1996) by Cambridge University Press. Published in Italian (1927) Casa Editrice Monanni.

Rutte, M. (2025). *Speech on building a better NATO* delivered at Chatham House, London 09 June. Accessed August 5, 2025, from https://www.nato.int/cps/en/natohq/opinions_235867.htm

Schmitt, C. (1932). *Der Begriff des Politischen.* Duncker & Humbolt.

United Nations. (2008). *UNSCEAR report: Sources and effects of ionizing radiation Volume 1. Report to the General Assembly with Scientific Annexes A and B.* United Nations.

Index[1]

[1] Note: Page numbers followed by 'n' refer to notes.

P. O'Sullivan et al., *Overcoming Gangsterism and Geo-Political Anarchy*, https://doi.org/10.1007/978-3-032-22438-5

GPSR Compliance
The European Union's (EU) General Product Safety Regulation (GPSR) is a set of rules that requires consumer products to be safe and our obligations to ensure this.

If you have any concerns about our products, you can contact us on

ProductSafety@springernature.com

In case Publisher is established outside the EU, the EU authorized representative is:

Springer Nature Customer Service Center GmbH
Europaplatz 3
69115 Heidelberg, Germany

www.ingramcontent.com/pod-product-compliance
Ingram Content Group UK Ltd.
Pitfield, Milton Keynes, MK11 3LW, UK
UKHW020925220926
475692UK00010B/76
* 9 7 8 3 0 3 2 2 2 4 3 7 8 *